by Stefanovski
and a 1 act

With introductory texts by
Chris Torch and Slobodan Unkovski
and translations by
Patricia Marsh-Stefanovska

Egret playwrights
Chapel Hill, North Carolina
2025

Cover and book design by Maxine Mills

Printed in the United States of America
First Edition

PUBLISHER CATALOGING-IN-PUBLICATION DATA

Names: Stefanovski, Goran, 1952 – author. | Marsh- Stefanovska, Patricia – translator.

Torch, Chris – author of introduction.

Unkovski, Slobodan – author of introduction.

Plays. Selections.

Title: 4 by Stefanovski and a 1 act / with introductory texts by

Chris Torch and Slobodan Unkovski

and translations by

Patricia Marsh-Stefanovska.

Description: Chapel Hill : Laertes Press, 2025.

Other titles: Dramatic works. Selections. English.

Identifiers: LCCN 2024951545 | ISBN 9781942281368 (softcover : alk. paper)

Classification: LCC PG1196.29.T58 A6 2025

www.laertesbooks.org

CONTENTS

STUBBORN DIGNITY

by Chris Torch

I WAS INTRODUCED to Goran Stefanovski in 1992. In the heat of the siege of Sarajevo, we were brought together by a common friend (critic, dramaturgist, and political philosopher Dragan Klaic) for an impossible mission: to shift Europe's gaze from the terror and tragedy of the Bosnian war to the soul of a city being drowned in blood, by creating a touring production, a mourning song, which Goran entitled *Sarajevo — An Oratorio for the Theatre*.

It was the beginning of a dynamic decade of collaborative projects. It changed me. It changed us both. That we practically lived together during those 10 years and maintained our co-creative energy was to a great degree due to Goran's immense integrity and stubborn dignity. We continued to clash and inspire one another until his life ended abruptly, just as we were starting preparation of a new major project, commissioned by two European Capitals of Culture, Rijeka 2020 (Croatia) and Timisoara 2021 (Romania).

Since then, I find myself starting sentences, fully expecting him to finish them, as it had always been. Now I struggle to complete a thought. There is no echo. And both I and the Europe that formed us are less lucid without his voice.

Allow me, American readers, to introduce you to a writer and thinker, a European cynic and a Balkan joker, a master playwright and a fearless experimenter.

GORAN THE PLAYWRIGHT

In this volume, the reader is privileged to be presented with a unique cross-section of Stefanovski's plays, all written during an extremely productive period of his life.

This anthology bridges two banks of recent Balkan history: 3 plays were written ***before*** the bloody breakup of the Socialist Federal Republic ofYugoslavia, 2 plays were written ***after***, when his world was hacked to pieces and he had already begun his slow emigration from a context he never left but instead carried with him in his mental backpack, until his life ended, far too soon.

In one of our earliest conversations, as a response to my naïve question about how he defined his "nationality," he responded with a popular proverb: *"In the Balkans, no one is ever born and dies in the same country."* This was certainly true for him. But it also mirrored the personal histories of most people in the region: constantly shifting, always re-forming, repeatedly invaded, adjusting to new masters, adapting to new languages, traditions, and values. It was this cultural and political fluidity that defined much of Goran's maturing vision.

It is neither my intention nor my task to critically analyze the tools of his trade. But while rereading his immense body of work, made up of plays but also lectures, stories, and anecdotes, I am reminded of the diverse but consistent mosaic of themes he returned to again and again.

Of course, the ongoing trauma of migration — the loss of a homeland and the confusion that results — is often at the core of his work. In this way, he is a truly Balkan writer, formed by the chaotic history that defines the region. But the tone he refined throughout his career was one of distance, in the Brechtian spirit, spiced with self-irony and self-criticism. This is especially evident in his male characters, complex constructions of masculinity, both violent and ridiculous, both unreachable and fragile. He reveals the simple and secret forces at work under the surface. No one is exactly who they appear to be. Truth is unreliable. And human behavior is never rooted in logic.

But I'm sure that Goran would protest about any definition as a "Balkan" writer. In his later years, he often lamented the tendency to stigmatize writers, locking them into their root cultures, instead of cultivating the important connection between the "universal" and the "provincial." Goran's characters were formed in the Balkans. The conflicts they found themselves in were intimately informed by the Balkan context. But in fact, they are easily understood as reflections on the universal human condition. One could change the names and the places; the actions and the emotions fit nearly any geopolitical context. Goran gave a voice to simple people struggling with existence, desperate for love, bound by historical imperatives. He cared deeply for the people he put on stage. They were born "locally" but are recognizable "globally."

Most importantly, his characters are never "good" or "bad." Even the most vulgar are somehow sympathetic, even the most beautiful are damaged. This is the world as he knew it and as he chose to present it: We wander the earth with little security, always astonished but never surprised.

GORAN THE OBSERVER

His exceptional insight never fell into the trap of moralism; his stories are never lessons. He never allowed his voice to be manipulated, to become a tool for ideology, power structures, or opinions. He struggled, in an immensely politicized context, to sustain his freedom as an artist, a critic, and a sceptic. Towards the end of his life, he wrote:

> *"I'm not a politician. It's not my responsibility to take a side and have a prepared position on every issue. I'm a playwright. I'm interested in both the voice of the angel and the voice of the devil."*

In this way, he approached life informed by the Sufi teaching: *to be* ***in*** *the world, but never* ***of*** *it*. His work was always personal but never private. He was undeniably attached to the society around him but kept it at a distance, with humor, without sentimentality. He became a brilliant observer of the pivotal motivations that make things happen.

His plays therefore leave a wide margin for stage interpretation, at the same time never leaving the actors without a narrative, a roadmap.

GORAN THE GROUNDBREAKER

But Goran was much more than a conventional playwright, bound to the rules and regulations of Western drama. He allowed himself to be challenged, he embraced opportunities to redefine his role as a writer for the theater. This is where our paths crossed.

During our intense decade of creative action together, Goran engaged directly in the entire creative process, making himself vulnerable and at the same time essential. Our first work together, *Sarajevo* (1993), was written as a series of images, a love song to a dying city. It was written during the siege of the city, each day changing the course of history, each morning newspapers reporting new atrocities. It was, as he remarked, *"like trying to shoot at a moving target."* The script he delivered was exactly the prayer so badly needed, meant to heal the wounds that kept unexplainably bleeding, the only possible antidote to our collective helplessness.

This open format, meant to be filled and revised by multiple co-creators, was something entirely unknown. His work initiated the projects but did not dominate them. His generosity and curiosity inspired creativity rather than controlling it.

Our common projects that followed — *Bacchanalia* (1996), *Euralien* (1998), and *Hotel Europa* (2000–2001) — deepened this form of large-scale collective creations. He became the creator of myths; the storytellers (directors, actors, designers) then took over and found ways to engage with the audience. He provided the original impulse around which our collaborators could gather. He followed the work process, protecting the integrity of his original ideas but also generously adapting to the needs of theater makers.

This thread in Goran's legacy requires a more complete and separate treatment. But in order to fully appreciate the plays made available in this anthology, it is essential to see them as part of a body of work that flowed from a "man of the theater," not only a playwright.

■ ■ ■

What then makes Goran's writing relevant to the American scene?

The Balkans are more than a geopolitical region. They are a metaphor for chaos and broken dreams, for the desperate and never-ending human struggle for dignity, for the most brutal battlefields, and for the most sophisticated multi-ethnic laboratory Europe has ever seen.

And this mirrors the ongoing American trauma, now more visible than ever. The USA is a nation of diverse peoples, arriving from many places, carrying with them baggage from the motherland, and yet determined to invent a synthesis human history has never seen. As the American people struggle with this challenge, they might do well to listen to a voice that is rooted in a recent — and failed — experiment in cooperation and coexistence. The horror of emerging hate, the loss of cohesion, and the human forces that undermine the beautiful but still unrealized American dream can all be felt in the writings of Goran Stefanovski. His unsentimental exposure of our most base instincts is balanced by his profound love for humanity and its mysteries.

So, step back, America. Turn your gaze from your own confusion and let yourself be guided through the mythical, now lost, Balkan cosmos. You couldn't have a better theatrical pathfinder than Goran Stefanovski.

■ ■ ■

Once, many years ago, a colleague posed a question to my mentor, master, and director, Judith Malina (co-founder of The Living Theatre): how it felt to be growing old and approaching death. Her response: *"Death is a conspiracy, and I am not participating."*

If only that were true. If only I could have protected my friend and co-conspirator Goran from the inevitable crossing of the river Styx. We could have had more time. He could have told us more stories.

But the ones he left behind are already such gifts. They deserve to be given life again, to transform his words into living songs, to make us laugh and sigh and wonder.

WILD FLESH

Translated from the Macedonian
by Patricia Marsh-Stefanovska

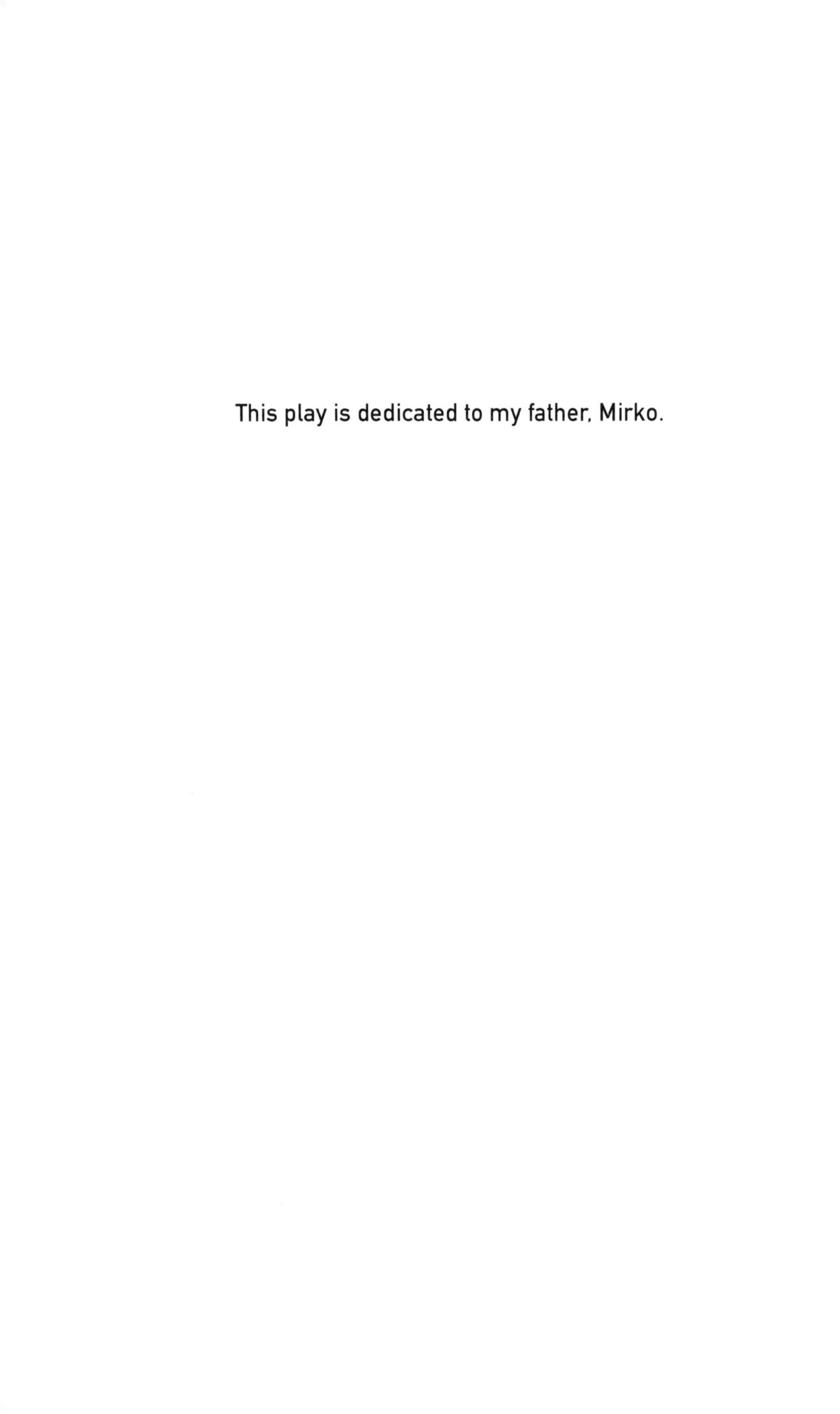

This play is dedicated to my father, Mirko.

CHARACTERS

DIMITRI ANDREYEVITCH 55, an invalid, former housebuilder

MARIA ANDREYEVITCH 50, his wife

ANDREI 22, their youngest son, assistant in a grocery store

STEVO 26, their second son, employee of an automobile dealership

SIMON 30, their eldest son, a waiter

VERA 25, his wife, a housewife

HERZOG 55, manager of the automobile dealership, a Jew

SARA 23, his daughter

HERMANN KLAUS 45, a visitor from Germany

SIVITCH 35, assistant manager in the automobile dealership

ATSO 23, a friend of Andrei's, a truck driver

WISE WOMAN

MIMI a prostitute

THE PRIEST

GUESTS at the reception

WORKMEN

CUSTOMERS in the railroad station café

The action takes place in Skopje, just before the Second World War.

SCENE ONE

[*The main room in the Andreyevitch's house with three other rooms and a kitchen leading off it. Dimitri is sitting in a wheelchair, reading the newspaper. Maria is sitting on the bed, staring into space. Silence. Pause.*]

DIMITRI. There's going to be war. [*Pause*] There's going to be war. [*Pause.*]

MARIA. We've had enough of this kind of peace anyway.

DIMITRI. What're you doing? Staring into space again? ***Do*** something.

MARIA. Like what?

DIMITRI. Make dinner. We've got people coming.

MARIA. It's all made.

DIMITRI. Make lunch.

MARIA. It's ready.

DIMITRI. If it's ready, I want to eat.

MARIA. Stop shouting at me! [*Pause*] It's our saint's day tomorrow.

[*Pause. Enter Vera, carrying an empty clothes hamper.*]

VERA. It's going to rain. Waste of time hanging the sheets out.

MARIA. Everything's a waste of time. [*Pause*] I had a dream I was cut in half. And there was a big worm where my backbone should be. And the worm had been cut in half, too, and it was writhing around. And then someone came and pulled it out. And it was agony, like having a tooth out.

VERA. You're always having dreams like that.

MARIA. They just come.

DIMITRI. Are we ever going to eat in this house?

VERA. They're not back yet.

DIMITRI. They needn't bother to come back, as far as I'm concerned.

VERA. Let's wait a bit longer.

DIMITRI. ***You*** can wait as long as you like. ***I*** want to eat.

VERA. You're eating me alive! [*Setting the table*] What should I do first? The cleaning, the washing, the cooking?!

DIMITRI. Teach your mother-in-law.

VERA. You leave her out of this.

DIMITRI. Have a daughter. ***She*** can help you.

[*Vera swallows hard. Dimitri eats. Silence. Pause. Enter Simon, drunk.*]

SIMON. You don't even wait to eat together anymore.

DIMITRI. When we waited, you didn't come.

SIMON. You can't say a thing in this house. I'll get a couple of gas cans and blow the place to kingdom come.

MARIA. Don't tempt Providence.

SIMON. I don't have to. Providence was tempted a long time ago.

VERA. Where have you been drinking?

SIMON. Wherever I could, to tell you the truth.

VERA. You're killing yourself.

SIMON. Something's going to kill me sooner or later. Don't put off till tomorrow what you can do today. It's easy for you.

VERA. It's easy for me. I have a really easy time of it.

SIMON. You afraid of the dark? No. ***I*** am. Afraid of the light? No. ***I*** am. I'm choking here, right here, I've got a lump.

MARIA. You've got a hair in your throat.

VERA. You're on your feet all day.

SIMON. If I could be a waiter sitting down, I'd sit down! I didn't say I'd got varicose veins from being on my feet all day. I'm choking, ***here***. I'm eaten up with worry. I can't eat. I can't sleep.

DIMITRI. But you can ***drink***. Let your father tell you something. Don't tell the world your problems. The world doesn't want to know. The world's got its own problems. If you're going to say something, say something nice, or don't say anything at all. So you're afraid of the dark. Who cares?

SIMON. It makes me feel better if I talk about it.

DIMITRI. But you're a pain to listen to. A real pain! You can't sleep. Dear oh dear. Your mother can sleep, but she has bad dreams. We could go on forever like that. Why don't you ask me how ***I*** feel?

VERA. Want your lunch?

SIMON. Give me a rakia.[1]

VERA. You've had enough.

---

1. Strong clear liquor made from grapes and drunk all over the Balkans.

SIMON. How do ***you*** know when I've had enough?

VERA. I just do.

SIMON. Everybody knows better than me. I spend my whole day serving people who know better than me. "Simon! Rakia!" Simon brings the rakia. "Simon! A glass of water!" Simon brings a glass of water. "Simon! Not ***this*** kind of rakia, ***that*** kind of rakia!" "Simon, get a move on!" "Simon, catch!" "Simon, fetch!" Simon everywhere. Simon for everything. Well, I've had enough. Simon isn't a machine. Simon has a soul, too, you know. You sit here and won't even give me a glass of rakia. And you find me a pain to listen to. Well, to hell with the lot of you. I'll get my hat and be off. [*He starts crying. Pause. Vera strokes his head. She pours him some rakia.*] That's right, give me a cuddle and make it all right!

DIMITRI. At least you've got your wife to make it all right. Who's going to make it all right for me, knowing I fathered you lot?!

MARIA. This is no way to go on. It's our saint's day.

DIMITRI. To hell with your goddamn saint's day! Look who you've got to celebrate it with! [*He goes back to his newspaper. Pause.*] Forgive me, Saint Iliya. But you can see for yourself what scum I live with.

[*Pause. Enter Andrei.*]

ANDREI. Hello, everybody.

MARIA. Hello, my boy.

ANDREI. [*Sitting down at the table*] Rabotnitchki won. Two zero. [*Pause. Vera gives him his lunch. Silence.*] Somebody die around here? [*Silence. Pause. He eats.*] When's the priest coming?

MARIA. Tonight.

ANDREI. How's it going?

MARIA. Just the baklava to do.

ANDREI. I've brought you some icing sugar.

MARIA. Bless you.

ANDREI. I was run off my feet today. The whole town was out shopping. And the boss was away. Just me and the boy. Had a hard time keeping up. It's not a small shop. [*Pause. To Dimitri*] What's in the papers today?

DIMITRI. Don't know.

ANDREI. How come?

DIMITRI. What's there for ***me*** isn't there for the likes of ***you***.

ANDREI. So what's there for ***you***?

DIMITRI. My business.

ANDREI. Oh, come on now, Dimitri, cheer up a bit!

DIMITRI. Dimitri'll cheer up in his grave.

ANDREI. Time enough for that.

DIMITRI. I don't know. We seem to be asking for it. [*Pause.*]

ANDREI. And how's my Vera today?

VERA. It's easy for me. I have a really easy time of it.

ANDREI. [*To Simon*] What about you?

SIMON. Just stop playing the fool, will you?

ANDREI. What's wrong with asking how you are?

SIMON. ***You*** know.

ANDREI. No, I don't.

SIMON. Don't make me tell you!

ANDREI. Tell me!

SIMON. Stop it!!

ANDREI. What's wrong?

SIMON. ***Stop it!!*** I'm older than you and I said stop it! And if I punch you in the teeth, your precious Russians won't save you!

ANDREI. Leave the Russians out of this.

SIMON. You're going to rot in jail, but ***I*** won't come and see you. Let your precious Communists bring you something to eat. If they're not all in jail with you. You just go on meeting after dark and writing in your diaries.

ANDREI. We're organizing a strike.

SIMON. My, my! You'll really scare the daylights out of them!

ANDREI. It won't be just any old strike. We're going to bite right down to the bone. Till the gangrene starts. The brewery, the cigarette factory, and the railroad men.

SIMON. You're just dribbling the ball all the time. What about a goal or two?

ANDREI. We're doing the training to last those ninety minutes on the field. The goals'll take care of themselves.

SIMON. When?

ANDREI. When you join us! That's the tough bit, isn't it?!

There're plenty like you sitting on the sidelines, nibbling sunflower seeds, and waiting to see a goal. But there's all that running to do. You've got to do some running!

SIMON. The doctor says running's bad for me. [*Pause.*] I could be a linesman, if you like.

DIMITRI. Politics is a card game. Strictly for whores and swindlers. It's all a big seesaw. First one of them's up, then the other. I dipped my finger in that pie once upon a time. I won't have any more talk of politics in this house.

ANDREI. What d'you mean, ***politics?!*** This is all just hot air! You're amateur politicians. What you call politics is what you overhear somewhere, or what you read in the evening paper.

SIMON. While you, of course, get it straight from God's balls! Come on, Andrei, don't get carried away. We've all been young once.

ANDREI. And you've grown up and still haven't got a brain!

[*Enter Stevo.*]

MARIA. Hello.

[*Stevo simply nods his head in greeting.*]

SIMON. It's too much of an effort for him to say hello.

DIMITRI. He's got other things on his mind. He's a philosopher. His head hardly fits on his shoulders after those two years of business school. If we'd let him go on to university, he'd probably've murdered us all in our sleep.

MARIA. Want your lunch now?

STEVO. I had some kebabs at Kantina.

MARIA. Don't you have a home?!

STEVO. I like eating out better. [*Pause*] And I won't be here this evening, by the way. I know it's our saint's day, I know all our relatives, neighbors, and friends are coming. I know they'll ask where I am. I've got things to do.

MARIA. You know this'll be the first time one of us isn't here for our saint's day?

STEVO. I'm going to a reception. [*Pause*] A reception. I was invited this morning. I could hardly say no. I knew it was our saint's day. I just couldn't say no. It's important. It means a lot to me.

MARIA. You're not going.

DIMITRI. How come they invite you at the last minute and you rush off to a reception, when you've got a family celebration at home?

STEVO. Like that.

DIMITRI. Like what?

STEVO. Just like that! The boss invited me. Mr. Herzog. There's an important guest coming from Germany. Everybody's going to be there. The cream of Skopje'll be there. Businessmen, bankers, men of the world.

SIMON. How come they invited you, then?

STEVO. Watch me.

SIMON. You going to sprout horns or something?

STEVO. No. Wings. You'll need a pair of binoculars to see me up there.

SIMON. Where are you going to fly away to?

STEVO. I've got a career ahead of me. Prospects.

ANDREI. Who's this German who's coming?

STEVO. A bigwig from Head Office in Berlin. Mom, press my black trousers, will you?

MARIA. I'm not letting you go and see any Germans. It's Saint Iliya's Eve.

STEVO. Vera, will you do it, for heaven's sake?

SIMON. First you ask ***me*** whether she can press your trousers.

STEVO. Can your wife press my black trousers?

SIMON. No, she can't. [*To Vera*] Don't you dare touch that iron. [*To Stevo*] Get your precious Lily to come and press them for you.

ANDREI. Has this German been here before?

STEVO. Dunno. No.

ANDREI. Why's he coming now?

STEVO. Dunno. On business.

ANDREI. What's his name?

STEVO. Hermann Klaus. What else would you like to know? What size underpants he wears? I don't know.

DIMITRI. And why the devil should ***you*** go to this reception?

STEVO. If you just happen to be in the right place at the right time, you can be sitting pretty for the rest of your life.

MARIA. I'm cross with you, Stevo. I really am.

STEVO. Well, you'll just have to be cross, Mom. There're some things I just can't explain to you anyhow.

MARIA. There's nothing ***you*** could ever explain to me if you tried.

[*A knock at the door. Maria opens it. It's the Priest.*]

PRIEST. Good afternoon.

MARIA. Good afternoon, Father. You're early.

PRIEST. Plenty of houses mean plenty of work. I can manage now, so I've come now.

MARIA. We're not ready.

PRIEST. What's not ready? Have you got the bread?

MARIA. We're not washed and changed.

DIMITRI. We said seven.

PRIEST. We did.

DIMITRI. Now it's three.

PRIEST. [*Looking at his watch*] A quarter after three. I know, Dimitri. There's no time like the present.

DIMITRI. I'm paying, and I want my priest here at seven.

PRIEST. Think of your soul, Dimitri. The praise of God is always and everywhere. It doesn't depend on a time or a place. Anyway, I don't think I can make it at seven.

DIMITRI. You'll make it all right.

PRIEST. Come now, Dimitri. Put yourself in my shoes.

DIMITRI. I am, Father, I am. But you put yourself in ***mine***.

You always do this to us. You go to the rich houses in the evening and come to us in the morning.

PRIEST. What d'you mean, in the ***morning***? Twenty after three in the afternoon!

DIMITRI. What about last year? Eight in the morning! Looked like you'd been sleeping on the front steps all night. We remember these things.

PRIEST. I swear, Dimitri, if I don't do it now, the Lord only knows when I'll be able to.

MARIA. ***Now***, Father. Please. We don't want to go without a blessing.

PRIEST. That's the spirit, Maria. Give me the bread now.

[*They bring him the special round loaf used in the saint's day blessing ceremony*.]

PRIEST. Render unto God the things that are God's. For many years to come. Honored be this day. May you celebrate it for another hundred years. All come round the table. [*They all gather around the table*.] Oh blessèd Saint Iliya, we pray you to help, guide, and protect us with your strength. Blessèd Lord, we beseech Thee never to abandon us, that he who is the enemy of our salvation may not come and cause our damnation. Say the names of the dear departed. Oh God our Father, we pray you to save and have mercy on the souls of our dear departed . . .

MARIA. Lena, Anastas, Spasia . . .

PRIEST. Lena, Anastas, Spasia . . .

MARIA. Georgi, Marko, Tryan . . .

PRIEST. Georgi, Marko, Tryan . . .

MARIA. Petri and Evda.

PRIEST. Petri and Evda.

SIMON. And Simon.

PRIEST. And Simon.

MARIA. Which Simon? Not Simon.

PRIEST. Not Simon. [*He takes the loaf and gives it to Dimitri. He takes Andrei's hand and places it on one side of the loaf. Andrei takes Simon's hand and transfers the loaf to him instead. The Priest makes an incision in the loaf in the shape of a cross.*] In the name of the Father, the Son, and the Holy Ghost, Amen.

ALL. Amen.

[*They all hold the bread, turning it round among them. They go round the table like this three times.*]

PRIEST. Free us, oh Lord, from unnecessary vexations to the spirit and may our joy be blessed in Thee. Give us strength in our weakness and grief. Be with us in our hours of trouble and sorrow, uncertainty, and trepidation, and relieve our tears and suffering. Heal our hidden pain and the wounds to our spirit, for only Thou seest them. All-loving God, we pray Thee, abandon us not.

[*The Priest leads them too fast and Dimitri has difficulty in keeping up in his wheelchair. He wobbles and the loaf falls, breaking into pieces.*]

MARIA. Oh no!!

DIMITRI. Can't you hold on properly, Simon? You drunk or something?

SIMON. I'm drunk all right, but I was holding on properly. ***You*** let it go.

PRIEST. Never mind, never mind. Father, Son, Holy Ghost, Amen. Many years to come. [*Pause. Silence.*] Come on, then. What're you waiting for? Pick up the bread.

MARIA. How could it break like that?

PRIEST. It fell and broke, that's all.

MARIA. How could it fall like that?

PRIEST. Don't worry, Maria. All that matters is to have God's blessing.

[*Maria picks up the pieces of bread.*]

DIMITRI. Is that it, then, Father?

PRIEST. That's it.

DIMITRI. Drop of rakia?

PRIEST. Don't mind if I do. [*Dimitri pours him a drink.*]

SIMON. A glass here, a glass there — don't do too badly, do you, Father? You can see God all the time. [*The Priest drains his glass in one go.*] Down the hatch! Think nobody'll notice if you knock it back in one go?!

DIMITRI. [*Giving the Priest money*] Next year at seven in the evening.

PRIEST. Say no more.

DIMITRI. Don't you "say no more" me! More ***will*** be said otherwise.

PRIEST. God willing, we'll still all be here next year. God be with you.

MARIA. And with you, Father.

[*Exit the Priest. Maria sees him out.*]

ANDREI. [*To Simon*] Why did you say your name with the dear departed?

SIMON. Just in case.

[*Maria comes back. Atso is with her.*]

MARIA. Come in, Atso, come in.

ATSO. I won't come in. I just wanted to have a quick word with Andrei.

[*Andrei goes up to Atso. They talk. Pause.*]

ANDREI. Mom, I'm going out.

MARIA. What, you too?

ANDREI. I've got to. It's just the way it's turned out.

MARIA. What d'you mean, the way it's turned out? Things are always turning out like this. Come in, Atso, don't stand in the doorway. It's our saint's day. Have some of the bread. Have a drink.

ATSO. We're in a hurry, Auntie Maria.

MARIA. I know you're in a hurry. You always are. Nobody ever seems to get things done any other way. Where are you going?

ATSO. It can't wait.

MARIA. You'll be back for dinner, won't you?

ATSO. I think so. I don't know. I don't believe we'll be long.

MARIA. You think. You don't know. You don't believe.

ATSO. [*To Stevo*] The truck I drive is in for an overhaul at your place. Do a good job, won't you?

STEVO. Don't give it a second thought. We're the best.

SIMON. You won't even recognize it when ***they've*** finished with it.

ATSO. That truck's my bread and butter.

DIMITRI. You're off to start a strike, are you?

ANDREI. That's right. Want to come? [*Pause*] OK. Bye.

[*Exit Andrei and Atso.*]

MARIA. Goodbye. [*Pause*] Looks like you're the only one staying home tonight, Simon. Why don't you give your wife a treat? Take her out dancing?

SIMON. I'm so drunk it doesn't make much difference what I do.

MARIA. [*To Stevo*] Lily came round.

STEVO. I'm not interested.

MARIA. She asked if she could help.

STEVO. I said I wasn't interested.

MARIA. She said to say hello. [*Stevo pointedly leaves the room. Pause.*] When you were little, I used to give you all a bath before Saint Iliya's Eve, put on your new clothes, and put you to bed. You couldn't get to sleep and would giggle together till all hours. You'd always be dipping into the food for the guests.

It simmered away in the pots all night. But now you don't laugh any more. And you eat out.

[*Pause. Dimitri is carving a piece of wood with a penknife. Vera is sweeping up. Maria sits and stares into space. Pause.*]

SIMON. [*Singing*]

Six for the months in half a year
Five for the fingers on a hand
Four for the teats on a cow
Three for the legs on a stool
Two for the eyes in a head
One for the nightingale that sings
Early in the month of May.

SCENE TWO

[*The railroad station café. Herzog is sitting drinking coffee. Pause. Sivitch comes up to the table, sits down beside him and picks up his drink.*]

SIVITCH. It's another half hour late.

HERZOG. Half an hour ago it was another half hour late.

SIVITCH. Trains. Have another drink.

HERZOG. I've had three coffees already. I'm ready to burst. People in this town are drinking, eating, and dancing as if tomorrow's going to be the end of the world. Which it might be, of course. The way things are going, we may well be at the end. The last great explosion. Planet Earth shot out from the gullet of a monster cannon. The last magnificent seconds in which everything will be possible.

SIVITCH. Everything's already possible now.

HERZOG. Not for me. I have terrible constipation. Spent half my life sitting on the john. You've no idea what I go through. Of course, it does give me time to reflect on things, but that's not altogether pleasant, either. I don't understand this visit from Mr. Klaus. I feel like a village schoolteacher with an inspector coming from the big city. I have a strange sense of foreboding about the whole thing. And I think I'm going to need your help.

SIVITCH. I'm at your service, Sir. [*Raising his glass*] Your good health.

HERZOG. And yours. Whenever I drink to someone's health in this smug way, I half expect someone to come up behind me and split my head open with a club.

SIVITCH. You have nothing to fear in this backwater.

HERZOG. Fear doesn't depend on real danger. I wonder why it doesn't say in the letter how long Mr. Klaus will be staying. If it was an ordinary visit, it'd last the usual three days. Did Stevo Andreyevitch look over the accounts?

SIVITCH. Yes. Rather carelessly. I had to go through them again myself. It's not the first time he's made mistakes which show he doesn't place much value on your goodwill towards him.

HERZOG. He seems an honest enough lad to me, and a bright one, too.

SIVITCH. You know best, Sir. I may be wrong. Though I'm not usually in these things. In any case, he gets on my nerves.

HERZOG. Well, at least the books are all right, aren't they?

SIVITCH. Yes.

HERZOG. I keep thinking something's not all right. I wake up in the mornings and I feel fine until I remember what's not all right for the day. There's always something for me to latch on to.

SIVITCH. You're overdoing things, Mr. Herzog. You need a rest.

HERZOG. Ah, if only I ***could*** take a rest. I need to have too much to do so I've got a reason for being so keyed-up all the time. Leave me with nothing to do for just two days and I'll go off into a panic.

SIVITCH. I could hold out much longer than that. Just keep the money coming in.

HERZOG. I give you enough, don't I? If you take care of Klaus, we can no doubt agree on a little extra. Sniff out what he wants. You're an old hand at that kind of thing. Your brother does it officially.

SIVITCH. Mr. Herzog, I like to know as much as possible. If I can sell that knowledge as well, so much the better. Nowadays everything's up for sale. Even things people think money can't buy. They're usually the cheapest of all.

HERZOG. Everybody must have arrived at home by now and be waiting. Everything'll be getting cold. There's something else on my mind, too, Mr. Sivitch. We haven't expanded the premises. We've been dragging our feet for six months now, even though we had definite instructions. We need an extra 400 square yards.

SIVITCH. I've brought the matter up several times, Mr. Herzog.

HERZOG. Should have listened to you. If we'd made that addition, the place might have made a better impression on Mr. Klaus.

SIVITCH. On the other hand, we may be overestimating this, Mr. Klaus. What if he's just a simple tourist nearing retirement, traveling through Europe on his expense account, without a clue in his head? He'll wonder how on earth he landed up in this backwater, pack his bags again, and go straight back home.

HERZOG. And what if he's a precise and cynical German with a couple of fangs sticking out of his mouth? Who I'm patiently waiting to meet at the station? All I need do now is prostrate myself before him like a red carpet. Please be so kind as to go and ask once more when this modern marvel of a train is due to arrive.

SIVITCH. [*Getting up*] Of course.

SCENE THREE

[*Herzog's house. A richly furnished drawing room. Sara is playing the piano. The Guests, glasses in hand, are listening to her. She finishes the piece and they applaud. Sara goes up to Stevo.*]

STEVO. Bravo. Wonderful.

SARA. It was abominable. Get me a drink. [*Stevo, somewhat embarrassed, pours her a drink.*] Cheers. Where does music live?

STEVO. I beg your pardon?

SARA. Literature lives on paper, paintings on canvas, but what about music? Where does music live?

STEVO. Well . . . er . . .

SARA. Well what? Don't tell me you know. What kind of music do you like?

STEVO. Beethoven.

SARA. What of Beethoven's?

STEVO. Everything.

SARA. What in particular?

STEVO. Hard to choose.

SARA. Exert yourself a little.

STEVO. Well, perhaps the piece you were just playing.

SARA. That was Chopin.

STEVO. Sounded like Beethoven.

SARA. It didn't bear the slightest resemblance to Beethoven. Where on earth do you live, Mr. Andreyevitch?!

STEVO. In Debarmaalo. Where your father's business is. I live right next door to it.

SARA. What's life like in Debarmaalo?

STEVO. Oh, it goes on. Much the same as elsewhere.

SARA. How long have you been working for my father?

STEVO. A year now.

SARA. And this is the first time you've been to our house?

STEVO. I've been here twice before. I brought some papers back for your father. I stayed for coffee once. I saw ***you*** that time, too. You were going up the stairs. You looked at me. I nodded to greet you, but you went on up as if you hadn't noticed me. As if you'd been looking right through me. I blushed. That's the way I am. Your father saw it all, but he pretended he hadn't. Your father's a wonderful man. He's helped me a lot to find my way in life, to find myself, if I may make so bold. When I remember that a year ago I was just an ordinary small-town boy, without work or prospects, and when I compare myself with what I am today, I can see how I've advanced. And it's mainly thanks to your father, Mr. Herzog. I do my best to justify his good opinion of me.

SARA. I don't find that in the least interesting. You were talking about prospects. What exactly would those prospects of yours be, Mr. Andreyevitch?

[*The main door opens. Herzog, Sivitch, and Klaus come in. The Guests get up and clap. They get into a receiving line. Klaus goes along it, greeting each in turn. A liveried servant presents them to him. Herzog and Sivitch go off to one side.*]

HERZOG. My worst predictions are coming true only too quickly. After all that time on the train, his first thoughts are of work. Hardly has he stepped onto the platform than he wants to see our premises. And the first thing he mentions is the expansion.

SIVITCH. Don't forget he's from Germany.

HERZOG. How could I ever forget ***that***?

[*They rejoin the guests just as Stevo is being presented to Klaus.*]

STEVO. How do you do. Stevo Andreyevitch. Office manager at the dealership.

HERZOG. One of my best men.

KLAUS. What did you say your name was?

STEVO. Stevo Andreyevitch, Mr. Klaus.

KLAUS. Stevo. That would be short for Stefan.

HERZOG. Well done, Mr. Klaus. You speak Serbian better than we do. This young man speaks excellent German. He translates most of our correspondence.

KLAUS. *Och, wirklich?*

STEVO. *Nein, nein. Mein Deutsch ist nicht gut.*

KLAUS. *Aber ich glaube doch. Möchten Sie etwas trinken?*

STEVO. *Rot Wein, bitte.*[2]

---

2. "Oh, really?" "No no. My German is not good." "But I believe it is. Would you like to drink something?" "Red wine, please."

[*Klaus pours him a glass of red wine. They raise their glasses to each other and drink.*]

KLAUS. You must have been to Germany?

STEVO. I'm afraid not, Mr. Klaus.

KLAUS. No? With such good knowledge of German you haven't been on any kind of internship?

HERZOG. You force me to reveal a little secret, Mr. Klaus. We are very seriously thinking of sending Mr. Andreyevitch on an internship to the Head Office in Berlin.

KLAUS. I hope you'll do so as soon as possible. So, how do you like working for Mr. Herzog?

STEVO. It's hard to find the words.

KLAUS. Is it so terrible?

STEVO. Oh no! On the contrary! On the contrary!

[*They all laugh.*]

KLAUS. Good wine.

HERZOG. My own home brew.

KLAUS. That's not usually a recommendation. But this is good. I like good wine. I like everything good.

HERZOG. Who doesn't?

KLAUS. There are those who don't. Indeed there are. Such as Mr. Sivitch, who's not drinking anything.

SIVITCH. I'll have a glass with dinner, Mr. Klaus.

KLAUS. Oh dear. Of course. I'm keeping you from dinner. You must all be hungry by now. But it's not my fault. It's your

Royal Yugoslav Railroad. The transport system is in a sad state here. And this town doesn't seem up to much. True enough, I've only been here a couple of hours, and I have no right to say anything without knowing more about it, but from what I've seen so far, I'm not impressed. What's your opinion, Mr. Andreyevitch? You were born here, of course, and you have a different perspective on things. But the station and the streets — it's all dirty and smells of the farmyard. I'm taking rather a liberty in telling you my first impression, but there it is. Well, shall we sit down to dinner, gentlemen?

[*They take their places at the ready-laid tables. Klaus puts Stevo next to him and Sara sits on Stevo's other side. Herzog gets to his feet.*]

HERZOG. Ladies and gentlemen, it's my pleasure and honor to propose a toast to our guest from Germany, Mr. Hermann Klaus.

[*They all rise, raise their glasses, and drink.*]

SCENE FOUR

[*A room. Darkness. The door opens. Enter Sara. She turns the light on. Stevo follows her in.*]

SARA. This is my room. We met only two hours ago and here we are already, alone in my very own room. How do you like that? [*Pause*] You give me a knowing smile. That explains you very well, Mr. Andreyevitch. It tells me more about you than you could yourself.

STEVO. And what exactly does it tell you about me?

SARA. What I'd already heard about you from my father.

STEVO. Your father's talked to you about me?

SARA. Better not ask what he said.

STEVO. Something bad?

SARA. Bad? I don't know what you'd call bad in such a context.

STEVO. Feel free to tell me.

SARA. Oh! You said that in such an offhand way, it sounds as if you couldn't care less what my father might have said about you. Very well, then. He said you were a typical Balkan barbarian. [*Pause*] No comment?

STEVO. What is there to say? [*Pause*] I think he's right.

SARA. Why are you like that, Mr. Andreyevitch? Why don't you stick up for yourself? If someone says something nice about you, you have grave doubts whether you deserve such praise and you brush it off easily. Whereas if someone attacks you, you immediately think they're right, and you retreat and throw in the towel. Why? Why should my father be right? What does my father know about you to be able to say anything at all? Why don't you have a higher regard for yourself? Why is it only someone who insults you who manages to win your genuine respect? I was lying to you. My father never said you were a barbarian. On the contrary. He once spoke of you as a capable young man from Debarmaalo who'll go far. That sounds a bit better, doesn't it? [*Pause*] Doesn't it?

STEVO. Much better.

SARA. I was lying again. My father's never told me anything about you. We're hardly on speaking terms. I didn't know you even existed until tonight. But now I know. And I wonder whether it might not prove some consolation.

STEVO. My food is pain, my smiles but tears,
Neither life nor death afford me respite,
You, lady, are the cause of my plight.

SARA. What was that?

STEVO. A poem.

SARA. Yours?

STEVO. Yes.

SARA. You write?

STEVO. A little.

SARA. How did it go? Say it again.

STEVO. That was just the end of a longer poem.

SARA. Recite the whole of it to me.

STEVO. I don't know it by heart. I've got it at home.

SARA. What kind of a poet are you, not carrying your poems about with you? All right. Recite the end bit again.

STEVO. *My food is pain, my smiles but tears,*
Neither life nor death afford me respite,
You, lady, are the cause of my plight.

SARA. Marvelous lines. [*Pause*] Pity they're not yours. That's the last tercet of a sonnet by Francesco Petrarch. [*Pause*.]

STEVO. You're the first one to recognize them. For years now I've been saying those lines to all the girls I meet.

SARA. That's the first honest thing you've said all evening. All the rest has been a lie which you use so often you've begun to believe it yourself. You've done enough trying to impress me with your intellectual abilities. You're no intellectual. Which doesn't mean you haven't got other qualities. Perhaps more important than the intellectual ones.

STEVO. Aren't you sort of jumping to conclusions?

SARA. Doesn't one always?

STEVO. Everybody has something which isn't immediately obvious.

SARA. Well, they can keep it to themselves. I'm not interested in what you think of yourself, but in what ***I*** think of you. Life is all at first sight. People fall in love at first sight. Murder each other at first sight. All wars are at first sight. Then there was Mr. Klaus. He took a liking to you at first sight and monopolized you. Didn't let me get a word in edgeways. [*Pause*] I had to touch you under the table.

STEVO. I thought I'd die. I was listening to Klaus but I couldn't take in a word he said. My mind was on you. I couldn't believe what was happening to me. I'm not worthy of you.

SARA. I was expecting you to say that. Your working-class inferiority complex wags its finger at you and warns you that Sara Herzog is forbidden fruit you don't deserve. Nobody is ever worthy of anything. Everybody grabs whatever they can lay their hands on. They're all vultures under their thin veneer of good breeding. Starting with me.

STEVO. It's just that I didn't expect you to behave like that.

SARA. Mr. Andreyevitch, if I were to behave as you expect me to, first of all, you wouldn't be here and, secondly, you wouldn't have the slightest chance of going to bed with me. So leave my behavior out of it and say something simple. Or just say nothing. That can be a relief in these nightmarish times. [*Pause.*]

STEVO. The same day I saw you that first time I broke off with my girlfriend, Lily. The next day I enrolled for dancing classes at the School in Aroesti Alley.

SARA. I like various pastimes, but not dancing. I go in for other forms of recreation. I asked you to say something simple, not that you fell in love with me at first sight.

STEVO. All right, then. It makes me happy to be here with you.

SARA. That's ***too*** simple. It may be honest, but that's what makes it sound pathetic. Nobody's happy. Everybody thinks someone else, in some other place, is happy, and using up the happiness meant for them. And they all smile in an ugly, affected way, and quietly drag their despair along behind them. And nobody can manage to love the people who are in love with ***them***, nor to win over the people who hate them. Do you masturbate often? [*Pause*] I do. Five times a day. I'd masturbate my life away if there weren't other boring things I have to do.

[*She uncovers one of her breasts, takes his hand and places it over the breast. Stevo looks flabbergasted. Sara closes her eyes and bites his hand. Then she opens her eyes and buttons up her dress again. Pause. They look at each other. Sivitch enters the room without knocking.*)

SIVITCH. Oh. Excuse me.

SARA. Why bother to excuse yourself when you don't even take the trouble to knock?

SIVITCH. I was looking everywhere for you . . .

SARA. And you didn't expect to find me in my room, of all places!

SIVITCH. Mr. Klaus is tired and wants to go now. He'd like to say goodbye. Especially to you . . . Mr. Andreyevitch.

SARA. We're just coming.

[*Exit Sivitch. He closes the door behind him.*]

STEVO. If he'd come a minute earlier . . .

SARA. Mr. Sivitch is old enough to have seen a naked woman before and I don't imagine the sight of a woman's breast would excite him much. Especially not mine. I hope one day they'll do ***it*** in the streets, and it won't be such a mystery anymore — which we have to waste so much time and energy over. Shall we go?

STEVO. When can I see you again?

SARA. Why do you think you have the right to see me again? After you, Mr. Andreyevitch.

[*Exit Stevo. Sara goes out after him, turning off the light.*]

SCENE FIVE

[*The main room in the Andreyevitch's house. Darkness. The door opens and Stevo enters. He turns the light on. Simon is sitting at the table, drunk, with a bottle beside him.*]

SIMON. [*Singing*]

Oh, moany, moany, moan and a-groany, groan
And a la-la-la, and a ha-ha-ha,
Oodle noodle noodle noodle, oodle poodle poodle poodle,
And a louse louse louse, Mickey Mouse.

STEVO. What're you doing?

SIMON. Trying to hatch some eggs.

STEVO. I thought you were afraid of the dark.

SIMON. I'm afraid of the light, too.

STEVO. How did it go?

SIMON. What?

[*Pause. Stevo sits down and pours himself a rakia. He starts reading the newspaper.*]

STEVO. All asleep, are they? [*Pause*] "National Theater. A performance of *The Migrant Workers* in honor of the Catering Association Congress." That was for you, and you didn't go. They must have canceled the whole thing. "People's University. Lecture on kidney stones, with slides." That was for Andrei. Good for general knowledge. "All-night pharmacy — Davchevitch, 42, King Peter's Street." "The Marger Inn. We are proud to announce the arrival of Madam Militsa Militchevitch, the famous singer of Russian ballads, classics, and love songs. Desirous of affording our customers the best possible entertainment without counting the cost, we have also engaged the services of Miss Katya Maturshka." It doesn't say what ***she's*** been engaged for. [*Throwing down the paper*] Simon, do you realize that we in the 20th century have a better life than all the billions of people who lived before us? In the 11th century, for example, or under the Turks? Now we've got newspapers, cars, electricity — and we take it all for granted. But in the 11th century they didn't have anything. Nothing at all! Just darkness and people living in the ground, like worms.

SIMON. Don't get too carried away.

STEVO. I'm suffocating here, Simon.

SIMON. Your precious 20th century will be the death of you. And your precious Herzog.

STEVO. Mr. Herzog will be my savior! A savior only appears once in your life. If you don't follow him, you're finished. That same Herzog made me office manager from a coffee-boy in a year! If he wants to be the death of me, then he seems to be going the wrong way about it! One year in the job, 1700 salary. You've been working all those years, and how much do you get?! You still think of Stevo as a kid. But I'm my own man now. I'm not the same Stevo you remember from ten years ago. You can forget about ***him***. Stevo's someone else.

SIMON. People are always the same. They're born one way and they die that way.

STEVO. OK. If I'm the same Stevo I was as a kid, how come I didn't know how to swim then and now I do?! If you'd thrown me in the water then, I'd've drowned.

SIMON. You'd ***still*** drown.

STEVO. Now I can swim.

SIMON. How long for? Ten minutes? Ten hours? Ten days? However long you can swim for, you'll still drown. Just the same as if you hadn't swum at all. [*Andrei comes out of an adjoining room, having just got out of bed. Pause.*] We're talking about the 20th century.

ANDREI. Oh, so ***that's*** why you don't want to go to bed. Afraid of oversleeping and missing the century?! Might be a better idea to get a bit of sleep and be sober when you're awake. [*Pause*] I met Lily. She asked after you. Says hello.

STEVO. I couldn't care less.

ANDREI. She knows. She said, "I know he couldn't care less, but say hello to him from me anyway."

STEVO. There. Take Lily for example. Nice girl. Housewife type. If I took it into my head to marry her, we'd have the wedding tomorrow. And the fact that I'm avoiding her and don't want to see her doesn't mean I've taken a hundred percent dislike to her. I may like her all of 49 percent. All very well, but if I happen to like some other girl 51 percent, that two percent difference will tip the scales and Lily loses out.

SIMON. Wicked little two percent!

STEVO. Two percent can mean a hell of a lot in life.

SIMON. Nobody loves anybody any more. Only the dogs and the gypsies are making love. The rest are working out percentages.

ANDREI. How was the reception?

STEVO. Wonderful. Champagne corks popping, women's

dresses rustling, eloquent toasts — culture, civilization, the 20th century!

ANDREI. In another hour or so the hungry workers will be setting off in their clogs across Stone Bridge to the cigarette factory. The unemployed will be waiting for work in the square. That's the 20th century too!

STEVO. Don't try to cast wool over my eyes with your social poetry! Why don't you go and get killed in Spain if you're so cut up about it?! I'll send you a postcard from Berlin. One day the newspapermen will be asking you if you knew Stevo Andreyevitch. And Stevo will be drinking his *Rotwein* in Hamburg, Marburg, or Würzburg. I owe it to myself. I often look at these hands of mine. And I feel what power there is in them! Know what I could do with these hands? Wonders. I could work wonders! And you want me to put them in my pockets, get married, make babies, and start going to pot. Well, the hell with the lot of you! I won't stop till I grab Fortune by the collar. OK, it's a risk, but you can't sit down to dinner without taking a risk. It's all or nothing. Stevo Andreyevitch from Debarmaalo now sits astride his white charger, his hair streaming in the wind, his lance at the ready, and gallops towards his prospects on the horizon. As for you, gentlemen, go on waiting at tables and flirting with revolution. Stevo Andreyevitch has no time left to consider your cases. He's too busy with his own. He therefore rises [*getting up*] and goes to take a well-earned rest.

[*Stevo leaves the room. Pause. Andrei gets up and leaves, too. Pause. Simon looks at his hands for a long time. Pause. Enter Vera. She puts her arms round Simon. He weeps and Vera strokes his head. He calms down and looks at her.*]

SIMON. Vera. Please. Give me a little baby boy.

SCENE SIX

[*Vera is at the house of the Wise Woman.*]

WISE WOMAN. Lie down. [*Vera lies down.*] Spread your legs. [*Vera spreads her legs.*] You said never once on purpose.

VERA. No. I can't keep it.

WISE WOMAN. What does the doctor say?

VERA. Stay in bed for nine months.

WISE WOMAN. Why don't you?

VERA. Somebody's got to take care of the house for nine months.

WISE WOMAN. Let your husband do it.

VERA. My husband can't even take care of himself.

WISE WOMAN. You should've come before.

VERA. Do something, for God's sake!

WISE WOMAN. There's nothing God can do here. [*She lights the fire under a cauldron full of water and opens her mouth wide over the water. She crosses herself and spits into the water.*] Heart on a stake. Heart on a pitchfork. Heart on a scythe. Open up the Great Eye to see, and what do you see? A worm slithering in the barren water. A sky of slime sticking to the roof of the mouth — neither here nor there. A fish bubble about to burst. A brain open to the ungodly winds. Devils, devils, on stumpy winged horses. Sinews bared and cut, wounds neglected and festering, hundreds of secrets untold. Enough to make you rip open your breast, put out your eyes. Bind the babe, hold the poor wretch up till its time comes to come out and rejoice. [*She puts out the fire and sprinkles Vera's stomach with a little water from the cauldron.*] Go down to the Vardar and tie rags to the bushes. Light a candle to Saint Petka, a big one. Take one of your husband's shirts to Kapishtets. And you owe me twenty dinars.

VERA. Will it do any good?

WISE WOMAN. I don't know.

VERA. So why bother with all this?

WISE WOMAN. To get it over with.

SCENE SEVEN

[*Stevo writing in his office. Sivitch comes in from the adjoining office.*]

SIVITCH. Hard at it, are we? We don't let the reins of our career out of our hands for a single moment, do we? Advancing daily, aren't we? But quick success has its drawbacks. Such as getting a bit too big for our boots. And thinking we can seduce the boss's daughter. None of my business, of course. None at all. Nor the fact that your brother'll end up in jail soon if you don't bring him into line. I mean the younger one, you understand, the Communist. Your elder brother drinks so much he's a lost cause, isn't he? I'm serious about Andrei, Mr. Andreyevitch. Some people I know have got him in their sights, and that could well prove dangerous. I suppose you're wondering how I know all this. Easy. You can hear what your parents are deciding to have for lunch today through this wall. These are thin walls. Easy to knock down. I mean literally. Even Herzog won't be able to save you then. Goodbye, Mr. Andreyevitch. Have a nice lunch.

[*Exit. Stevo looks pensive. Pause. He goes on with his work. There is a knock at the door.*)

STEVO. Come in.

[*Enter Atso.*]

ATSO. Hello, Stevo.

STEVO. Hello, Atso. What's up?

ATSO. I've got problems. I've come about the truck. It's a bad business.

STEVO. Sit down. Want a cigarette?

[*Atso takes the cigarette Stevo offers him. Enter Klaus. Stevo jumps up.*]

STEVO. Sir?

KLAUS. Has Mr. Sivitch left?

STEVO. Yes. A couple of minutes ago.

KLAUS. Never mind. You just carry on. [*He starts looking through some files.*]

STEVO. [*To Atso*] What did you say the problem was?

ATSO. We had the truck in for a complete overhaul and we paid for a complete overhaul, but they only put on a bit of axle grease and changed the plugs.

[*Klaus turns and gives Stevo and Atso a meaningful look. Then he turns back to the filing cabinet.*]

STEVO. Impossible.

ATSO. Unfortunately not. It's a swindle.

STEVO. Why didn't you submit a complaint when you came to pick it up?

ATSO. Why the devil should I? I saw it looking all shiny. You don't expect me to take the engine out and start making complaints, do you? Then this morning it starts rattling just like before. I know they all cheat, but you guys've really overdone it! You give me a bill for changing the piston rods, the gaskets, the bearings, the clutch, and the shock absorbers — and I open it up and there are all the old parts sitting there. All a pack of lies!

STEVO. I don't know how this can have happened, but we'll look into it.

ATSO. Look, Stevo, stop talking to me like a stranger and don't try to brush me off with these official phrases. Just tell me whose neck to wring for this business. My boss is really taking it out on me. I'm responsible for that truck. He says he paid for the overhaul, now it's my problem. I was supposed to drive to Vranje this morning. That's a whole day's pay down the drain. I've got a kid at home.

STEVO. Please don't make my position more difficult than it already is. I said we would see to it and sort it all out.

ATSO. Well, go on then! ***See*** to it and ***sort*** it all out!

STEVO. There's a set procedure to follow.

ATSO. I need a truck I can count on!

STEVO. All right. Just don't start shouting, because, if we look at it from the strictly legal point of view, you accepted receipt of the truck and that's where our responsibility for it ends. You signed that everything was in order.

ATSO. But it isn't, is it? Now I'm supposed to pay for another overhaul out of my own pocket, am I? And stand over the mechanics to make sure they don't pinch any screws?

STEVO. Well, ***I'm*** certainly not going to foot the bill.

ATSO. There are about a hundred people in Skopje I've been meaning to blow to kingdom come, Stevo. You've just become number hundred and one.

[*Exit Klaus.*]

STEVO. Listen, Atso!

ATSO. Oh! So I'm Atso now, am I?! And while that creep was in here you didn't want to know me. What have you got to say?

STEVO. Look, Atso. I've got nothing to do with all this, honest.

ATSO. Well, you sit here preening yourself as office manager, you damn fool! And next time you offer somebody a cigarette, light it!

[*Atso throws down the cigarette and goes out, slamming the door behind him. Stevo looks disconcerted. Pause. Enter Klaus.*]

KLAUS. Having problems?

STEVO. No, Mr. Klaus. Everything's all right.

KLAUS. [*Looking at what Stevo has been writing*] The consignment's nearly ready, I see. Excellent. Remove these three items.

STEVO. How do you mean, Mr. Klaus?

KLAUS. Just that. Remove them. Cross them out. [*Pause*] Cross them out.

STEVO. [*Crossing them out*] Like this?

KLAUS. Like that. You see the power of the pen. What existed until a few moments ago exists no longer. And it has simply been crossed out.

STEVO. What will Mr. Herzog say when he sees it?

KLAUS. Why should he see it? [*Pause*] Business is a strange world, Mr. Andreyevitch. The most complex sphere of human activity. In the beginning was Capital. [*Looking at his watch*] Our working day is at an end. It wouldn't be a bad idea to try some of that homemade rakia you keep urging me to come and taste.

STEVO. Oh, Mr. Klaus!

KLAUS. Only I shall have to go and buy some flowers first.

STEVO. Oh, Mr. Klaus. There's no need.

KLAUS. It's the done thing.

STEVO. Oh, Mr. Klaus. You should have told me a bit earlier. They would have been better prepared.

KLAUS. I prefer the unprepared.

SCENE EIGHT

[*The Andreyevitch's house. Dimitri is carving his piece of wood, Atso and Andrei are talking together, Maria is playing Patience, Vera is washing some clothes, and Simon is asleep.*]

ATSO. And while that German was there, he didn't want to know me. Then he changed his tune.

ANDREI. Something's the matter with him.

ATSO. Something's the matter with all of us, but he's really overdoing it.

ANDREI. I'll talk to him.

ATSO. You can talk till the cows come home. What am I going to do without my truck?

ANDREI. We're going on strike anyway. We'll sort things out afterwards somehow.

ATSO. From bad to worse. Ah, Stevo, Stevo!

[*Enter Stevo.*]

STEVO. Mr. Klaus is coming! Vera, Mom, tidy the place up a bit. Ah, Atso. You're here. Simon, wake up, brother. He's gone to buy some flowers. He's coming for a rakia. Get some of last year's out. [*Exit Atso.*] Atso, don't go. Make some meze[3], too. Salad. We got any cheese?

SIMON. Who did you say was coming?

STEVO. Mr. Klaus, for a rakia!

---

3. An appetizer or snack to accompany drinking rakia, often cabbage salad, cooked meat, or cheese.

SIMON. Well, why do I have to be awake for him to have a rakia?

DIMITRI. And who invited him for a rakia?

STEVO. I did! D'you mind?

DIMITRI. No, I don't exactly ***mind***. I'm just not ***overjoyed.***

MARIA. Who's coming?

STEVO. I ***told*** you, Mom. Mr. Klaus!

MARIA. Why out of all the world is he coming to see ***us***?

STEVO. Change your scarf, for heaven's sake! Put another one on!

[*Maria goes to another room.*]

ANDREI. What shall ***I*** wear?

STEVO. Leave me alone, Andrei, for the love of God.

ANDREI. Why didn't you leave Atso alone?!

STEVO. I'll explain later.

ANDREI. I get it.

STEVO. No, you don't.

ANDREI. You're the one who doesn't get it.

STEVO. Get up, Simon! Go and get washed!

SIMON. Why don't you take that Kraut to some family you like better?

MARIA. [*With a different scarf on*] Will this one do?

STEVO. ***Yes***. Vera, get something sweet out, too.

SIMON. Get your own wife to fetch and carry for you.

VERA. Just this once, Simon.

SIMON. Just this once, just this twice, and life's gone by.

DIMITRI. Perhaps he'd like to stay for lunch, as well? I don't mind. He can stay for supper, too. And breakfast tomorrow morning.

[*Stevo looks at himself in the mirror and combs his hair. He sits down and looks at his watch. Silence. Pause. They all wait.*]

MARIA. Who are we waiting for?

DIMITRI. The devil.

MARIA. You don't wait for the devil. You shoo him away. Shoo! Shoo!

[*Pause. Silence. They go on waiting.*]

DIMITRI. You can wait for Saint Haralampi himself if you want to.

[*Dimitri goes towards the door in his wheelchair. At that very moment there is a knock at the door. Dimitri goes back to his place. Stevo jumps up and opens the door. Enter Klaus.*]

STEVO. Please come in, Mr. Klaus. Come in. This is my mother, Maria.

KLAUS. How do you do, Mrs. Andreyevitch.

[*Klaus gives Maria the flowers he is carrying, and she takes them, looking bewildered.*]

STEVO. My father, Dimitri. [*Klaus nods his head to Dimitri.*] My brother, Simon. [*Klaus nods to Simon, and Simon nods back.*] My brother, Andrei. [*The same procedure.*] And my sister-in-law, Vera. [*The same procedure.*] Please sit down.

KLAUS. Thank you. [*He sits down.*] Stevo has been so kind as to invite me to visit you several times, and I've at last managed to find the time. So this is your home. [*Looking around*] Very nice. How do you occupy yourself, Mr. Andreyevitch?

DIMITRI. Pardon? Er, I'm making a whistle.

STEVO. My father was a well-known housebuilder. My elder brother's a waiter and my younger one is an assistant in a grocery store.

KLAUS. [*To Andrei*] Where?

ANDREI. In the Jeftinotcha grocery and delicatessen.

KLAUS. By Mr. Ristitch's house? I think I saw you in there once. [*Vera is serving rakia and salad.*] Ah, so this is the famous rakia, is it? [*Taking up his glass*] Not drinking with us, Mr. Andreyevitch?

DIMITRI. No. I've already had my lunch. I have lunch early.

KLAUS. [*To Andrei*] What about you?

ANDREI. I don't drink.

KLAUS. [*To Simon*] Aren't you going to have a drink either?

SIMON. Well, just this once. Let the pig into the mosque. [*He takes a glass.*]

STEVO. To your good health, Mr. Klaus. Welcome to our home. The best of health.

KLAUS. Cheers. [*Drinking*] It really ***is*** good. Where has Mrs. Andreyevitch gone?

[*Stevo gets up to look for Maria. Maria is standing in the kitchen with the flowers still in her hand. She is trembling.*]

STEVO. What's the matter, mom? What is it?

MARIA. Wild flesh.

STEVO. What do you mean, wild flesh?! Come back. We've got a guest. [*Stevo goes back to Klaus.*] Have some meze. Please, help yourself. Perhaps you'd like something sweet. We have some excellent quince jam.

KLAUS. No, thank you. I'm fine.

STEVO. What else can we offer you?

SIMON. We could give him a song and dance.

KLAUS. Yes, indeed. I have noticed how well people sing and dance here.

SIMON. You're right. Trouble is, everybody thinks that's ***all*** we can do.

STEVO. My mother has a wonderful voice.

KLAUS. I should love to hear her sing. Might she be persuaded?

STEVO. Mom! Mom, come and give Mr. Klaus a song.

[*Maria comes out of the kitchen as if in a trance.*]

MARIA. [*Singing*] *Were I but pure clear water, Mother,*
Were I but pure clear water, oh Mother dear,
I'd know where to run.

[*Pause.*]

MARIA. Wild flesh.

[*Maria goes back into the kitchen. Pause.*]

KLAUS. Wild flesh?

STEVO. No offence meant. My mother's tired.

KLAUS. What does wild flesh mean?

STEVO. It's an old wives' tale. A silly belief that if somebody gets a hair stuck in their throat, flesh will grow around the root of the hair. Flesh which isn't human. And it'll grow so big that it'll choke them.

KLAUS. Interesting. [*Andrei downs a glass of brandy in one go.*] I thought you said you didn't drink.

ANDREI. That's right.

[*Pause. Dimitri cuts his finger while carving. He swears under his breath and sucks at his finger.*]

KLAUS. You cut yourself.

DIMITRI. Yes.

[*Dimitri drinks some rakia from the bottle and spits some back onto his finger.*]

KLAUS. I've noticed you don't speak pure Serbian.

ANDREI. We live in the Vardar Province. We speak Vardar Provincial.

KLAUS. How do you like your work in the grocery? I suppose the pay's a mere pittance and the work's hard.

ANDREI. There are plenty of unemployed.

KLAUS. Does that mean that you suppress your own dissatisfaction by comparing it with what other people have to put up with? That's rather a conservative way of looking at things, isn't it?

ANDREI. How do you like ***your*** job, Mr. Klaus?

KLAUS. Hmm. Not much. I'd prefer not to have to do any work at all. Just travel and read books.

ANDREI. That's a typical bourgeois way of thinking.

STEVO. Not now, Andrei.

KLAUS. You're right. I ***am*** bourgeois. I always have been. And I'm not ashamed of it. We're all what we are, and we have to resign ourselves to the fact.

ANDREI. On the contrary. We should all try to become what we could be.

KLAUS. That's often difficult.

ANDREI. Difficult, certainly. But feasible. Under the Turkish Empire people thought for five hundred years that they could never dream of toppling such a power, but then it rotted and fell just like a worm-eaten beam. It's true it took five hundred years, but it fell in the end. Or take Austria-Hungary. That great empire collapsed in 1918 as if it had never existed. And Mr. Ristitch's mansion on the square, which we think of as being solid and built to last forever, it'll vanish one day as if it had never existed.

KLAUS. That's what's called a dialectical interpretation of history!

SIMON. More rakia, Mr. Klaus? [*He pours himself another.*]

KLAUS. No, thank you. Well, if it took five centuries for the Turkish Empire to collapse, how long will it take for Mr. Ristitch's mansion?

SIMON. A couple of hours bashing away with picks and shovels.

KLAUS. And who's to wield the picks and shovels?

ANDREI. I, for one!

KLAUS. What have you got against Mr. Ristitch?

ANDREI. Nothing in particular. But a lot against his kind in general.

KLAUS. What exactly?

ANDREI. They drive cars.

KLAUS. That's not a sin.

ANDREI. They pass by behind their misted-up windows and look at us as if we've just crawled out from under a stone. They're always in a hurry. After breakfast they're off to lunch. And they pass by. They've been passing by us for centuries. They keep us intimidated with their speeches and rituals and dogmas. They keep us in dread of having the bread taken from our mouths, of having our houses knocked down, of having our faces smashed in. And we in our fear make way for them and tip our caps to them. And as long as we fear them, they can walk all over us. Only when we overcome our fear will we find our freedom. Freedom will be when we turn out all the chests from the damp attics, shake out all the fusty eiderdowns, wipe out all the cockroaches, cellar rats, and malaria mosquitoes. When all the houses will be painted white, all the windows thrown open, all the clothes boiled and washed in spring water, and put out in the May sunshine to dry.

SIMON. Hear, hear! And when ***I*** sit at a table in the restaurant and the boss serves ***me***!

KLAUS. That's revolution!

KLAUS. You're a poet. What you have just declaimed sounded so impressive I thought for a moment you must have learnt it by heart. [*Looking at his watch*] Well, I must be getting along. I'm expected for lunch. I don't know whether this is the best moment to mention this, but I don't see why not. Perhaps I should have talked to you about it first, Stevo. It's about the dealership premises. We're in dire need of expansion. We're under pressure from the competition. We need to face onto the main street. Your house is on the main street and is right next door to the dealership. We'd like to buy it. For a good price. I'd be grateful if you'd consider my offer.

DIMITRI. It's out of the question. [*Pause*] Out of the question.

STEVO. Just a minute, Dad.

DIMITRI. It's out of the question.

STEVO. We'll give the matter some thought, Mr. Klaus. Of course we will. We'll see.

DIMITRI. You stay out of this.

KLAUS. It was a great pleasure meeting you. Thank you. Goodbye.

STEVO. I'm sorry if anything wasn't right.

[*Klaus goes out. Stevo sees him to the door. Pause. Silence. Stevo comes back.*]

DIMITRI. When did you and he hatch ***this*** up?

STEVO. I didn't know anything about it. This is the first I've heard of it. I swear.

DIMITRI. You sell off what you've paid for and built yourself. Don't you dare touch this! This is ***mine***.

STEVO. They'll pay us for it. Over the odds.

DIMITRI. Nobody can ***pay*** me. Who's going to ***pay*** me for these legs of mine? It was ***this*** roof I fell from.

STEVO. We're not talking about your legs.

DIMITRI. Oh yes we are. I think it's precisely my legs we're talking about. And only them.

STEVO. Look. Let's be reasonable.

DIMITRI. I don't need any of your reason. Leave me alone.

STEVO. You leave ***me*** alone! All of you! I'm sick to death of you! Goddamn peasants! You cling to some worn-out old principles and customs of yours like a blind man to his stick. You made me feel ashamed in front of the man! You looked at him as if he might give you some terrible disease. You treat anything unfamiliar as cursed — alien and hostile. The main thing's to keep to what you know, stick together, be one of ***us***. But ***Europe*** is calling me, ***Europe***. While not one of you in this shitty place gives me so much as the time of day. If I could only get out of your clutches, I'd fly.

ANDREI. They'll put up a statue of you by the bridge. King Peter on his horse, King Alexander on his horse, and Stevo Andreyevitch on . . . ***his*** horse.

STEVO. You can talk. We heard ***your*** speech. You want them to throw me out of my job because of your half-witted political posturing? We've seen who ***you*** are!

ANDREI. Then let's see who ***you*** are! If you ***are*** anyone, that is! You're in with that spy.

STEVO. Klaus isn't a spy.

ANDREI. He knows Skopje better than any of us who were born here! No, no. He's not a spy — Simon is!

SIMON. Why am I a spy? I'm not a spy!

[*Enter Maria.*]

MARIA. You can't breathe with your throat swollen up, you can't sing. The flesh must be rooted out with the fingernails, and the wound burnt with red-hot embers. But all you do is quarrel. You couldn't care less. I look at you and I don't know who you are. I don't recognize anyone anymore.

STEVO. I am your son, Stevo, and this is your husband, Dimitri, and for Christ's sake tell him to let us sell this house so we can get a decent amount of money and set ourselves up somewhere else!

MARIA. Where are we moving to?

SIMON. Mars.

MARIA. Where's that?

SIMON. Over the other side of town.

STEVO. My career depends on my every move. At this moment it depends on this rotten old house.

DIMITRI. You can stuff your goddamn career up your ass! And leave this rotten old house to fall down on my back.

STEVO. What do you know about having a career, you old sod? You spent your whole life as a laborer. At the age of 26, I've got my own office!

DIMITRI. I was a master builder.

STEVO. A master builder who falls off the scaffolding! Take a look at this house you built!

DIMITRI. I built it as well as I knew how. And if you want to knock it down, get out of here and don't come back, you thankless bastard!

STEVO. Are ***you*** going to throw me out? Come on, then, get up and throw me out!

[*Stevo propels the wheelchair with Dimitri in it against the wall. Andrei goes for Stevo and punches him. Vera runs up and separates them.*]

SIMON. Leave them to it. Let them kill each other.

[*Pause.*]

DIMITRI. If I'd known how you were going to turn out, I'd've jerked off instead. You and your bloody youth. You'll lay all to waste. You don't heed God or the Devil. No order in your bodies or your minds. Any wind can take you, like headless flies. You think if it moves, you can eat it. ***Europe*** is calling you. Europe doesn't give a ***fart*** about you! You pine for Germany! And your father who lost his legs to make a home for you is pig shit, who doesn't know a thing, and is stopping Europeans making a career! You don't know how to take care of yourselves. You live on installment plans. You'll die in some hole, covered in cobwebs, your names will be forgotten, no trace will be left of you. I don't have tears to mourn you enough.

[*Andrei gets up and quickly goes out.*]

MARIA. ***Andrei!!***

SCENE NINE

[*A room in Sivitch's house. A knock at the door. Sivitch comes out of an adjoining room in a dressing gown. He opens the door.*]

STEVO. Good morning, Mr. Sivitch. I wonder if I might come in for a moment? I'd like to ask a favor of you. [*Sivitch makes way for him to enter.*] Thank you. [*Pause*] My brother's been arrested. During the strike last night. I've been to the police station. They said they haven't even counted how many have been arrested, let alone know which one Andreyevitch is. I spoke to Mr. Herzog a little while ago and he sent me to you. [*Sara comes into the room in a nightdress. She stands behind Stevo and he has not noticed her yet.*] He told me your brother works there. I did speak to Andrei when you warned me what was going on, and he promised to turn over a new leaf. I don't know how all this with the strike came about, but if you can do something now, I'm sure it won't happen again. I'll personally vouch for him. Please, Mr. Sivitch. The situation at home is unbearable. My mother wept in my arms all night. They think I'm involved in some way. As if I'm the one who had him arrested.

SIVITCH. Sara, why don't you go back to bed? Mr. Andreyevitch and I have an important matter to discuss.

[Stevo *turns round and looks at Sara in dismay.*]

STEVO. Miss Herzog.

SARA. Do sit down, Mr. Andreyevitch.

STEVO. Excuse me. I didn't know.

SARA. What didn't you know?

[*Sara goes up to Sivitch and puts her arms round him. They look at Stevo. Pause.*]

STEVO. Do you think you can help me, Mr. Sivitch?

SIVITCH. No.

STEVO. Isn't there anything you can do?

SIVITCH. No.

STEVO. Please, Mr. Sivitch.

SIVITCH. No.

[*Pause. Stevo looks at them for a few moments and then leaves. Pause. Sara makes to kiss Sivitch, but he slaps her face. She presses herself against him to avoid another slap.*]

SCENE TEN

[*Klaus's hotel room. Stevo and Klaus. There is a bottle of cognac on the table in front of them.*]

KLAUS. [*Pouring Stevo some cognac*] Actually, why not leave your brother in jail for a while?

STEVO. No more, thank you, Mr. Klaus. I've had enough.

KLAUS. Come on, young man. Have some more. Relax a little. You're very tense. As I was saying, why do you think he's better off out of prison? Perhaps he ***wants*** to be in there. Perhaps he's been deliberately working to that end. You may find it unlikely, but life is full of surprises. I've known several cases of such paradoxical logic, the inversion of normal reasoning. After all, don't forget one important factor — he's a Slav. That provides a simple answer to the question of why anybody would want to stay in jail. I call it the Slavic Masochistic Soul syndrome. When nothing is as it should be, but nobody so much as lifts their little finger to improve the situation. They even find some kind of perverse pleasure in it. And nothing has ever been as it should be in the Balkans. For as far back as twenty thousand years. If anybody has ever tried to make something of your predicament, their help has never been gratefully received. Quite the contrary. It has been rejected with suspicion. And the state of decline has continued. You are condemned to live in a state of decline. Not ***collapse***, because that's a definitive state, and not well-being — you're a long way from that — but ***decline***. A continual declining. Always in the same way. Making the same mistakes. Again and again. Stubbornly and persistently. Never learning from experience. It's becoming quite ridiculous. Why, even a performing bear can learn to ride a bicycle! You spend your youth nibbling sunflower seeds and looking at girls. You never read anything more taxing than comics about pirates. Your heroes are those idiots who committed suicide listening to that song "Sad Sunday," and that petty criminal, Kiro Atevitch. You lounge around bars all day and yet you don't know how to drink. Your eyes go all glazed after a couple of rakias, you start hugging and kissing each other, and shaking your fists at the whole world. You don't see what people are doing behind your backs any more. Either don't drink, or learn to take alcohol better. Your brother Andrei fits this classification to a tee — and you're not far removed from it, though you are a slightly different matter. You must do something with yourself. You must free yourself from the fetters of your masochism and let your heart lead you. The heart is never masochistic — it's full of joy. The ***head*** is what causes the problems. I'm aware, of course, that there's something else gnawing at you: you don't know exactly what it is your heart wants. But it's a false dilemma. You've never let it ***tell*** you. You keep it smothered in your inside pocket and then complain about not being able to follow your innermost instincts. Leave your heart free to breathe and it'll reveal itself to you. Then, of course, there'll be a string of ***other*** complications. Such as your lack of a feeling of belonging, of tradition. How far back can you trace your family tree? What were the names of your great-grandparents? I don't suppose you have the faintest idea. Whereas I do. My family tree has been meticulously recorded since the 14th century. People may think those are not important differences, but on the other hand . . . on the other hand, tradition and culture belong to the whole world, to all of humanity. Goethe is just as much ***yours*** as mine. And you are a handsome, bright young man, marked out for success. We'll go back to Germany together. You can perfect your German staying on my estate by the Rhine. And your taste, too. After a couple of months, you'll be able to distinguish the slightest nuances of bouquet between two wines which are almost exactly the same. You can get your body into shape swimming and playing tennis, improve your mind with selected readings. You will relish it all. And stop being afraid of yourself. You'll become mature and sophisticated, sure in your opinions and decisions — in your every move. And I'll be there with you, following your progress. We'll make a triumphant return to Yugoslavia. You try to write poetry. But how do you expect to have the muses smile on you in the dirt and squalor of Skopje? I believe simplicity and rusticity can be an inspiration, but only when filtered and purified through education and culture. In other words, one should by all means keep one's innocence, but enhance it with experience. You're still in the stage of ***naïve*** innocence. You haven't yet lost your hymen. That's rather a vulgar sexual image to use, but it's precise, nevertheless. You need to be raped. You find this embarrassing, but I mean to embarrass you. You need somebody to grab you by the hair, break your bones, open up your eyes and ears and nose, stir you up, mince you, pound you, and remold you into a new human being. You already have eyes, ears, and a nose, but you don't ***use*** them. They're simply there for decoration. You don't see anything or hear anything. You live in a moronic, hypnotized, provincial state of semi-consciousness, waiting for a revelation, a miracle, for the great moment when your life will finally begin. And you doubt more and more whether that moment will ever come. Years go by — today, tomorrow — and suddenly life is over. You look around you and see a wasteland. The revelation never came and you are stuck fast in a rut. So off you go to the nearest bar and drink with whoever happens to be there. Drink to your blurred visions of what you might once have been. But I'm offering you something else. I'm offering you the chance of severing the umbilical cord tying you to this tribe of yours and of rising to achieve an identity of your own. And then you can return to the tribe and lead it to heights it could never have achieved on its own. I'm offering you my humble assistance. I'm offering you my hand.

[*Klaus takes Stevo's hand. Pause. They look at each other. Pause. He takes hold of Stevo below the table. Pause. Stevo is dumbfounded.*]

STEVO. I'll have to be going now, Mr. Klaus. [*Pause*] I have to go. [*Pause*] Mr. Klaus. [*Pause*] Let me go, Mr. Klaus. [*Pause*] Please let me go. [*Pause*] Please let me go, Mr. Klaus.

[*Klaus releases him. Stevo gets up and leaves the room in a daze. Pause. Klaus finishes his drink.*]

SCENE ELEVEN

[*The visiting room of a prison. Andrei and Stevo. Andrei has been badly beaten.*]

STEVO. Hello, Andy. [*Andrei nods his head.*] You all right? [*Andrei nods his head.*] I couldn't come before. They're not allowing visitors. I had a hard time just getting these five minutes. It smells funny in here. I've been finding out the best people to see to get you out of here. Everything'll be all right. [*Andrei nods.*] Mom and Dad are bearing up. They send their love. And some food and cigarettes. I had to leave them at the door. They'll give them to you later. [*Andrei nods.*] Guess what. Vera's expecting. She's decided to stay in bed and make sure she doesn't lose it this time. We'll be having a nephew . . . or niece. They've given Simon the sack. I suppose he was drunk. He won't say. He's not in Skopje. He's gone on an army training exercise. They're always having exercises and maneuvers these days. I'm afraid they might haul ***me*** in for one soon. I'm sure they'll let you out in a day or two. We'll go down to our beach and have a swim.

[*Andrei tries to say something.*]

STEVO. What did you say? I didn't get that.

ANDREI. [*Speaking with difficulty*] They're sending us to a prison camp. Atso's here, too. He said to say hello and no hard feelings. Under the threshold of the front door at home you'll find a revolver and a thousand pamphlets I hid there. Give them to Milo down the road. Give my love to Mom and Dad. And Vera. And Simon, when he gets back. [*He starts crying.*] I must hold out. I must hold out to the end. I've swallowed a hair, too. I must spit it out! [*He pulls himself together.*] There's going to be a war soon. We'll be able to see things more clearly. We'll meet again in another time. Goodbye. Be brave.

STEVO. ***You*** be brave.

ANDREI. You're the one who needs to be brave. I've made my choice.

[*Andrei turns and goes out*.]

SCENE TWELVE

[*Herzog's office. Klaus is sitting behind the desk and talking on the telephone.*]

KLAUS. Thank you, Mr. Zhivkovitch. Yes, yes. I have all the documents. It's just that this is an urgent matter. It must be done as soon as possible. This evening, if possible. I know that's asking a great deal, Mr. Zhivkovitch, otherwise I wouldn't require your assistance. Yes. [*Pause. Enter Sivitch.*] Yes. Excellent. Mr. Sivitch will be coming to pick up your authorization paper. Excellent. I am forever in your debt, Mr. Zhivkovitch. I shall have to find some way to repay you. Goodbye. Goodbye then, Mr. Zhivkovitch. [*Replacing the receiver*] Send twenty men with picks and shovels to knock down number 18 this evening. When I come into this office tomorrow morning, I want to see an empty space out there on my right. [*Tossing an envelope to Sivitch*] Fifty thousand. Give it to them. They're on their own now. We tried being nice.

SIVITCH. What's Mr. Herzog going to say?

KLAUS. What business is it of his? We're not knocking ***his*** house down. At least, not ***yet***. With all the girls to choose from in Skopje, why on earth did you decide to have an affair with his daughter Sara? She's a ***Jew***, for heaven's sake. Why are you looking at me so stupidly? You don't read the papers, Mr. Sivitch, the papers. If you want to stay in my employ, you'll have to be better informed.

SIVITCH. In ***your*** employ? What about Mr. Herzog?

KLAUS. Mr. Herzog is now a senile retired Jew.

SIVITCH. Who's retiring him?

KLAUS. The Third Reich.

[*Klaus shows Sivitch a letter.*]

SIVITCH. [*Reading*] What about Stevo Andreyevitch?

KLAUS. I am personally retiring ***him***.

[*Enter Herzog.*]

HERZOG. What's going on, Mr. Klaus? You phone me at this hour and give no explanation whatsoever. I thought there must be a fire. I have trouble with my stomach, you know. I'm not at anyone's beck and call. Sivitch, make some coffee.

SIVITCH. ***I*** think we've run out, Mr. Herzog.

HERZOG. ***So***, Mr. Klaus?

KLAUS. So, Mr. Herzog, I've been going over the documents of this dealership in the last few days.

HERZOG. Who gave you permission?

KLAUS. Nobody.

HERZOG. Mr. Klaus, to the best of my knowledge, you came here on a simple business visit.

KLAUS. To the best of ***your*** knowledge! But to the best of ***my*** knowledge, Mr. Herzog, you have been remiss in representing the company's interests. Very remiss.

HERZOG. Really? Has anyone asked you for an opinion?

KLAUS. Yes.

HERZOG. May I inquire ***who***?

KLAUS. No, you may not.

[*Klaus gives Herzog the letter. Herzog reads it. He goes white.*]

HERZOG. You've had this letter from the beginning.

KLAUS. There's a certain pleasure in keeping a secret which might turn out to be useful.

HERZOG. What am I supposed to do now?

KLAUS. Have a cup of coffee with us. Would you make us some, Mr. Sivitch?

SIVITCH. Certainly, Mr. Klaus . . . Sir.

SCENE THIRTEEN

[A brothel. Simon in a room with Mimi, a prostitute. He is lying with his head in her lap, dressed in a soldier's uniform. She is stroking his hair.]

SIMON. [*Singing*]

Red are the ribbons, tied all in a bow,
Give them to Simon Boshkovitch and Co.,
Simon, Simon, when you go to town,
Mimi will love you till the sun goes down.

Red are the ribbons, tied all in a bow,
Give them to Mimi Boshkovitch and Co.,
Mimi, Mimi, when you go to town,
Simon will love you till the sun goes down.

MIMI. Ah, Simon! You're just as sentimental an old fool as I am.

SIMON. At this very moment all the privates and corporals and lieutenants and captains are out scouring Skopje for Private Simon Andreyevitch of the reserves — and Simon is dozing away in Mimi Boshkovitch's lap! I don't give a damn. They were trying to kill me. I felt this lump in my throat here again, right here, and I go to the Captain and I say, Sir, it's like this, Sir, and so on and so forth, and can I see the doctor, and he says, No, you damn well can't, this is an army maneuver, not a goddamn school picnic. And I say, I can't breathe, I'll die. Go on then, die, he says. Well, I'm damned if I'm going to die. Let ***him*** die. So I sneak out under the wire. It's still cramping my breathing, right here.

MIMI. You've been drinking a lot. Why don't you go home and sleep it off?

SIMON. How can I go home? It's dark outside. I'm too damn scared to go home, damned if I'm not!

MIMI. What are you scared of?

SIMON. I'm closed in.

MIMI. Well, go outside, and you won't be closed in anymore.

SIMON. Doesn't matter ***where*** I am. I'm closed in between the earth and the sky. There's no way out of that. Put old Simon on a wide open plain and he'll still be shut in. Simon can't get away from Simon. Simon's going to die like a dog.

MIMI. I'll come with you.

SIMON. You're a goddamn whore. Can't be seen with you. I've got a wife at home. She's going to have a baby. She's going to give me a son. You don't mind me calling you a whore, do you? What else can I call you when that's what you are?! And I'm one, too. A bigger whore than you. The biggest whore in the world. The world's a brothel, and I'm the biggest whore in it. Oh, God, I feel terrible. I'm choking. I feel terrible. I want to go home. What am I doing here? Let me see your yellow book. When's the last time you went for a check-up? You're trying to give me the clap. Only I'll get treatment. Permanganate. Private Simon Andreyevitch of the 21st infantry reserve down with the clap, Sir. Request 10 days' sick leave to take the permanganate treatment. Where did I get it? At Mimi Boshkovitch's. You don't know her? My God, you're ignorant, Sir! Mimi, get the band up here to play for me. Tell Militch, the one who plays the drums, tell him I want him to play for me.

MIMI. He's busy downstairs at the moment.

SIMON. Tell him. I'll pay.

MIMI. He's playing in the bar. It's full of customers. I can't call him away ***now***.

SIMON. You tell him Simon wants him. He's a friend of mine. He'll come.

MIMI. I can't do that.

SIMON. All right, then, ***I*** will. [*He gets up and nearly falls over. He lies back on the bed.*] Oh, my God!

MIMI. You stay there. I'll go and get him.

[*Exit Mimi. Pause.*]

SIMON. [*Singing*] *Six for the months in half a year*
Five for the fingers on a hand
Four for the teats on a cow
Three for the legs on a stool
Two for the eyes in a head
One for the nightingale that sings
early in the month of May.

[*Pause*] Oh my God.

[*Pause. Enter Mimi with Stevo.*]

MIMI. Your brother's here.

SIMON. Stevo. Get the hell out of here! How do you know my brother?

MIMI. Militch knows him. He pointed him out to me. He can't come up. The boss won't let him.

SIMON. Well, my brother's no good to me! ***He*** can't play the drums. You know how to play the drums, Stevo? Eh? No, he doesn't. Nobody plays the drums as well as I hear them in my head.

STEVO. You're supposed to be on an army exercise.

SIMON. Yes, I am. I'm on an army exercise. I'm not here. You ***think*** I am, but I'm not. I'm there. Come on, Stevo, you're the one with the education, give me an explanation. How come I'm alive? I speak. I see. If you say something, I'll hear you. How come? Why don't I just fall into a faint, for instance? What is it keeps me upright? And when I walk, first one leg goes in front, then the other. How come I can breathe? Why can't I see my own eyes? Ah, Stevo, it's all your fault, Stevo. All your fault.

STEVO. Yes, Simon. Let's go home now.

SIMON. Andrei getting arrested, that was your fault. Vera not being able to have a baby, that was your fault. Mom's mind going, that's your fault. Dad losing his legs, your fault. And me slowly choking, that's your fault, too. Klaus came to have lunch in my restaurant. Instead of going to one of the classy places, he has to come to us. He ordered dozens of dishes and I had to serve him. Went and spilled the lot all over him. How come? First time I've ever spilled anything. I'd been drinking all right, but I knew what I was doing. And then he begins to scream and shout at me. And the boss comes up and goes down on his knees apologizing and then it's "Out, Simon!" No job for Simon anymore. Ah, Stevo, Stevo. It's all your fault. Like you knew everything, but didn't let on. Didn't want to tell.

STEVO. Tell what?

SIMON. The secret. You were hiding the secret.

STEVO. What secret?

SIMON. The secret. There's only one secret. And if you know it, but don't let on, you bring down a whole load of bad luck on your head. It's choking me. Here. And the Captain wouldn't believe me. You're not going to the doctor, he says. Die. And you don't believe me, either.

[*Simon dies. Pause.*]

STEVO. ***Simon!!!***

SCENE FOURTEEN

[*The Andreyevitch's house. Dimitri is carving his whistle. Vera is lying down and Maria is sitting beside her.*]

MARIA. Would you like some lemon barley, or a bowl of cereal? They're both good when you're expecting. ***I'll*** get it for you. You lie here. What are we going to call the baby? I was thinking about it all night. We should think up a new name. Not one of the old ones. Something better. I'm going to be a grandmother. Andrei'll be back by then. I'll sing to the baby in the evenings:

[*Singing*]

Bleat, bleat, billy-goat,
Leave your droppings in the road,
Just like buttons for a coat,
Grannie's going to take them all,
Thread them all, and sell them all
To the tailors round the corner —
They will pay for each a quarter.

[*There is a knock at the door. Dimitri wheels himself over to the door and opens it.*]

SIVITCH. Good evening. My name is Sivitch. I'm from the Schneider company next door. Can I come in? [*Dimitri makes way for him. Sivitch comes in, takes the envelope out, and puts it on the table.*] There's 25,000 dinars for you. I'm afraid you'll have to leave the house as quickly as possible. I have an order for immediate demolition. The workmen are ready and waiting outside. I know this leaves you no choice, but I'm simply doing my job. The order has been signed by the Chief of Police, and I must see it is carried out forthwith. This house was scheduled for demolition six months ago.

DIMITRI. ***Out!!!***

SIVITCH. I have the order here, Mr. Andreyevitch. [*He takes out the authorization paper.*]

DIMITRI. [*Grabbing the paper and tearing it up*] No, you haven't. Get out!!

SIVITCH. The original is in a safe place. If you're not out of here in five minutes, we'll start demolition. Then you'll ***have*** to get out.

[*Exit Sivitch. Long pause. Vera starts weeping.*]

MARIA. Don't cry, my dear. Don't get upset now. [*She puts a scarf on her head and gets some bread and salt*[4]*. She opens the door.*] Come in. Come on. Have a rakia before you start work. And something to eat. Nothing special, I'm afraid. Had we known you were coming, we'd have given you a better welcome.

---

4. Bread and salt are traditionally served to welcome a guest into the home in many Slavic cultures.

SCENE FIFTEEN

[*Herzog's house. Sara is playing the piano. Enter Stevo. He listens to her for a while. Pause.*)

STEVO. Where's Sivitch?

[*Pause.*]

SARA. He's gone. He said he was leaving me.

[*Pause. Sara goes on playing.*]

STEVO. Where's your father?

SARA. He's gone. He said he was going to hang himself.

[*Pause. Sara goes on playing. Stevo takes out a piece of paper and puts it on top of the piano.*]

STEVO. I've written you a poem. I didn't copy any of it from anywhere.

[*Pause.*]

SARA. Do you want to kiss me?

[*Pause. Sara goes on playing. Exit Stevo. Pause.*]

SARA. Nobody wants to kiss me anymore.

SCENE SIXTEEN

[*Klaus in his hotel room. There is a knocking at the door.*]

KLAUS. Who is it?

[*Silence. Pause.*]

KLAUS. Who is it?

[*Louder knocking at the door.*]

KLAUS. Who's there?

[*Pause. Silence. Klaus opens the door. Stevo rushes in and pushes Klaus up against the wall. He holds a gun to him through his pocket.*]

STEVO. Hands up!

[*Klaus puts his hands up.*]

KLAUS. What do you have in mind, Mr. Andreyevitch?

STEVO. To kill you! I have in mind to kill you.

KLAUS. Wait, Mr. Andreyevitch.

STEVO. What? What shall I wait for? For you to suck my blood? Put me up on a stake? What else shall I wait for?

KLAUS. We can clear all this up.

STEVO. What's not clear about it?

KLAUS. Why have you come?

STEVO. Why didn't you leave me to go on my own way? To sink or swim? Everything thrown in the water must reach the shore. You think your truth about me is the only truth? Well, it isn't. My heart beats in a different way.

KLAUS. Please, Mr. Andreyevitch. Please.

STEVO. Please what? One of my brothers is in a prison camp, the other is lying dead fifty yards from here. Please what? Scared? Your family tree's not worth a brass farthing at this moment. And I made my mother sing for you so I could be like you. If I kill you, will your rotten, powdered skin rub out that shame? How can I rub out that shame?

KLAUS. I beg you, Mr. Andreyevitch, don't. Don't kill me!

STEVO. I've got nothing to kill you with. [*He takes his empty hand out of his pocket*.] If I had, I wouldn't have done any talking. I'm going to get a real gun. If I come back for you, it means I haven't killed ***myself***.

[*Exit Stevo*.]

SCENE SEVENTEEN

[*The ruins of the Andreyevitch's house. Dimitri sits in his wheelchair with his whistle in his hand. Vera is lying down. Maria is collecting all their belongings up into one place. Stevo comes back. He looks at the ruins. Pause.*]

MARIA. When the workmen built the house they shouted:

We've raised high the roof-beams
Now may God bless this house
And grant its owner a good long life
And health for all his family.

[*Maria goes on with her task. Stevo finds the pamphlets and the revolver. He puts the pamphlets in his pocket and sits down. He looks at the revolver. Long pause. Dimitri starts playing his whistle, producing atonal, disconnected sounds.*]

VERA. I think I can feel his heart beating.

[*Stevo fires into the air.*]

CURTAIN

THE FALSE BOTTOM

A passion for the theater in three movements with a coda

Translated from the Macedonian by Patricia Marsh-Stefanovska

CHARACTERS

JACOB 30

BOZHO 60

CHRISTINE 25

NOVEY 30

PARASKEVA 55

Note:
The play should be performed without intermission.

FIRST MOVEMENT
(ART)

[*The not-too-distant future, say 1999. An underground concrete shelter. A heavy metal door with a lock. Low ceiling with a round hole in it with a metal cover. Weak neon lighting. Stifling atmosphere. Three beds. Suitcases full of clothes and household equipment. Bozho and Paraskeva are sitting up in their beds and staring ahead. Christine is lying in the corner of the shelter with her face turned to the wall. Pause.*]

BOZHO. Are you asleep?

PARASKEVA. I don't know.

[*Pause. Bozho takes out a pill. He gives it to Paraskeva. She takes it and swallows it. Pause.*]

PARASKEVA. Is it Thursday today?

BOZHO. Friday.

PARASKEVA. How the days fly! I've got used to it. [*Pause*] What time of day is it?

BOZHO. Morning.

PARASKEVA. Good morning. [*Pause*] Good morning, Christine. [*Pause*] Christine? [*Pause*] She's been stuffing herself with pills all night.

BOZHO. You shouldn't take more than the dose we've been prescribed. Otherwise, what's supposed to save you'll kill you.

Moderation in all things. And self-control. That's the ultimate wisdom. Who said you could sleep on the floor?

PARASKEVA. She hasn't opened her eyes for months now. [*Pause*] She's hiding. [*To Christine*] You can't hide in a hide-out! [*Pause*] The ventilation grille needs spraying. I saw a six-ounce cockroach.

BOZHO. You should be glad you're in a ministerial shelter. Who knows what it's like in other places.

[*Pause.*]

PARASKEVA. Shall we get up?

BOZHO. What for?

PARASKEVA. To brush our teeth.

BOZHO. Europe's dead.

PARASKEVA. So?

BOZHO. So our teeth can rot too.

[*Pause. There's knocking at the door.*]

BOZHO. Who is it?

JACOB. Jacob.

BOZHO. Jacob who?

JACOB. The artist.

BOZHO. The artist?

JACOB. Yes, the total artist.

BOZHO. I don't know you.

JACOB. Well, let's get to know each other, then!

[*Bozho opens the door. Jacob is standing in the doorway. He is dressed in bright colors. Sunglasses. A saxophone round his neck.*]

JACOB. Good afternoon.

BOZHO. It's morning.

JACOB. Oh, is it? [*He comes in.*] So you are Mr. Bozho, man of letters and Minister of Culture. I've been wanting to meet the man who's in charge of me for a long time. I've read your books. They were in the syllabus at school. You wrote about freedom. So I'm interested in how you look on life now. What you're writing now. I had a hard time getting to you. From pipe to pipe like through a beehive. Plus keeping out of the way of the guards.

BOZHO. There's a law against movement through the corridors.

JACOB. Oh, the law and I don't take each other very seriously.

PARASKEVA. Your eyes are blood-red. You haven't combed your hair for months. Your nails are like eagle's claws. What are you doing to yourself?

JACOB. Putting up with myself. You must be his lady wife. A housewife, I suppose. All the wives of literary ministers are housewives. Your daughter?

PARASKEVA. Christine. A ballerina.

JACOB. She's got her eyes closed. Depression. Logical product of this kind of parental combination.

BOZHO. You're overwrought, young man. The law requires you to take tranquilizers.

JACOB. I don't take them. I want to know just how untranquil I am.

BOZHO. What line of work were you in?

JACOB. I was studying to be a student. [*Pause*] History of art. [*Pause*] And psychology. [*Pause*] And political science. [*Pause*] And acting.

BOZHO. What did you finish in?

JACOB. What can you finish in other than life?

BOZHO. Here's a partner for you, Christine. An artistic soul. Your sort were never sober. Screwing around wherever you got the chance with whoever gave you the chance. Farting at the whole normal world. We should've put you on the barbecue before it was too late, cooked you to perfection, and served you with spring onions and some nice white wine and soda. But the times have caught up with you anyway. Now it's survival that matters. A clean slate, you might say. The wheat over here and the chaff over there. Now we know exactly who's doing what. There's no culture any more. No bluffing. Everything's out in the open. You're all rotten inside. In my village the church bell used to toll every three days because some child had died. And that was a good thing. The sick should be left to die. None of this taking him to the doctor's, getting him half better with injections. Then his head swells and his body dries up. To say nothing of the childhood trauma. All of it added together equals an artist. And then you don't know what to do with him. You've eaten more sugar in your lifetimes than I've had bread. Well, now the balloon's burst. Millions've been wiped out. Now let whoever's got the guts survive.

JACOB. Mr. Minister, Sir, you think like a grocer. I thought you were guarding the essence. I came so we could coordinate our activities, so I could ask your advice. How I can be useful, how I can be an artist in these clouded times.

BOZHO. There're no such luxuries any more.

JACOB. Everything we were hiding before comes out now.

BOZHO. You were obviously born with it out.

JACOB. And now what?

BOZHO. Adapt.

CHRISTINE. We'll embroider a tapestry, Jacob. A six-ounce cockroach on a grey background.

JACOB. You're not crying, are you? [*Pause*] Don't. [*Pause*] Stopped now? [*Pause*] Shcrumvlertsturfkiush.

CHRISTINE. What?

JACOB. Shcrumvlertsturfkiush.

CHRISTINE. What's that?

JACOB. A word nobody in the world has ever said before. I thought it up on my way here. It's a gift from me to you.

BOZHO. Such a pity it doesn't mean anything.

JACOB. It can mean anything you like. That was what the tranquilizers were called which the citizens of Mesopotamia had to take after the fall of the Sumerian civilization. They were prescribed by the Government of National Salvation. Once they kept people sober by law. Now they drug them by law. Pill in the morning, pill at midday, pill in the evening. Snack pills as required for the hypersensitive.

BOZHO. They're just temporary measures.

JACOB. Oh yes, of course. The Sumerian civilization was temporary, too. We'll discontinue these measures ourselves when we die, when we conk out, when we croak, when we kick the bucket, when our vital functions terminate.

BOZHO. Go and sleep!

JACOB. Who says I'm awake? The whole nation is anesthetized.

BOZHO. Keep your voice down. They check up on us.

JACOB. I've had enough of talking so no one can hear.

BOZHO. You'll pay a high price for that.

JACOB. I'm the only problem you've got left, aren't I? You've solved all the others. Now just the question of me to answer. What can you do to me? Shut me away? Any more than I am already? We're all shut away now. [*To Paraskeva*] What're you doing, Madam? Just sitting and staring? Waiting for bedtime? Why don't you read something?

PARASKEVA. I can't concentrate. It's the pills.

JACOB. Stop taking them.

PARASKEVA. I wouldn't have a moment's peace. [*Pause*] What is there to read, anyway?

JACOB. Yes. You've already read all your husband's works.

PARASKEVA. So you've come to tell us how to live our lives, have you?

JACOB. [*Smacking his own face*] Stupid boy! You keep trying to make people live, and they're so happy being dead. What right have you got? I'm sorry, I'm most terribly sorry. Please accept my sincere apologies. I *do* apologize.

PARASKEVA. The situation is deadly serious.

JACOB. I'm the jester from the folk tales. I'm supposed to make some dirty jokes the night of the wake.

CHRISTINE. I'm bleeding. My womb is falling apart. I keep dreaming I'm pregnant. I have babies before their time. Deformed scarecrows, disabled in all kinds of ways. Not just one. Not two. Whole regiments, armies of them. Whole open spaces full of unusable human material. Don't say anything. I'm not interested in what you think. How you feel about me. Whether you sympathize. I don't want to communicate. I'm just thinking aloud. Help me.

BOZHO. Who's she talking to?

PARASKEVA. Comfort her, Jacob.

JACOB. How?

PARASKEVA. You're a man of the arts, aren't you? Do something entertaining!

[Jacob jumps into Christine's bed and closes his eyes. Then he opens them again.]

JACOB. Good morning. [*He jumps out of bed.*] Here I am. Ecce homunculus! A few breathing exercises. [*He breathes deeply.*] Push-ups. [*He does some push-ups.*] Wrists. [*He does wrist exercises.*] Ankles. [*He does ankle exercises.*] Coffee. [*He mimes drinking coffee.*] Shave. [*He mimes shaving.*] Goodbye, dear. [*He kisses Christine on the cheek.*] I'm going to work. You sweep up, feed the cat, the canary, and the children, make a three-course lunch with a nice soup, perm your hair, make yourself up, have a little wash and put on some black stockings with a black suspender-belt under your silk dressing gown, so I can let you have it as soon as I walk through the door. And don't let anyone in the house. No postmen, no plumbers. [*Christine smiles.*] Ah, smiling, are you, you whore?! You're hiding something. Ah, what intuition I have! So the smell of sex on you is not from me. I'm going to take sick leave then. I'll stay here and wait behind the door with a sawn-off shotgun to see who pays you visits early in the morning. *Dixi.*[1]

BOZHO. That's enough of that over there!

JACOB. It's so cramped in here there's no one ***over there***. Everything is ***here***.

BOZHO. You're obsessed with sex.

JACOB. Yes.

BOZHO. These times require restraint all round.

JACOB. These times suit frigid people. I've got sperm dripping out of my ears.

BOZHO. And you're proud of it?

JACOB. Should I be ashamed?

BOZHO. Of course you should.

JACOB. Sir, I have no need whatsoever of your bourgeois respectability. My still calling you "Sir" is, of course, tongue in cheek. I don't believe anything wonderful is going to change my life all of a sudden. Nothing's worth three good fucks any more.

BOZHO. That's too much!

---

1. I have spoken.

JACOB. All right. Two good fucks, then.

BOZHO. You come here sowing dissension, breaking the law, spreading controversy, disturbing the peace, demoralizing us, and hurting our deepest patriotic feelings.

JACOB. I'm just decaying naturally. I'll grow out of it. If I grow at all. Don't take me seriously, though. I'm just a drifter. Let's kiss and make up. [*He offers his hand.*]

BOZHO. I'm old enough to be your father.

JACOB. Be my father.

[*Jacob goes over to Bozho and kisses him on the lips. Bozho hits him hard across the face.*]

BOZHO. Get out of here! Out!!!

[*Jacob bangs into the wall opposite. He covers his face with his hands. Pause. He uncovers his face. He smiles.*]

BOZHO. Still got that grin on your face?

JACOB. That's only how it looks to you.

BOZHO. Young man. We have lived through a cataclysm unparalleled in the entire history of mankind. The world no longer exists as we knew it. The very components of life have been upset. The Government is making superhuman efforts to supply us with food and water. Each day is a matter of life and death. If you really believe that you are contributing to the indispensable normalization of the situation with this chaotic behavior of yours, then I'm afraid you are gravely mistaken. I'm older than you. I've been around on this planet a little longer than you. What do you want of us? You want us to act out a little play here? Behave like a load of neurotics? We all have reasons for being distressed and desperate, but that doesn't mean we have to start devouring each other. A little more self-control won't do anyone any harm. With patience and understanding on the part of everyone, we'll be able to overcome this misfortune.

JACOB. Patience isn't going to overcome this misfortune. You're full of sedatives. You don't know what you're talking about.

BOZHO. I'm an honorable and loyal citizen of this country.

JACOB. The world is falling apart from all the honorable and loyal citizens. You'd live honorably and loyally in a kingdom ruled by a hundred-headed dragon. Honor and loyalty are relative concepts.

CHRISTINE. Please come out onto the veranda. It's nice and quiet there. And the air is cleaner. That's because of the fountain. And the lake's not far away. Jasmine tea? Yes, those are nightingales among the pomegranate trees. Sugar?

[*Christine starts winding up an alarm clock.*]

JACOB. Just six spoonfuls for me. [*Silence. Pause.*] Don't wind that clock up too much.

CHRISTINE. It mustn't stop. It's bad luck if it stops.

JACOB. The spring'll snap and then it won't work at all anymore.

CHRISTINE. There's still snow on the mountains. They're high. The streams are fast-running and cold. There're trout in them. We'll go there on Saturday. We'll roll up our trouser-legs and paddle. Splish, splash, splish, splash!

PARASKEVA. She gets like this. It comes in waves.

JACOB. She's dreaming of a better tomorrow. She has fine hallucinations. An example to us all. Full of self-control. She takes her pills regularly. You brought her up to be totally dependent with your credit cards, your hard currency, your winter sports, your summers by the sea. Why should she open her eyes now when there's only sand left for ostriches to bury their heads in?

BOZHO. Just who do you think you are? Some kind of supreme judge? Who asked you here?

JACOB. I don't wait for official invitations anymore. I take what I need.

BOZHO. What do you need?

JACOB. What I take.

BOZHO. I still have power, you know.

JACOB. Burn me, then. Throw my ashes into Lake Ohrid from the Church of St. John of Caneo. The church is in ruins, of course, and the lake's dried up, but it would be something at least.

PARASKEVA. You're obsessed with death.

JACOB. Because I'm alive. You don't care one way or the other. [*Pause*] People long to die. Children at primary school long to be in high school. High school kids long to be at college. College students long to get jobs. Those who have jobs long to get married. Married couples long for a place of their own, and for the children to grow up so they can have a peaceful retirement. And in retirement they long for health. And all of them long to be dead. And the dead long to be reborn, so they can be kind of alive again. Again be out of step with themselves.

BOZHO. Come down from the clouds.

JACOB. I'm ten yards underground. I have to reach for the clouds to stay on the surface.

[*Jacob does a headstand.*]

BOZHO. What is it now?

JACOB. Just an ordinary headstand. Nothing metaphorical. Got any better ideas what to do? [*Pause*] You've got none of your own, but you don't like mine. The blood circulates, the brain pumps blood, the hands produce formic acid. The bottom becomes the surface. Post-conceptual artism. The aesthetics of despair. Cave art for art's sake. [*He returns to his feet.*] I'm not happy to be alive. I have to distract myself with whatever turns up.

BOZHO. Go out for a walk and distract yourself. And shut the trapdoor so there's no draught.

CHRISTINE. I've got an appointment at the beauty salon for a facial and a wax.

BOZHO. Stop it, Christine! Open your eyes!

PARASKEVA. She can't remember how to open them.

JACOB. You have to remember freedom. We're always forgetting. And we always blame someone else.

PARASKEVA. You can't escape what's written.

JACOB. I'm free inside. Within what is written for me. [*He sprays red paint on his face. It leaves a mark on the wall.*] This is what I write. This is under my control. I determine it.

PARASKEVA. You use your art to open Christine's eyes, then, my boy.

JACOB. Mommy! [*Pause*] Mommy Christine!

CHRISTINE. Who's that?

JACOB. Your daughter.

CHRISTINE. I haven't got a daughter.

JACOB. Well, whose daughter am I then?

CHRISTINE. What do you want?

JACOB. I'm lost. I lost my way. I've forgotten my name. What's my name, Mommy? When I was little you taught me my name and address so I'd know what to say if I got lost. But now I've forgotten. Some people are asking me my name. What shall I say? Quick. They'll go away.

CHRISTINE. Your name's Christine.

JACOB. And what's your name, Mommy? They want to know your name, too. They want to know where to take me. What's your name, Mommy? They've got work to do. They're getting impatient. What's your name, Mommy, ***please?!***

CHRISTINE. Christine.

JACOB. And where do we live? Where should they take me? How can I tell them where we live?

CHRISTINE. By the river.

JACOB. What river, Mommy? The people say there's no river. There aren't any rivers anymore. They think I'm just playing with them. What shall I tell them? Where do we live?

CHRISTINE. I don't know.

JACOB. What do you mean, you don't know? Look and tell me. Quick, quick!

CHRISTINE. Here! We live here!

JACOB. Where?

CHRISTINE. Tell them to bring you here!

JACOB. Where's here? This is an underground shelter.

CHRISTINE. No-o-o!

JACOB. Yes. And there's no way out. No river. But I'm here. I'm home. I'm saved. Here I am.

[*Christine opens her eyes. Jacob kisses her eyelids. Bozho claps. Then he realizes applause is inappropriate. He stops. Pause.*]

BOZHO. You've got no common sense.

JACOB. Common sense is what you need to bet on a point spread in football pools and count your change.

[*Pause.*]

CHRISTINE. Jacob? [*Pause*] I can see.

JACOB. People usually can with their eyes open.

CHRISTINE. [*Looking at herself*] I'll never be able to dance again. Look at me.

JACOB. That's what we all look like. Normal people are now the invalids. We'll send the ones who aren't for spa treatments to get special hormonal disturbances. So they look like us.

CHRISTINE. There won't be any ballet anymore. There won't be anything anymore.

JACOB. Sssh. They listen in. Get up and walk.

CHRISTINE. I can't get my balance.

JACOB. Walk and you'll get it.

CHRISTINE. Where?

JACOB. Round in circles. If there's anywhere to go, tell me and we'll go there. [*He kisses her hands. He tries to lift her up.*] Get up, Christine. Move. Please. You're in charge of your life. It's like a fire. You have to tend it. It's not just you. There're sacred, heavenly principles at stake. I don't know how to explain it to you. I kiss you and I beg you and I love you. Get up. Walk. The world will fall apart. Nobody does anything.

[*Christine gets up. She walks around with Jacob in a circle. Pause. The upper trap-door opens. Novey lets himself down. He is wearing a gas mask and a black plastic cape. Pause.*]

NOVEY. Good evening. [*He takes off his mask.*]

CHRISTINE. So it's evening. We thought it was morning.

NOVEY. It's all a bit mixed up. What're you doing here, Jacob? I haven't seen you since college.

JACOB. I was just asking the Minister to take me on as special culture consultant.

NOVEY. I'm his special culture consultant.

JACOB. Then I'll go to the Forestry Minister — I've just come from the Transport Minister. [*Pause*] Have you finished your epic poem?

NOVEY. I'm working on it.

JACOB. You've been working on it for five years.

NOVEY. [*He puts down some letters. To Bozho*] Strictly confidential. [*He takes out a packet of pills and offers one to Jacob.*] Special sedatives. From government stock.

[*Jacob shakes his head. Novey offers one to Paraskeva.*]

PARASKEVA. Well, I've just had one. But ***I*** wouldn't like to refuse you. Cheers.

JACOB. How are you special consultants paid now? Do you get special benefits? A shorter working life?

NOVEY. The working conditions are tougher now. We're mostly in the field. It's not easy.

JACOB. What's the situation like?

NOVEY. Complicated.

JACOB. Why? Everybody's in holes, aren't they?

NOVEY. Yes, but it's seething in there.

JACOB. I thought now we're all separate we'd be calm enough.

NOVEY. Let's talk about something else. They check up.

JACOB. They check up on you, too, do they?

NOVEY. Of course.

JACOB. They check up on us, too.

NOVEY. I know.

JACOB. I didn't know they checked up on you, too.

NOVEY. Not half.

JACOB. What about the ones who check up on you? Does anyone check up on them?

NOVEY. Too much knowledge makes your head ache.

JACOB. Whenever they answer your question with a proverb, it means they don't know the answer. How long're we going to be living underground? Will the air outside clear?

NOVEY. They're working on it.

JACOB. Who?

NOVEY. There're special departments for that.

JACOB. Which departments?

NOVEY. You ask a lot of questions. Can't help asking questions, can we? You're an angry young man. If there'd been cities you could've organized some urban guerrillas. As it is, all you could organize is a nice private little suicide.

BOZHO. Jacob. I accuse you of treason.

JACOB. Instead of just singing its praises, now you're creating freedom on the spot. Poet, know thy duty.

BOZHO. Something not clear? We're in a paradoxical situation. You protest that people are shut in, but if we let them out, they'd suffocate. If we left them without drugs, they'd be a danger both to themselves and to others. You're a good example. Freedom in such circumstances is only possible in prison. A dialectical contradiction. But you've heard somewhere that artists demolish prisons, so you want to demolish something, too, eh? ***What*** exactly?

JACOB. The wall inside your head. I refuse to be alive by inertia, to breathe through gills. I refuse to wait like a lamb for Easter, like a turkey for Christmas. I refuse to stroll around with my guts in my hands, to watch how badly you operate on me. How inexpertly you cut and sew. How my wounds fester. I refuse to wonder how much it's going to hurt when I start to recover. I don't want any sedatives. I'm not a heap of protoplasm. I have a will and a mind, and I take responsibility for my own life.

BOZHO. Mind, will, responsibility. Such concepts! Such luxuries! The freedom you're blathering about is just a fiction. It only exists now in the theaters and brothels — under strict control, of course. Otherwise it gets rooted out like a contagious disease. People long for slavery. Greyness. Death. People only ask a little bread and salt and, if possible, to avoid a thrashing. And you want them to smear their faces with paint and dance ritual dances, each in their own little shelter.

[Jacob starts turning over the beds and suitcases. He makes a complete mess. Novey makes to stop him, but Bozho holds him back.]

BOZHO. Leave him alone. There's nothing else left to him.

JACOB. In each of your words, each one of your movements, your whole past, present, and future show up like in a crystal ball. I don't come under any regulations, any stated policies, any rules, appendices, paragraphs, contracts, or clauses. I'm here to announce the false bottom! The egg is too small for the chicken. Its beak is already tapping against the shell. The chicken's going to emerge into the greater egg.

CHRISTINE. Jacob, take me with you.

BOZHO. What false bottom?

JACOB. You don't know? Shame on you! Grown people. How can I explain it to people like you, who only accept answers of yes or no? Who divide colors into just black and white? And people into friend or foe? I swear on my faith, my conscience, and my honor that I will work for the liberation of the spirit with all my power and means, and that I will never betray the secrets of the act of revolution. Should I do so, let me be killed with this revolver or this dagger which I kiss. To everything there is a false bottom.

[*A distant rumble is heard. It grows louder*.]

BOZHO. What's going on?

JACOB. Sssh! It's too late for questions.

[*Thunder. Music. The false bottom is revealed. Chaos*.]

SECOND MOVEMENT (MADNESS)

[*The recent past, say 1911. An expensively-furnished drawing room in Bozho's house. Bozho has just finished reading a manuscript. Paraskeva and Christine are seated. They are dressed in expensive clothes in the fashion of the time. Jacob is standing. He is wearing an unlaced straitjacket and is barefoot. Pause.*]

BOZHO. [*Reading the title of the manuscript*] "The False Bottom — a passion for the theater in one movement." [*Pause*] There! We've read your play as you asked us to. Happy now?

[*Jacob looks at them fixedly. Pause.*]

BOZHO. Do you want something to eat? [*Pause*] Thirsty? [*Pause*] Then thank you for coming to see us.

[*Jacob doesn't budge.*]

BOZHO. Now go back to the mental hospital and everything'll be all right. [*Pause*] Agreed? [*Pause*] Do they know you're not there? [*Pause.*]

JACOB. They didn't know I ***was*** there.

BOZHO. Go. [*Pause*] Let's not argue about it. [*Pause*] We've read what you think of us. That's enough. What more do you want?

JACOB. What else can madness do except show what it thinks of you?

[*Long pause. They look at each other.*]

PARASKEVA. [To Bozho] Bozho, he's going to attack us.

JACOB. I'm mad, Ma'am, but I'm not deranged. My madness is of a responsible kind.

CHRISTINE. Why does the action of your play take place in the distant future?

JACOB. Unfortunately, the action hasn't taken place at all for a long time.

PARASKEVA. Christine, don't talk to him and don't look him in the eye.

CHRISTINE. Why did you choose ***our*** family to write about?

JACOB. I saw you on a courtesy visit to the mental hospital. Your father gave a reading. You danced some ballet. And your mother fluttered her eyelashes. Our library has two hundred copies of his collected works in leather-bound editions, donated for the purposes of education and edification. Your father is a soap manufacturer, a national man of letters. A monument to culture in this town. And I'm a patient in the asylum which has the honor of bearing his name. What other family would I write about?

PARASKEVA. Why do you show yourself as an artist in the play, when you're really a lunatic?

JACOB. What's the difference?

CHRISTINE. What's the matter with you exactly?

JACOB. Schizoaffective psychosis with auditory hallucinations present, and a strong depressive component. [*Pause*] I was involved with the essence, and the essence scorched me. I'm a figment of the imagination. We're all just figments of the imagination.

CHRISTINE. How can we be figments of the imagination when we exist?

JACOB. We've been imagined in order to exist.

CHRISTINE. Who imagined us?

JACOB. The Great Dramatist. Some people call him God. We're characters in his plays. He's cruel. He doesn't like people. He writes bad plays.

CHRISTINE. Which parts do we play?

JACOB. You're the keepers of a dead world. Which you think is finite.

CHRISTINE. What about you?

JACOB. I've given up my part. I've left the play. I've turned my back on the Great Dramatist. Why should I be just his echo? His shadow? Why should ***I*** think up ***his*** fictions? I've become one with the false bottom. [*Pointing to himself*] And this is the price.

CHRISTINE. How can I get out of the play, too?

JACOB. Stop playing the part they make you play. Play the one you want to play. The world is covered in snow. Take off your clothes and make a hole in the snow with the warmth of your body.

PARASKEVA. You've got no shoes on. You'll freeze.

JACOB. Konstantin Miladinov and I had no shoes on when we walked around Moscow in January.

BOZHO. You knew Konstantin Miladinov?

JACOB. Oh, yes.

BOZHO. Well, just how old are you, then? Miladinov died in 1863.

JACOB. So what?

BOZHO. Well, it's 1911 now.

JACOB. What've dates got to do with it? I'm a figment of the imagination. I knew Bakunin, the anarchist, too. He was chained to the wall in Switzerland for five months. Then another seven years in Siberia. We met in Paris after they'd thrown him out of the First International. The passion for destruction is a creative passion. Walt Whitman read me his pornographic poems in Brooklyn. I drank absinthe in Ethiopia with Rimbaud — Arthur Rimbaud. The disorder of the senses. I've been alone and an outcast all my life. I've reached something which is more than transience, but still not eternity.

BOZHO. Get out of here! Out!!!

CHRISTINE. That's a line from the play. What a strange coincidence!

BOZHO. There aren't any strange coincidences anymore, my dear. It's all ulterior motives. This fellow's written a play today. Tomorrow he'll stab a knife into us. It all starts with literature and ends with blood.

JACOB. Ladies and gentlemen, I came here to offer you madness classes. All the mad things you've wanted to do but been afraid to — you can try them all out in front of me. Or on me. Or with me. Or I'll do them for you. Use me as the sweep for your mental chimney. It's my lot to collect your soot on me. Should I fail to give satisfaction, I'll refund your money. Discretion guaranteed. First because I don't remember anything, and secondly because I have no moral values, and fail to discriminate between good and evil. You can have individual classes or group ones. The first introductory class is free and I suggest we have it here and now.

PARASKEVA. Done.

BOZHO. Don't be taken in. This is a game. A provocation.

PARASKEVA. The game doesn't fascinate me. And I can return the provocation. Can I tie you up? [*She ties the sleeves of the straitjacket behind Jacob's back.*] I'm tying you loosely. I leave you the hope of escape. You don't take the opportunity. You understand these things. You're an artist. It's best to be tied. That way you can dream of freedom. If you escape, you'll get lost in the big wide world. Real freedom will paralyze you. I've been to Egypt, Persia. I know. Better to stay here so we can go on rubbing up against each other. At least we know each other like old coins. But what if I turn the other side of the coin overnight? What if I tie you tightly? What if I teach you not to play with madness? Just as my mother taught me not to pee in my pants? She gave me a wooden spoon and sent me to ask the neighbors for some salt. I went, but I didn't know they'd made an agreement about what to do when I got there. I knocked on the door. They opened it, took the spoon and started hitting me about the head with it, and shouting "So you're the one who does her wee-wee in her pants, are you?" [*She hits Jacob on the head.*] They didn't give me any salt. [*She grabs hold of him below the belt.*] You're mine. I'm holding you tight. I'm giving you an erection. Don't pretend it's sent from heaven. Stop struggling. I can twist them off. But why make a big martyr of you? I can do that when I like. For the moment I need you as an alibi. As an identity card for my humanism and renaissance. You're the make-up for my face. I allow you to break the rules so people know what the rules are. They, of course, will stay the same. You, at best, will get a little posthumous notoriety. You think you're breaking the rules, but you're just reinforcing them. Who can give madness classes to whom here? We know who we are and what we are better than you do. You can't show us anything new.

CHRISTINE. Run away, Jacob. Be careful. You don't know who you're dealing with. They'll make your madness mad. She makes me do modern dance, be talented. She wants to have a salon for poets, suicides, weirdos of all kinds, and she wants me to serve them tea and brandy. She wants to be close to art, salons, make-up, perfumes, beautiful people, bouquets, gloves, applause, applause, gifts, receptions, trips. Rome, London, Paris. I can't take it anymore. I can't take it anymore. Go. Be normal. Take care of yourself. You can't fight them with reason or with madness. Nor with truth or with acting. Comb your hair. Put some clothes on. Nothing is in the heart. It's all in the face. Change the wild animal into a cow chewing the cud. Why do you have to show who you are night and day? You don't have to wear your heart on your sleeve. The need to tell the truth all the time is a primitive one. You're literate. That's the sin that got Adam and Eve thrown out of Paradise. You're ruining yourself. It's easy to be as free as a bird. Be as free as a human being. You know what it takes to be normal. You break the rules so often, you know them perfectly. Go against yourself. If you want to hurry, slow down. If you want to move, sit down. If you want to live, die. That's what good manners are all about. Jacob with the snakes in his hair, the Holy Spirit in his eyes, Jacob who drinks dew and eats wild honey, has put a spell on Christine. She could have seduced any of the consuls. She speaks French and Greek like a native. Christine who does embroidery on a frame and eats off silver plates. Whose father uses camels to trade in Africa and Asia.

[*Christine and Jacob look into each other's eyes.*]

JACOB. What are you trying to tell me?

CHRISTINE. I'm normal!

JACOB. What are you trying to tell me?

CHRISTINE. That I'm normal!

JACOB. Look me in the eye!

CHRISTINE. I'm afraid of going mad!!

[*Jacob seizes her from behind by the forehead, as if she were about to vomit.*]

CHRISTINE. My hands shake. I blush for no reason. I sweat. I go dizzy. I see double. I'm lethargic. I can't get out of bed in the mornings. I can't go to sleep. My heart beats fast. I'm afraid of death. Of life. Of people. Of animals. Of still life. I'm afraid of fear. I choke, can't breathe. My eyes look inside. They go off in different directions. I get cramps in my legs. I'm being followed. I'm being plotted against. I'm being laughed at. My head's as small as a fist. It's as big as a pumpkin. My ears buzz. I hear voices. There's someone else inside me. I feel like shouting. I feel like laughing. I feel like being silent. I see images. My brain gets stuck to my skull. I make the same movements for days. I don't make any movements for days. Now I'm a head of cabbage. I'm not here.

JACOB. [*To Bozho*] Have you noticed these symptoms in your daughter, Sir? You know she locks herself in her room and does ballet. Knocking herself from wall to wall. Or you don't know she's alive. You understand these shades of meaning, these nuances, as an experienced observer of life, don't you?

[*Jacob leads Christine in a silent waltz. Pause. Novey comes into the room, wearing a police dress uniform.*]

NOVEY. What's going on here?

JACOB. That's a good question.

NOVEY. [*To Bozho*] Do you need any assistance, Sir?

JACOB. In my old schoolfriend's parlance, that means should he break anybody's back with his baton.

NOVEY. Just give the order, Sir.

JACOB. If they ordered you to kill me, would you do it?

NOVEY. Yes.

JACOB. You wouldn't have a guilty conscience?

NOVEY. No.

JACOB. Not about killing someone?

NOVEY. I've killed before and I didn't have a guilty conscience.

JACOB. On orders?

NOVEY. I wouldn't kill a fly without orders.

JACOB. And when they order you to kill your own children tomorrow? D'you know why I'm in an asylum?

NOVEY. No.

JACOB. D'you want to know why they lock people up?

NOVEY. No.

JACOB. Don't you wonder whether I'm normal or not?

NOVEY. Once you're in the looney bin, you're a looney.

JACOB. Why don't you think for yourself once in a while?

NOVEY. Why?

JACOB. So you can understand what's going on around you.

NOVEY. Why? So they can lock ***me*** up, too? It'd be a good idea if the whole world were a big prison. So there was no outside and inside. So everyone could keep an eye on everyone else. Then there'd be a bit of peace and quiet. They could abolish all books. There could be just one book to read. Say, *Little Red Riding Hood*. That'd be quite sufficient. It's all crystal clear. The wolf's bad. Little Red Riding Hood's good. That's it. [*To Bozho*] No disrespect intended, Sir. I'm not referring to you. You're a great man. You're head of the literary circle. You bring the young intelligentsia together. You give lectures on religion. Revolution. The place of the artist today. Hats off to you, Sir. There could be just one of ***your*** books, actually.

JACOB. Why not your epic poem? Have you finished it?

NOVEY. I'm working on it.

JACOB. For the sixth year? [*Pause*] Novey, you're an extremely normal person. You're not subject to fits of passion. Let's make a bet.

NOVEY. What bet?

JACOB. [*Taking a gold coin out of his shirt*] I've got a gold coin saved. It's yours if you manage to stand in one place with your eyes closed and without swaying. Close your eyes.

[*Novey closes his eyes.*]

JACOB. I'm going to poke you from behind with my finger. You can't open your eyes and you can't sway. Let's have a trial run.

[*Jacob pokes Novey. Novey stays as he is.*]

JACOB. That's the way. Well done. Let's have another try. [*He pokes Novey, who stays rooted to the spot.*] If I lose, you get the coin. If ***you*** lose, I bite your ear. All right?

NOVEY. [*Turning to Bozho with his eyes closed*] Sir?

JACOB. Don't ask permission for everything. Get ready now. Remember: it's all in your head. Ready?

NOVEY. Ready.

JACOB. [*Whispering in Novey's ear*] Novey! Novey! You're standing on the edge of a precipice. It's a 1,000-foot drop. You're standing with just your heels on solid ground. There's nothing but thin air under your toes. There won't be so much as one little bone left of you.

[*Jacob pokes Novey with his finger from behind. Novey staggers. He opens his eyes. Jacob jumps on him and bites his ear. Pause.*]

NOVEY. Can we have another round?

JACOB. You want a new life for old stupidity?

BOZHO. You can be taken to court for this sort of thing. There is law and order in this country.

JACOB. There's also my own way of doing things in this country.

BOZHO. That's why you're in an asylum.

JACOB. Mr. President of the Literary Circle, Mr. Soap Manufacturer, Mr. Vice-President of the Town Council, Mr. Secretary of the Franco-Slavonic Friendship Society, Mr. Honorary Member of the Philatelists' Association, why, in your mature phase, should you have so much hatred for a mad dilettante?

BOZHO. If you actually consider yourself a writer, you'd better learn to write. [*Pointing to the manuscript*] What's this inane rubbish? Who needs this? Choose a popular theme from village life, something to do with the liberation from slavery.

Some patriotic subject which will help the national cause. It's the artist's duty to educate!

JACOB. If he's educated himself. You can't distinguish between night and day. But you're educating the people. ***I*** am the people. I forbid you to write about me. Who gave you the right to represent me? I take back your letters of credit. From today I represent myself.

BOZHO. If someone is to judge me, it'll be history. Not you!

JACOB. I only fart at you. History will shit all over you!

BOZHO. Take that back!

JACOB. I could never say another word from now on, but I can't ***not*** have said what I already have. You can. You're like a fingernail. Dead tissue. You cut yourself all the time and it doesn't hurt.

[*Jacob starts turning over the furniture as if in a fit of madness. Novey starts towards him. Christine restrains Novey.*]

NOVEY. Look what he's doing!

CHRISTINE. He's on a pilgrimage.

BOZHO. Where to? [*Stamping on the floor*] This isn't like the floor in your play. This is solid.

JACOB. Everything is like in my play.

BOZHO. Nothing is like in your play. Everything is like in my reality.

JACOB. I swear on my faith, my conscience and my honor that I will work for the liberation of the spirit with all my power and means, and that I will never betray the secrets of the act of revolution. Should I do so, let me be killed with this revolver or this dagger which I kiss. To everything there is a false bottom.

[*A distant rumble is heard. It grows louder.*]

BOZHO. I trust the false bottom is not about to occur.

JACOB. Life is passing while you wonder whether you're alive or not.

[*Thunder. Music. The false bottom is revealed. Chaos.*]

THIRD MOVEMENT (REVOLUTION)

[*The recent present, say 1983. A luxuriously furnished living room in Bozho's house. Bozho sits at his desk. Christine and Paraskeva are sitting on the sofa. Jacob is standing center-stage, dressed in a long, dirty raincoat and boots. Bozho has just finished reading a manuscript. Pause.*]

BOZHO. [*Reading the title of the manuscript*] "The False Bottom — a passion for the theater in two movements." [*Pause*] Whatever I say, it'll sound like what this character of yours with my name says here. [*Pause*] Are you an artist or a madman?

JACOB. A revolutionary.

BOZHO. A revolutionary?

JACOB. A total revolutionary. What you've just read is the case against you. I've come to try you. By court martial. Summary process.

BOZHO. What a witty chap you are!

JACOB. I do my best.

BOZHO. Have we met before?

JACOB. I've been to one of your readings. You were celebrating your thousandth anniversary as a writer. I asked a question. They threw me out. An everyday sort of thing. You wouldn't remember.

PARASKEVA. How do you know our family? We haven't been on any courtesy visits to lunatic asylums.

JACOB. I read an article on your idyllic family life in a magazine. Each of you with your hobby and at your place of work. Charming.

PARASKEVA. And is that a reason to malign us?

JACOB. No. Just a pretext. The reasons are complicated. I just happened to pick on you. I could've chosen others. You're not the only ones of this ilk.

PARASKEVA. Leave this house immediately.

JACOB. I've got nowhere to go.

PARASKEVA. How do you mean?

JACOB. Literally. Can I take over your second floor?

BOZHO. Is this part of your play, too? Is this dialogue of ours written somewhere as well?

JACOB. Art precedes reality. For twenty-five centuries our civilization has been unraveling the knots tied by Plato and Aristotle. Christine, bring a glass of water and a little hammer.

CHRISTINE. And a live turkey.

JACOB. Why a live turkey?

CHRISTINE. Why a glass of water and a little hammer?

JACOB. Just get them!

CHRISTINE. I demand to be tied up in a sack with a sanitary pad in my mouth in accordance with all the principles of terrorism.

[*Exit Christine. Pause.*]

PARASKEVA. You think she's on your side?

JACOB. She's not on yours. And whether she likes it or not, she has to be on somebody's.

PARASKEVA. Whose side am I on?

JACOB. Nobody's. You don't know what it means to be on a side.

BOZHO. Jacob considers us as authority and himself as art. All this is a flimsy allegory on that theme. You're playing with dangerous things.

JACOB. Playing with harmless things is flattery.

PARASKEVA. If I may say something . . .

JACOB. No, you may not!

PARASKEVA. Thank you.

JACOB. Don't mention it. What could you possibly add to what has already been said on your behalf in my play? I explained you better than you could to yourself.

[*Enter Christine. She is carrying an ordinary metal hammer and a glass of water.*]

JACOB. I meant a little wooden hammer. How can a court sit with a hammer like this? [*He strikes it on the desk. He sips some water.*] And you didn't let the water run long enough.

BOZHO. Now would you be so kind as to leave my house immediately? Don't make us use other methods.

JACOB. [*Taking a machine-gun out from under his raincoat*] Why not?! [*Pause*] First I was an artist. I didn't get involved. I despised you from afar. I thought that was enough. So I fell into depression, fits of madness. Now I'm taking radical measures. I've done enough interpretation. I'm starting the change. I've done enough simmering in a revolutionary ferment. Now I'm taking over. I'm making the leap from the kingdom of necessity to the kingdom of freedom. Expropriation. Death to bureaucracy, especially in art.

BOZHO. [*Pointing to the gun*] Where did you get that from?

JACOB. South America.

BOZHO. What were you doing in South America?

JACOB. Carrying on my father's Spanish traditions.

BOZHO. That's not true.

JACOB. But it's not unlikely.

BOZHO. You're a madman.

JACOB. Plus an artist, plus . . . [*Opening up one side of his raincoat which is lined with ammunition and grenades*] a revolutionary. [*Taking out a grenade*] Hand-grenades are projectiles of various shapes made with explosive, inflammable, smoke, or chemical means, constructed in such a way as to be able to be thrown by hand up to a distance of forty yards. Intended for the annihilation of animate enemy forces at close quarters, in trenches, shelters, or ambushes. [*Opening the other side of his coat*] Some samples from our chemical warfare range: nerve gases, vesicants, lung irritants, sternutators, psychochemicals, sarin soman, tabun, yperite, lewisite, phosgene, diphosgene, cyanic acid, cyanogen chloride. Our explosives include trinitrotoluene—TNT to you, dynamite, mercury fulminate, lead azide, trotile, camentite, vitezite, and lead tricinate. I need all this for you finally to take me seriously. If we are all concentrating sufficiently now, let's start. With your books, for example.

BOZHO. So you've read them?

JACOB. So I've read them.

BOZHO. Well?

JACOB. I think they're a load of garbage.

BOZHO. You came to that conclusion after one reading?

JACOB. You think I read them through to the end?

BOZHO. What kind of literature do you like, then? Homer, Dante . . .?

JACOB. I only read living writers.

BOZHO. Why?

JACOB. Because I'm alive alongside them. I look to see what they write about my life. Nothing.

BOZHO. Yes, but a Dante, now . . .

JACOB. . . . speaks to me, too, with his universal messages? Why don't living writers speak to ***me***, not to Dante's readers? Actually, for your part you don't even do ***that*** much.

BOZHO. Are you always so ferociously honest?

JACOB. You only ***find*** me ferocious. You're used to a language which says nothing and to people who say everything and avoid saying anything at all.

PARASKEVA. Are you saying my husband is an idiot?

BOZHO. Stop defending me, Paraskeva.

PARASKEVA. Christine, say something!

JACOB. Christine, say something!

CHRISTINE. Christine, say something!

BOZHO. Are you sure you know me so well?

JACOB. I don't have to eat dung to know what it smells like. That was unwarranted and insulting. I just say what I think. Especially if I get a good image in my head.

BOZHO. Are you sweating? Nervous?

JACOB. Yes.

BOZHO. Other people in your position wouldn't admit it. I train my mind and body not to sweat in any situation. Nothing is worthy of my sweat. I have a whole theory against sweating.

JACOB. As witnessed by your dry books.

BOZHO. You think you need balls to write?

JACOB. I use mine for other things. I'm not a writer.

BOZHO. You've written a play.

JACOB. You've written thousands of pages. So what?

BOZHO. All the romantic geniuses died before they were thirty. You'll have to hurry if you want to catch the last train.

JACOB. How many years ago did you miss your last train? You're a prose writer, a playwright, a literary historian, a linguist, a critic, a theoretician, a publisher, a member of the government, a consultant — and in fact you're on the borderline of functional illiteracy.

PARASKEVA. What does functional illiteracy mean?

JACOB. Literate illiteracy. The worst kind of illiteracy.

BOZHO. Don't get involved in this, Paraskeva.

JACOB. Get involved, Madam. Bring a little humor into our hermetic dispute. Christine, swear to tell the truth, the whole truth, and nothing but the truth.

CHRISTINE. So help me God?

JACOB. I'm an atheist.

CHRISTINE. I'll have no other atheists but Thee.

JACOB. Have you read your father's books?

[*Pause.*]

CHRISTINE. I have.

JACOB. Have you read them to the end?

CHRISTINE. No.

PARASKEVA. Christine! You have your own personal copies with special dedications!

JACOB. Thank you. The bench has no further questions.

BOZHO. [*To Jacob*] Isn't it terrible? You really can't stand me, can you?

JACOB. It's terrible for me. You couldn't care less.

BOZHO. I've always assumed there must be people who didn't appreciate my work, who didn't agree with my opinions. But that there were people like you whose hatred for me had reached a pathological passion — I'd never even dreamt that for one moment! You've obviously been thinking about me for months. I've been eating into you like an acid. I don't know you, but I'm the center of your obsession and trauma. It's easy for you to say "I'm not a writer. I just happened to write something. I'm not responsible."

JACOB. Why don't you do that, too? Why spend your whole life defending your works like a little child? It's a real infection here. People are either illiterate or they're men of letters. Or both. You haven't got one useful thought in your head, so you prove that water is wet. Give up. Confess. Half of it will be forgiven.

PARASKEVA. He has a different idea of his work, whatever you may think of it.

JACOB. So much the worse for him. He'll bear the full responsibility for his guilt.

BOZHO. Stop it, Paraskeva!

PARASKEVA. I also take this as a personal insult.

BOZHO. [*To Jacob*] You think you're better than me in every respect?

JACOB. There's no comparison between us. We're like apples and pears, chalk and cheese. Though I'm not exactly a paragon of virtue, of course. Your faults bother me, which means I must have them myself. I know how to attack myself as well. Very effectively and logically. But that's not what this particular scenario is all about.

BOZHO. As far as you're concerned, I'm a bad writer, a petty politician with double standards, stifling young hopefuls. I have an intellectual monopoly. I travel with a generous expense account, I give speeches and seminars for special occasions. And you believe you can dislodge me with fifty pages of infantile cynicism? Look at it from the other side. Don't you think all my posts and responsibilities might be a burden to me? You think I enjoy being torn in all directions? Ask yourself what price I pay. You despise me for not being a "pure" man of letters. For the fact that I'm at the center of vital ideological and political ferments at the same time. That every day, every hour, I have to make important decisions which history imposes on me. Which can't wait and which won't be excused. Do you know what kind of pressure that is? But it has to fall on someone. Someone has to shoulder the burden. Why don't you offer your assistance? Why not help in that battle? It's your battle, too.

JACOB. Yes, it is. That's why I'm here. I'm helping.

BOZHO. You don't see future prospects. You don't believe in a tomorrow!

JACOB. I have certain hopes for the day ***after*** tomorrow, though.

BOZHO. That's irresponsible pessimism.

JACOB. A balance to your irresponsible optimism. I match your extremes with my own. I find it boring to be always keeping the balance. What right do you have always to be the scales and I'm always the weight? You always the gunner and I always the one giving the ammunition?

BOZHO. It's easy to put your hand to your forehead, a cravat around your neck, and float off into *Weltschmerz* and *ennui*.

JACOB. And what's so difficult about putting on a bowtie and writing recitals? Any old drunken bohemian is more interesting than a sober philosophy professor. If I were the very best, you wouldn't even admit me as your equal!

BOZHO. You think you're a film star or something? You look at yourself in the shop windows when you walk down the street. You think everyone should follow your example.

Why can't you understand you're acting a role which has been planted on you? What you think of as your own free choice is just blind acceptance of what others offer you.

JACOB. They offer me various things. It's not that I don't choose.

BOZHO. All the confused, soft, and naïve romantics talk like you. Behind their rebellious phrases they simply hide their inability to find a place in the world they live in. The world is made of steel. It's a razor. A system of blades. Without me in the world, you'd cut yourself in three seconds. You bark at me but you don't bite. Because if I didn't exist, you wouldn't know what to do on your own. As long as I'm ***here***, you can try to stay ***there***. I fix your angle of deviation from me. You only exist as my opposite. You haven't got a real life of your own. You're my paid opposition. You sentence me to death at the same time as you beg me for clemency.

JACOB. [*Making a vulgar sign*] This to your logic, your reason, and your syllogisms! It's all theater! The best acting is in the best pretense.

PARASKEVA. Jacob, you won't get away with this.

JACOB. Of course I won't.

PARASKEVA. You don't know what you're doing, what you're saying!

JACOB. What about you, Madam? Do you know what you're doing and what you're saying? Why you're alive? Answer me! Why are you alive?

PARASKEVA. What do you mean, why am I alive?! What right have you to ask me such a thing?

JACOB. What right have you not to know the answer? You've packed fifty-five years away up your rear end and you don't know why you're alive! You've never given any thought to that particular problem. Something more important was always cropping up. Think of an answer! Here and now!

PARASKEVA. I've lived for art!

JACOB. You, too?!

PARASKEVA. I've lived for beauty. Music. Theater.

JACOB. Who gave you permission? You think ***anyone*** can love art and the theater? You think, come on, let's all love art and the theater! You have to be deserving! You ***play*** at culture. You think this is where the fewest responsibilities lie. Well, what the heck! Bash away! Nobody's going to bite me. From this moment I forbid you to love culture and the theater. Do you have any example, any illustration of your love? You must have learnt some poem, some tragic soliloquy by heart. If suddenly it's the end of the world now and only you remain alive, and some little green men come along, what experience of life will you convey to them? What art will you talk to them about? I'm listening. [*Pause*] Say something, Madam, we haven't got much time. We've still got a lot to do.

PARASKEVA. What do you want of me?

JACOB. A song, a poem, anything.

[*He puts the gun to her head.*]

PARASKEVA. I don't know anything.

JACOB. That's impossible. Your husband's been dragging you around the culture scene with him all your life. Think of something. You must remember some poem or other you learnt at school. Do you know "Three Blind Mice"? [*Pause*] Do you know the song "Three Blind Mice?" Answer the question. [*Pause*] Sing it. [*Pause*] Sing it!!

PARASKEVA. [*Singing*] Three blind mice, three blind mice . . . [*Pause.*]

JACOB. Yes? [*Pause*] Is that all? [*Pause*] "See how they run"? D'you only know one line? It's not possible. Dear oh dear. The Lord is my witness. The theater, did you say? What theater? [*To Bozho*] Why have theater, Sir? Close the theaters, the culture clubs, the schools. Everything! Why should we need horseshoes for frogs? There's no theater! In our lumpen-proletariat fantasies we see ourselves as middle-class citizens, as bourgeois thinkers. There's no art! Now we're going to split up our provincial awareness into its component parts. We're going to peel off the false glaze and be reduced to our indivisible core. To what will remain of us. If anything does remain. And if nothing remains, we'll have to think of something better! Come on, run!

BOZHO. What?

JACOB. Run!

BOZHO. Where?

JACOB. On the spot!

BOZHO. Why?

JACOB. So you can sweat a bit. A disciplinary measure. [*Bozho looks at him.*] Something not clear? [*Bozho starts running on the spot.*] Faster. [*Bozho runs faster.*]

[*Pause. Enter Novey dressed in a paratrooper's uniform.*]

NOVEY. What's going on here?

JACOB. Well, here's another special man of the arts who doesn't understand what's going on here. What's this paramilitary uniform for, then?

NOVEY. I do skydiving.

JACOB. I put you in uniform in my play. But I never thought life would so outdo art.

NOVEY. What play?

JACOB. What life? Finished your epic poem?

NOVEY. I'm working on it.

JACOB. He's been writing an epic poem all his life about humankind from prehistoric times to the present. The Iliad is his prologue. He's written twenty-four lines so far. It'd be best never to finish it. That way you'll be an eternal, promising new face. First put in a request for permits, grants, prizes. Why rush things?

NOVEY. I don't understand a thing.

JACOB. Yes, we've already established that much.

NOVEY. A few days ago Jacob came round to my house one evening. I was watching TV. I asked him what he wanted. He didn't answer. Then he got up, looked at me, and said "You're watching TV." And went away. My mother was upset. I couldn't explain to her what had happened.

JACOB. Now tell us, my dear fellow student, why you were always trying to play up to me in college. Tell us, sweetie.

[*Pause.*]

NOVEY. They called me in. They asked about you. I just told them what I knew. I didn't make anything up. They knew it all anyway. You can't blame me for anything.

PARASKEVA. Who knew it all anyway?

JACOB. ***They*** did. One doesn't name ***them***. Do not take the name of the Lord Thy God in vain.

PARASKEVA. What did they know?

NOVEY. That he took it upon himself to give lectures to the students in the breaks between classes. That he came to classes in a gas mask. He went on a hunger strike because the toilets weren't clean. He interrupted student meetings with comments that were out of order. He wore way-out clothes. He stood outside the maternity ward at the hospital shouting to the pregnant women to refuse to bring children into this kind of world. He went barefoot in the streets in winter. An egomaniac. He found it as easy to make as to break friendships. They knew he wrote graffiti on buildings saying "To everything there is a false bottom."

BOZHO. Well done. Less talented people would need more than three lifetimes to make such a shambles.

JACOB. Everything I did I wanted to do. I did it of my own free will. [*To Novey*] Say the alphabet.

NOVEY. What?

JACOB. The alphabet! Say it!

NOVEY. Why?

JACOB. Firstly, so I don't shoot. And secondly, because you're a writer.

NOVEY. A, B, C, D, E, F, G, I, J . . .

JACOB. Wrong. Start again.

NOVEY. A, B, C, D, E, F, G, I, J . . .

JACOB. Wrong. Start again.

NOVEY. Where did I go wrong?

JACOB. Don't you know?

NOVEY. Why do I have to know the alphabet if I'm a writer?

JACOB. In your case, actually, you don't have to!

[*Pause*.]

CHRISTINE. Well, that leaves me. How are you going to enlighten me?

JACOB. Are you a good dancer?

CHRISTINE. I don't know.

JACOB. That's something you feel in your bones.

CHRISTINE. Yes, I am.

JACOB. Of course you are. If you're bad, you're nothing.

[*Jacob ties Christine with a long black rope from head to foot, like a mummy*.]

JACOB. If you're a real ballerina, you'll dance tied up. With no arms or legs. No music. No spotlights. Don't say "I won't," "I can't." For "I can't" you go to hospital. For "I won't" you go to jail. [*He ties a knot in the rope*.] Now grow into a butterfly, my dear larva. Mind you don't break anything while dancing. When they put down this republic of mine in blood, the ideological side won't weigh against me as much as the material damage.

CHRISTINE. To everything there is a false bottom.

JACOB. The false bottom is a cellar in your head. That's where we hide all our contingency plans. Such as which woman to marry if our wife should die in a car accident. Such as how to transfer our brother's savings account to our name if he should meet a sudden death. That's where all our secret adultery is. All that we've kept quiet about. Everything we've forgotten on purpose. It's clear there who we hate and how much we hate them. That's where we hide all our lack of faith in what we swear in public we believe in. And all our faith in what we publicly refute. That's the warehouse of vanity and passion. Of our darkness and defeat. There we have no makeup, no false teeth, no corsets. There we are ugly. But among that rubbish and waste matter in our heads lie shackled in a deep sleep our truth and our freedom, our innocence, and our human dignity. States and civilizations have their false bottoms as well. Nobody cleans them out. They grow. They strain against the nine heavy portals, each with its nine bolts and padlocks. We smuggle our own selves into the false bottom and look on our smuggling like customs men — who see it all, but who can't believe that anyone could be so brazen as to carry their very own self in a suitcase over all permissible borders against the law. Your head can break the portals of the false bottom. With the artistic psychosis, or the schizoaffective psychosis, or the revolutionary psychosis. Your head breaks and bleeds like the champagne bottle when a ship is launched. The history of the world is the history of the bottoms that have been pierced through. One day the bottom and the false bottom will finally be one. Then there won't be any mad artists or terrorists anymore.

[*Jacob takes Bozho by the hand and leads him to a large mirror.*]

JACOB. Look yourself straight in the eye.

[*Jacob counts the seconds off with his hand. After a certain time Bozho turns his head away.*]

JACOB. Seven seconds.

[*Jacob fetches Paraskeva and carries out the same procedure.*]

JACOB. Thirteen seconds.

[*The same with Novey.*]

JACOB. Fifteen seconds.

[*Jacob gets Christine up off the floor. She is crying. She goes on looking into the mirror without turning her head away.*]

JACOB. That terrifying thing we see in the mirror when we look at ourselves is the false bottom. Only Christine will be one with it. Only she will free herself. She's not afraid. She doesn't turn her back on it. And now, ladies and gentlemen, Christine, the promising young ballerina, will with a little assistance give us a brief performance entitled "Who I am, what I am, what I have done, and what I should do to prepare for the future."

[*Jacob holds Christine in front of him like a puppet.*]

JACOB. Come, my cocoon. Find the right place for you. Look for it! You can't stay here. Here you're in the center. You're nothing. A conservative position. [*He turns her in a circle.*] This is anarchy. [*He leads her to the left.*] Here you're a lefty. No way! [*He leads her further to the left.*] Here you're an ultra-lefty, if not a terrorist. [*He leads her to the right.*] Here you're the right wing. No good. [*He leads her further to the right.*] The extreme right. Fascism. Let's get out of here! [*He throws her to the floor.*] You're a nationalist! [*He drags her forward.*] A liberal, eh? Want to be a little leader, do we? [*He drags her backwards.*] You're pulling back, you dark reactionary!

CHRISTINE. Where should I be?

JACOB. In the right place!

CHRISTINE. Where's the right place???!!!

JACOB. I'm not telling you. I'm going to live another thousand years. Why should I betray the secret ahead of time? Find out for yourself. And if you chance to find it, I'll lie and tell you it's not right. That you haven't found it! Look for it! By your own example, your readiness to fight . . .

JACOB. Consistency, decisiveness,	**CHRISTINE.** . . . integrity, perseverance,
clichés, opportunism,	hypocrisy, passivity,
socialism, communism,	statism, hegemonism,
capitalism, fascism,	irredentism, nihilism,
dogmatism, technocracy,	clericalism, nationalism,
degeneration, mutation,	frustration, carburation,
Freud, Nietzsche, Hegel,	affirmation, negation,
Kafka, Shakespeare, Dostoevsky,	Christ, Einstein, Chaplin,
then blank, blank, blank,	then blank, blank, blank,
and then in the end	Jacob!
Christine!	Who?
You!	And you!
Me?	Me?

[*Jacob unwinds the rope around Christine as if she were a spinning top. Christine starts weeping and falls down.*]

JACOB. You're not going to cry ***now***, are you? Your parents kept you bound up all your life. You didn't object. You thought that was how it was supposed to be. You thought you were fine.

BOZHO. Is this your idea of revolution, then? A diabolical concoction of art, anarchy, and adolescent madness. An apocalyptic vision with cyclical time. Atomic bomb shelters in the future and lunatic asylums in the past. This is just flirting with fashion. A diversion of a subtle kind of shape. Where is the humanist commitment in this? There's no greater ideal, no greater mission for a man of the arts than serving the people. A wide field of activity is open to all artists. All the noble sources of inspiration are open. And you imbibe from them only phantom-like inventions, inflated lampoons, black-and-white posters, pamphlets, and allegories — even though they use real names. Anyone can do that! Anyone knows how!

JACOB. You talk like some mythological god! You've taken on his form. You've put on his mask. You've become inviolable, untouchable. The anointed pharaoh. I strike you and you cry "Do not strike him." I want to embrace him and you cry "Embrace me. I am he." But you're just a devil who's jumped onto God's back and is driving him like a chariot. I'll peel you away from God. I'll scour you off like burnt pastry in a pan and I'll make the bottom shine with a wire pad. You teach me that the past doesn't exist, that the future has taken place. I have to sniff out for myself on the dung heap of the world who I am. I return your ready-made products. I want the tools back. All churches are false. Only faith is real. You're a finely affecting and easily affected poet with watery eyes, puffy from your literary drinking bouts. You walk around at night with your hands in your pockets. Whistling. You fiddle with your little prick. You positively die of beauty in a dogmatic slumber and in drooling rhymes. And from your perfect frog's eye view, you inform us how you feel and what plans you have for the world. People have gone into space. But here before you, in the jaws of death, I have to prove to you that the Earth revolves around the Sun. I'm going to take your world, empty out all the waters, put the mountains in their places. Everest in the Pacific. I'm going to crumple them all up together with all the flora, fauna, nations and nationalities, and flick them away with my two fingers like so much snot. *EPPUR SI MUOVE.*[2]

[*Jacob starts turning the furniture over. Pause.*]

BOZHO. What now, eh? Where can you run to now?! What false bottom are you going to hide in now? This is final. Nothing is like in your play. Everything is like in my reality.

[*A distant rumble is heard. It grows louder.*]

BOZHO. Impossible!!

JACOB. Yes! The time has come for ***that***, too!

[*Thunder. Music. The false bottom is revealed. Chaos.*]

2. And yet, it moves.

CODA
(THEATER)

[*The stage. Empty. Bare walls. A door backstage opens. Jacob comes out. He is stripped to the waist. He behaves like a private individual. He is taking off his make-up with one hand and carrying a manuscript in the other. He slowly walks towards the proscenium.*]

JACOB. Time future, time past, and time present make up time theatrical. What is time theatrical to me, and what am I to do with it? [*He looks at the manuscript.*] "The False Bottom — a passion for the theater in three movements." [*He throws the manuscript up in the air. Pages fly all over the stage.*] Nothing is like in my play. But I don't know what my reality is. [*He touches the wall.*] I swear on my faith, my conscience, and my honor that I will work for the liberation of the spirit with all my power and means, and that I will never betray the secrets of the act of revolution. Should I do so, let me be killed with this revolver or this dagger which I kiss. To everything there is a false bottom. [*Silence. He strikes the wall.*] To everything there is a false bottom. [*Silence. He strikes harder.*] To everything there is a false bottom. [*Silence. He looks ahead of him. He turns, exits quickly, slamming the door behind him.*]

THE END

3

TATTOOED SOULS

Translated from the Macedonian
by Patricia Marsh-Stefanovska

This play is dedicated to the shade of my mother, Nada.

CHARACTERS

VOYDAN 30

TSIBRA 33

STREZO 60

ALTANA 55

KOLYO 60

RUZHA 26

MARE 25

CLAUDIA 35

THE TATTOOER

THE DANCER

THE MAN

THE BOY

THE PASSER-BY

THE BODYGUARD

GANGSTER I

GANGSTER II

MUSICIANS

PEOPLE IN THE BAR

AUTHOR'S NOTE

Most of the personal names, geographical references and general "local color" in this play are Macedonian. There is no objection to their being changed to suit any other nation which may find parallels in the text with its own situation in a foreign culture.

TRANSLATOR'S NOTE

I am very grateful to Mr. William Shine of the USIS Center in Skopje for having "Americanized" my original British English translation of the text.

SCENE 1

[A big city in the United States. Night. A street. A passer-by is standing under a streetlamp, either drunk or drugged. He is gazing blankly ahead of him. Pause. Enter Voydan, carrying a suitcase. He glances at the passer-by and goes past him. Then he stops and turns.]

VOYDAN. Good evening. [*Pause*] I wonder if you could help me. I'm lost. This is my first day in America. [*Pause*] Do you understand what I'm saying? [*Pause*] Everyone in this part of town speaks our language, so I'm told. [*Pause.*]

[*Passer-by nods his head.*]

VOYDAN. I've been trying to find this address for hours. And now it's dark.

[*Passer-by nods his head.*]

VOYDAN. Well . . . [*Pause*] Goodbye. [*Pause*] I'm from Yugoslavia. [*Leaving.*]

PASSER-BY. [*Letting out an inarticulate cry*] Nnnh!

VOYDAN. [*Turning*] Excuse me?

PASSER-BY. I don't give a fuck . . . if you're from Yugoslavia.

[*Passer-by stares blankly at Voydan. Voydan quickly goes away.*]

SCENE 2

[*A hamburger bar with a counter and some bar stools, wooden tables and benches, a pinball machine. Altana is sweeping the floor with a long broom and smoking a cigar. Pause. Enter Kolyo. He is wearing a suit with cuffs on the trousers and a hat.*]

KOLYO. Good evening.

ALTANA. It's after midnight.

KOLYO. I can't sleep. [*Sitting down*] Through for today?

ALTANA. Yeah, just. I've been feeding the scum of the suburbs. [*Pause*] They don't even say thank you, but at least they didn't smash the place up this time.

[*Pause.*]

KOLYO. I've got a new way of getting there. [*Taking various airline schedules out of his pocket*] A Pakistani airline. They fly from New York to Abu Dhabi via Frankfurt. 400 dollars to Frankfurt. A hundred dollars cheaper than the way I told you about yesterday. Every Thursday at 7 pm. Six-hour flight, six time zones. I'd be in Frankfurt at 7 in the morning. [*Pause*] The connecting flight for home isn't much good, though. Seven-hour wait at the airport. [*Pause*] What d'you think? [*Pause*] So what if it's a Pakistani line? Flying's the safest way of traveling these days. More people die on bicycles. [*Pause*] I'd get on a snail's back if it'd get me back home.

ALTANA. Oh, Kolyo. D'you know you say the same thing every single day?

KOLYO. Yes?

ALTANA. Well, say something else for a change.

KOLYO. OK.

ALTANA. OK what?

KOLYO. I'll say something else for a change.

ALTANA. You do that. [*Pause*] What's new?

KOLYO. New? Huh! My sons want me to make some of the old meat pies from home. Let's eat some decent human food, they say. When they pushed me out of the shop, I was too old, I didn't know anything. Now they'd like some of the old pies. Well, that's too bad. We could have swamped America with all our special rolls and buns from the old country. We could've started a company. They didn't want anything to do with it. So if they didn't want it then, they're not having any of the old pie now. Let them eat plastic. [*Pause*] I take my grandchildren to school in the mornings. I say something to them, they don't understand. They say something to me, ***I*** don't understand. [*Pause. He is weeping.*]

ALTANA. Don't start.

KOLYO. I won't. [*He pulls himself together.*] I'll dress you up in a white dress, put a ribbon in your hat, me in a captain's uniform with all the braid, and arm in arm onto the ship over the seas and far away. [*Pause*] When are we going to get married?

ALTANA. Yesterday.

KOLYO. The snail setting out on a pilgrimage knows he's not going to get to Jerusalem, but he feels happy that at least he's on the Sacred Way.

ALTANA. I'm all washed up.

KOLYO. Who knows what you must have been like. In that regard.

ALTANA. Who knows?

KOLYO. You're not to be passed over.

ALTANA. Who says?

KOLYO. I do.

ALTANA. I thought you had taste. [*Pause*] Nobody even dares rob me. They see me through the window and cross over to the other side of the street. [*Pause.*]

KOLYO. When I think there's somebody dying at this very moment who desperately wants to live. And here am I living for nothing.

ALTANA. Don't start.

[*Enter Voydan, carrying his suitcase. They look at each other. Pause.*]

VOYDAN. Good evening.

ALTANA. We're closed.

VOYDAN. I'm Voydan Ivanovski. Strezo's son. From the old country. I'm a researcher.

ALTANA. Strezo?

VOYDAN. Strezo Ivanovski? You know him? I found this address on an old letter. I wasn't planning to come here. That's why I didn't let you know. [*Pause*] Am I in the right place? [*Pause*] If I'm not welcome, I'll go.

ALTANA. You'd better go. [*They look at each other. Pause.*]

SCENE 3

[*Night. A street. Tsibra staggering along drunk. He stops at a corner and urinates. Pause.*]

TSIBRA. America!!! [*Pause. He finishes and zips up his fly.*] Good night, America. [*Pause. He goes off.*]

SCENE 4

[*Altana's bar. Altana is sitting, staring in front of her. Pause. Enter Tsibra. Pause. They look at each other.*]

ALTANA. You're all I needed. [*Pause*] This guy just turned up. His name's Voydan, says he's Strezo's son. He's sleeping in your old room. [*Pause.*]

[*Tsibra goes to the refrigerator and takes out a can of beer. He sits down, opens it and drinks.*]

ALTANA. I didn't know Strezo had a son. Strezo didn't say he had a son. [*Pause*] Want something to eat? [*Pause*] He just appeared out of nowhere. He's on some kind of a grant. [*Pause*] What're we going to do? [*Pause*] What am I going to do? [*Pause*] Go home to bed. [*Pause*] You said you didn't want anything to eat?

[*Pause. She gets up and exits through the door leading to the back part of the house. She turns out the lights. Tsibra remains sitting in the green neon light of the bar window. He drinks his beer. Pause.*]

SCENE 5

[*A room. Voydan is asleep. Enter Ruzha, carrying a cup of coffee. Pause. She looks at Voydan. Silence.*]

VOYDAN. Good morning.

RUZHA. You scared me. I thought you were asleep.

VOYDAN. You woke me up.

RUZHA. I'm Ruzha. Altana's my aunt. She told me you were here. I wanted to meet you before I go to work. Coffee. No sugar. I don't take sugar either. I sleep in the room next door. I hope the radio didn't bother you. It's on all night. I always sleep with it on. I like listening to voices. Not music. Voices. This is my brother Tsibra's room.

VOYDAN. Where is ***he***?

RUZHA. Where he likes. I work in a supermarket. What about you?

VOYDAN. I'm a research assistant.

RUZHA. You're from the old country. Is it really as great as they say over there?

VOYDAN. I don't know what they say.

RUZHA. That it's heaven.

VOYDAN. Who says?

RUZHA. Altana. Kolyo. Everybody.

VOYDAN. They're lying. Why don't you go and see for yourself?

RUZHA. I didn't think you could actually ***go*** there. Like a fairy tale land: "Once upon a time in a far distant land . . ." [*Pause.*]

VOYDAN. Do you sell calculators in your supermarket?

RUZHA. What are they?

VOYDAN. You work in a supermarket in America and you don't know what calculators are?!

RUZHA. I'll ask.

VOYDAN. Check what kind of prices they have. Don't forget. [*Pause*] Why're your cheeks so red? What're you so embarrassed about?

RUZHA. I've got to get to work.

VOYDAN. Are you doing anything this evening? Would you like to go out somewhere with me?

RUZHA. They wouldn't let me.

VOYDAN. Who wouldn't?

RUZHA. Altana.

VOYDAN. But you're not a child. [*Pause. He looks at her.*] The patriarchal model par excellence.

RUZHA. Excuse me?

VOYDAN. I'm making a diagnosis. [*Pause*] You going?

RUZHA. Where?

VOYDAN. To work. If someone tells me they're in a hurry to get somewhere and then stays where they are, I start hurrying instead. If someone tells me they want to go to the bathroom, and then they don't go, it makes ***me*** feel like going.

RUZHA. I'm going in for the Miss Macedonia of America Contest. D'you think I got a chance?

VOYDAN. Yes.

RUZHA. Liar. How d'you know what the others'll be like? Am I pretty?

VOYDAN. Yes.

RUZHA. Liar.

VOYDAN. No, I'm not.

RUZHA. Cross your heart and hope to die.

VOYDAN. Cross my heart and hope to die.

RUZHA. You'll die when I count to ten if you're lying. One, two, three, four, five, six, seven, eight, nine, nine and a half, nine and three-quarters . . . [*Pause*] . . . ten. [*Pause*] You're still a liar. Even though you're not dead. I didn't die either. I said to my mother: "If there's a God, let me die when I count to three. One, two, three." My mother used to spit on the ground where I'd been standing to save me from my blasphemies. It didn't work. Look at this nose of mine.

VOYDAN. What's wrong with it?

RUZHA. It's ugly.

VOYDAN. It's not ugly.

RUZHA. But it's not pretty either.

VOYDAN. How d'you want it to be?

RUZHA. Different.

VOYDAN. In what way?

RUZHA. Not like this.

VOYDAN. Well, why don't you go and have plastic surgery, then?

RUZHA. You want me to go and have plastic surgery. [*Pause.*] So you ***admit*** I'm ugly.

SCENE 6

[*An open space. Tsibra is shooting a pistol at a target. Enter The Boy.*]

TSIBRA. What d'you want?

THE BOY. You're Tsibra. I want to be your assistant.

TSIBRA. Assistant for what?

THE BOY. For everything.

TSIBRA. What do you know?

THE BOY. I know all the makes of guns.

TSIBRA. Yeah?

THE BOY. Winchester, Ithaca, Remington, Browning, Steyr, Ruger, Heckler, Koch, Smith & Wesson, Wetherby, Bereta, Marlin.

TSIBRA. Is that all? Go back home.

THE BOY. I haven't got a home.

TSIBRA. Well, go . . . somewhere else. Go to the movies.

THE BOY. I want to watch ***you***.

SCENE 7

[*Altana's bar. Altana is smoking a cigar. Enter Voydan from living area of the house.*]

ALTANA. Good morning.

VOYDAN. I feel like shit. I could hear the radio blaring all night. I'd just gone off into a really deep sleep when Ruzha woke me up. Brought me a cup of coffee. Bitter as aloes. The light bulb in the bathroom's dead. [*He sees the pinball machine and gives it a try.*] These are only good for getting you all riled up. I don't know how some people can spend all day playing them.

ALTANA. You hungry?

VOYDAN. I helped myself in the kitchen.

ALTANA. Make yourself at home.

VOYDAN. You got hundreds of cactuses in the back garden. Why cactuses and not flowers?

ALTANA. Cactuses are flowers, too.

VOYDAN. They flower once in a hundred years. I heard you talking to them. They all got names? [*Pause*] I was supposed to go and stay with a girlfriend of mine in New York. I met her at the beach last year. She fell in love with me. I went straight to her place from the airport yesterday. And guess what — she lives with two blacks. I didn't even go in. Didn't see the point. I said to myself, I'll go to my own people. So here I am. I won't stay long. Just 'till I get my bearings. I could go to a hotel, but this suits me better. Cheaper, too. [*Pause*] Why's Ruzha so shy? Is it because of me? She say anything to you?

ALTANA. No.

VOYDAN. I don't want to get involved in any sort of emotional shit. I've had some bad experiences. What's her brother do?

ALTANA. Tsibra has a grocery store.

VOYDAN. Typical of immigrants from our country. Not rich, not poor. Not one thing or the other. I'm an ethnologist. Ethnology is the science of the lives, beliefs, and customs of a people. [*Pause*] So my father used to live in this house, did he? When did he die?

ALTANA. Ten years ago.

VOYDAN. What of?

ALTANA. Heart attack.

VOYDAN. Not that I have any particular feelings about him. I was just a child when he left us. He used to send money at first, write. Then he stopped. My mother didn't expect him back. She didn't write to him. She died last year. That's probably why I chose this profession. Sort of like the son of crazy parents becoming a psychiatrist to protect himself from the family illness. I'm writing my Master's thesis on "The influence of migration processes on the mental and physical constitution of Macedonian immigrants in the United States of America." To put it simply, it's about how migration affects your health. I've got a whole methodology worked out, questionnaires, graphs, stats. I came over here more to get away from home than to do any real research. I've got a clear picture already.

ALTANA. What picture?

VOYDAN. About our people here. I've got an exact image of who they are and what they're like. You're not married, are you?

ALTANA. No.

VOYDAN. Why not?

ALTANA. Yeah, why not? [*Pause*] Your father was a friend of my brother's. We came over together. They worked together.

VOYDAN. I spent my whole childhood dreaming about America. I pictured my father as a big, well-built man, his black hair sleeked down with brilliantine, a detective's hat on his head, a suit with padded shoulders and cuffs on the trousers, black and white shoes, a carnation in his button-hole, a Colt under his arm, driving a Chevrolet, holding Marilyn Monroe's hand, them listening to jazz on the radio, drinking Coca-Cola, and smiling, smiling.

ALTANA. Your father was a skinner. It's a hard, stinking job. People used to go miles out of their way to avoid going past that slaughterhouse. It stank to high heaven. Our men prided themselves on being able to put up with the horrible smell.

VOYDAN. Anything's better than living in a village back home.

ALTANA. If you're just an onlooker. Not involved.

VOYDAN. At least the pay's ten times higher. And the prices are the same as back home. And then I was looking at some pocket calculators in New York yesterday. Three dollars each in a shop down the street. I found some for two and a half. You can get them even cheaper if you shop around. They cost three times as much back home. I'm going to buy a dozen of them. [*Pause*] As presents.

ALTANA. What're these calculators for?

VOYDAN. Calculating. Have to go with the times. You always smoke cigars?

ALTANA. Yes.

VOYDAN. I find it strange. An old woman with a cigar. The smoke bothers me a bit. Never mind, though. Keep smoking, it sets you apart. [*Pause*] Of course, I'm ready to pay for staying here.

ALTANA. Don't overdo it.

VOYDAN. Thanks. I'm somewhat of a journalist, too, you know. I can write a series of articles about your lives here. I'll send you copies. You can cut them and frame them. I could maybe even make a book out of them. A novel or something.

[*Enter Kolyo.*]

KOLYO. Good morning.

ALTANA. You haven't slept, you haven't eaten — you haven't even taken your shoes off. Ready to leave at any moment.

KOLYO. Never know what a day has in store for you. May never get another chance.

VOYDAN. Hey, it's great you came! I wanted to ask you something. [*He takes out some forms.*] This is a questionnaire I put together with my Social Psychology professor. It's the first in a series of seventeen questionnaires for testing types of mental effects experienced by subjects exposed to the stress of migration. We could have a little trial run. It's quite simple. You have to circle one of the possible answers — that is, the alternative which is ***your*** answer. For example. Number one. "I cook national dishes a) every day; b) once a week; c) once a month; d) not very often." Or question Number Two. "I dream about the old country a) every night; b) once a week; c) once a month; d) not very often." [*Pause*] Would you like to fill it out on your own, or should I help you? [*Kolyo begins to cry. Pause.*] What's the matter?

ALTANA. He's crying.

VOYDAN. Why's he crying?

ALTANA. Why shouldn't he cry? What do you want him to do?

VOYDAN. But why cry? These questions are purely of scientific interest. [*Pause*] I'm going out.

ALTANA. Be careful.

VOYDAN. Be careful?

ALTANA. This is a big city.

VOYDAN. I come from a big city, anyway. I'm not a country cousin. I've seen a bit of life.

[*Exit. Pause.*]

KOLYO. Just when I start believing there are only little princes of men left in the old country, some damn fool like this turns up! The folk back home make a little money, too, but they don't spend it on the right things. They buy themselves a horse, a fine, high-stepping one, and then instead of spending a bit more for a good saddle, they go and put one of those wooden mule's packsaddles on it. [*Pause*] I think I'll stay on that plane right through to Abu Dhabi.

SCENE 8

[*Pornographic peep-show booths. Tsibra is waiting outside. Voydan comes out of one.*]

TSIBRA. Voydan Ivanovski! [*Voydan turns.*] Good afternoon.

VOYDAN. Who are you?

TSIBRA. Your passport.

VOYDAN. Excuse me?

TSIBRA. Give me your passport.

VOYDAN. Why should I?

TSIBRA. I want to see if you have a visa.

VOYDAN. Of course I do.

TSIBRA. I want to see it. [*Voydan gives him the passport.*] Why are you giving me this?

VOYDAN. You asked for it.

TSIBRA. I could've asked you to jump off the Empire State Building. You think there's nothing wrong in just giving travel documents to strangers, in a foreign country, ***and*** in a place like this? Now I'll just burn it. You won't legally exist in this country anymore. I'll just take all your money, too. And leave you as naked as the day you were born. Like your father when he first arrived.

VOYDAN. How d'you know my father?

TSIBRA. Are you Strezo's son or the Secret Service's? What're you doing in America?

VOYDAN. I'm a research assistant. I'm writing about you. That is, you and us. All of us.

TSIBRA. Writing, are you? Or looking at naked women? You don't have these booths in Macedonia, do you? There aren't any whores there, are there? You're all saints. High moral standards. First you jerk off and then write about family ethics and strict, simple, national customs.

VOYDAN. I was just passing by. I didn't know what was in there.

TSIBRA. Let's have a look at your hand, then.

VOYDAN. What for?

TSIBRA. Your hand!

VOYDAN. Leave me alone!

[*Tsibra grabs Voydan's hand and looks at his palm. He takes out a paper handkerchief and puts it in Voydan's hand.*]

TSIBRA. You should do it in a Kleenex or a rubber. You can buy them over there for 50 cents. But you're saving your money, of course! "Just passing by," eh? I've been following you for three days. You "pass by" here twice a day! You know someone has to clean out this booth now? [*Pause*] Huh? [*Pause*] Someone has to put on a pair of rubber gloves, get a bucket of water, a cloth, and go down on their knees to wipe up what types like you leave behind them. You know what it's like, that kind of job? You know what human dignity means? What're you shaking for? Like a rabbit in front of a python! You're a coward. That your own personal trait, or is it a national one? Huh? That's what you're studying, isn't it? You should know. You all just kiss the other's guy ass. When there's nobody looking. And then you're all heroes. How did that poor country ever put up with you? [*Pause*]

What now, eh? Who's going to save you now, you, the big hero, the good guy, from me, the bad guy in this scene? You going to think up some clever way of escaping at the last minute, or are you waiting for the cavalry to turn up from somewhere? That only happens in films. Not in real life. It didn't happen to my father, or your father, and it didn't happen to me. So why should it happen to you? Why should you be the exception?

VOYDAN. [*Starting to cry*] Leave me alone. Please.

TSIBRA. Leave you alone? Why should I? Why don't you leave ***me*** alone?

VOYDAN. I haven't done anything!

TSIBRA. And you think that's not a crime? Not to have done anything at ***your*** age? Why don't you do something? You come on to Ruzha. You ask Kolyo if he has dreams not very often or never. You clean out Altana's fridge. You sleep in my bed. I'm Tsibra. Welcome to the new world.

VOYDAN. Come on . . . Is this any way to . . .?

TSIBRA. I was checking up on you. I have all types trying to get close to me.

VOYDAN. This isn't fair.

TSIBRA. Ah, the gentleman is concerned about fair play?

VOYDAN. And what did you check up on exactly? Who am I?

TSIBRA. You know very well.

VOYDAN. I'm shaking all over.

TSIBRA. I'll treat you to a beer.

VOYDAN. I don't drink. [*Pause*] Make it Coca-Cola.

SCENE 9

[A bar full of people. Enter Voydan and Tsibra. Everybody stops talking. Silence. They make way for Voydan and Tsibra, who go up to the bar.]

TSIBRA. Two beers.

VOYDAN. Coca-Cola.

TSIBRA. Two beers and a Coke.

VOYDAN. With ice.

[One by one the people start to leave the bar. Only two men in cowboy hats remain by the counter. Tsibra gives them a look. They look at each other and then leave. Voydan does not notice any of this.]

VOYDAN. I was shaken. I thought you were one of those extremists. I was given orders and instructions about keeping away from that type. Of course, immigrants from our country don't usually go in for extremism, but there's the occasional one or two. Anyway, it all had a happy ending, like a good old Hollywood movie. [*Pause*] So you knew my father.

TSIBRA. Your father was my teacher. [*Pause*] About life and death. [*Pause*] I wanted your father to be ***my*** father, but he couldn't be — because he was already ***your*** father, which I didn't know.

VOYDAN. What? [*Pause. He notices that there is nobody left in the bar.*] What happened?

TSIBRA. What?

VOYDAN. Where've all the people gone?

TSIBRA. What people?

VOYDAN. There were a lot of people when we came in!

TSIBRA. I didn't notice.

VOYDAN. What d'you mean, you didn't notice?! It was full!

TSIBRA. Full, yes. Full of animals. You call them ***people***?

SCENE 10

[*The open road. A parked car with the doors open. The sound of crickets.*]

TSIBRA. Are we feeling more ourselves now?

VOYDAN. You're not right in the head.

TSIBRA. You mean you don't like my driving.

VOYDAN. You don't drive. You fly low.

TSIBRA. You really want to live, don't you?

VOYDAN. Should I want to die? The life-wish is a natural instinct. We learned that in the first year. [*Pause*] What're we doing here? [*Pause*] Where are we? [*Pause*] How far are we from the city?

TSIBRA. You always want to be close to something?

VOYDAN. What've we come here for?

TSIBRA. We're safe here. We're nowhere here. If we're somewhere, they can always find us.

VOYDAN. Who's after us?

TSIBRA. There's always somebody for some reason or other.

VOYDAN. You're making it up.

TSIBRA. I made up one guy who stuck a knife in under my shoulder-blade.

VOYDAN. Can I see where?

TSIBRA. You don't believe me. [*Pause*] You don't believe me, do you?

VOYDAN. What are you doing to me? Playing some kind of game? Why did those people leave the bar? You're hiding something.

TSIBRA. Yes. [*Pause*] Aren't you? [*Pause.*]

VOYDAN. Let's go.

TSIBRA. You afraid?

VOYDAN. I don't exactly feel at ease.

TSIBRA. That feeling of uneasiness is usually called fear. Which year do you learn about that?

VOYDAN. How d'you want me to feel in the middle of nowhere? There's just the moon and the crickets.

TSIBRA. Shall we pray?

VOYDAN. Who to?

TSIBRA. The moon.

VOYDAN. How?

TSIBRA. Like coyotes. [*He howls like a coyote.*] Now you.

VOYDAN. No thanks. [*Tsibra howls again. Pause.*] You'll get over it when you get married. [*Pause*] If you don't feel like going, I'll start walking.

TSIBRA. Listen!

VOYDAN. What is it?

TSIBRA. Ssssh! Someone's coming.

VOYDAN. Who can it be? [*Pause*] Who can it be?

[*Enter Mary, pushing a carriage with two babies in it. She is carrying a picnic basket.*]

VOYDAN. Who are you?

MARY. Who are ***you***?

TSIBRA. This is my wife, Mary. This is Voydan. A research assistant from the old country.

VOYDAN. What're you doing in the middle of nowhere in the middle of the night?

MARY. I live here.

VOYDAN. Where?

MARY. Over there.

VOYDAN. A house. How come I didn't see it? How is it possible I didn't see it?

MARY. [*To Tsibra*] Did you get the diapers? [*Tsibra gives her some bags full of groceries.*] Sugar? Detergent?

TSIBRA. Everything you ordered. [*Pause*] How're the kids?

MARY. Alive.

[*She takes some sandwiches out of the basket and gives them to Tsibra and Voydan.*]

VOYDAN. What's this?

MARY. You ordered supper, didn't you?

[*Pause. They eat.*]

VOYDAN. The last supper.

MARY. What?

[*Pause.*]

VOYDAN. [*Looking into the carriage*] Boys?

MARY. No.

VOYDAN. Girls. Never mind. Goo, goo!! They're asleep.

MARY. I know.

VOYDAN. Do you live here all the time?

MARY. All the time. Just for a while. I don't know. I don't have my own opinions on anything. [*With heavy irony*] I'm just a candle in the wind.

TSIBRA. Did anyone call?

MARY. No.

TSIBRA. Anyone come?

MARY. No.

TSIBRA. The gas man?

MARY. Yes.

TSIBRA. Isn't he somebody? Did he ask any questions?

MARY. No.

TSIBRA. You watched him while he was working?

MARY. Yes.

TSIBRA. You sure?

MARY. I'm not even sure what my name is.

TSIBRA. Sure?

MARY. I watched him as much as I could. I've got two kids to watch as well. What're you so frightened of? Them putting in microphones? They've got better ways for you. Don't you worry!

VOYDAN. What's all this about?

[*Silence. Pause.*]

VOYDAN. Nice sandwiches.

MARY. I didn't put any cucumbers in them.

TSIBRA. I don't eat cucumbers.

MARY. That's why I didn't put any in. [*Pause. To Voydan.*] Would you like some more?

VOYDAN. No, thank you.

TSIBRA. What're you thanking her for? Just say "no" and leave it at that. [*Pause.*]

VOYDAN. Are you really husband and wife?

MARY. I often wonder myself.

VOYDAN. I was interested, from a strictly scientific point of view, how a typical marriage functions over here.

TSIBRA. Go on, tell the man. He asked you a question.

MARY. Once a week he howls out here like a vampire. Deposits food. I look after two kids. I'm expecting a third. A cow for breeding purposes. I'm producing a tribe for him. I live in a prison with air-conditioning, color TV, and a dishwasher. All on credit. He promises me a nice barbed wire fence next. He keeps me two hours' drive away from the closest habitation. Meanwhile he's mixed up in something shady in the big wide world. I expect them to bring him home in a metal coffin one day. Every night I dream I'm lying with my legs apart on the freeway. I get screwed by whoever comes along. I squeeze my breasts in front of the mirror. I play with cucumbers.

[*Tsibra slaps her face.*]

VOYDAN. What d'you think you're doing?

TSIBRA. Something not to your liking?

VOYDAN. Why d'you hit her?

TSIBRA. Why didn't you stop me?

MARY. [*She takes out a revolver.*] While one baby's just shat all over the place, the other one's just thrown up. The milk's boiled over, the telephone's ringing, Tsibra wants supper at dawn. Mary jumps out of bed and is careful not to put cucumbers in the sandwiches. The scientist asks how it functions. How ***what*** functions? Go and ask your own wife at home! Or your sister, if you haven't got a wife! Or your mother, if you haven't got a sister! Get the hell out of here!

VOYDAN. But I'm on your side

MARY. [*Slapping his face*] Get out of here!

TSIBRA. Come on, Voydan. You don't know her. She'll shoot.

SCENE 11

[*Voydan's room. Voydan is lying in bed with the covers over his head. There is a knock on the door. Voydan looks out.*]

VOYDAN. Who is it?

THE MAN. [*Opening the door a little*] Can I come in? [*Enters*] Good morning. I hope I'm not disturbing you. You're Voydan. Tsibra's new assistant.

VOYDAN. Excuse me?

THE MAN. News travels fast.

VOYDAN. What d'you mean, "assistant?" I don't understand.

THE MAN. I don't even understand myself anymore, either. I'm Simon Delimitovski. My wife is Svetanka Delimitovska, née Verskova. Mr. Tsibra knows her well. She's his mistress. I wanted to ask you if you could ask him not to bite her so hard. It leaves bruises. They don't get better for weeks. If he could just be a little more careful. I can't bear to look at her like that. She's all I got. I wanted to get my revenge on him, but he's stronger than me. I know this sounds funny. Svetanka laughed when I told her I was going to come. She doesn't believe I would. She won't believe me when I tell her I've been, either. Will you promise me you'll let Mr. Tsibra know about this?

VOYDAN. I've got nothing to do with him.

THE MAN. No, of course you haven't. Thank you.

VOYDAN. What for?

THE MAN. For everything.

VOYDAN. This is a madhouse.

THE MAN. Precisely. No better word for it.

[*Exit. Voydan pulls the covers over his head again.*]

SCENE 12

[A gymnasium. Tsibra, in a track-suit, is practicing with a punching bag.]

VOYDAN. He also said, if he ever got the chance, he'd have his revenge on you.

TSIBRA. Somebody else'll have their revenge on me for something else, so he'll get his way in the end. He'll see me dead, he don't have to worry. Tell him his wife's not much good anyway. She spits it out when I come in her mouth. Doesn't want to swallow it.

VOYDAN. It's none of my business to tell him!

TSIBRA. I don't know who this Svetanka Delimitova, née Verskova, is. Never heard her name before. I get blamed for everything. Who knows who's screwing his wife, but it's me he's got it in for.

VOYDAN. Why don't you tell the man?

TSIBRA. The more you try to convince people, the less they believe you. You tell him.

VOYDAN. What's it got to do with me? I'm not your assistant.

TSIBRA. No, you're not. [*Pause.*] You're the devil's.

[Enter Claudia and the bodyguard. Claudia is wearing expensive tasteful clothes. The bodyguard is large and simple-minded. Pause.]

CLAUDIA. Tsibra?

TSIBRA. Who let you in here?

CLAUDIA. At last.

TSIBRA. [*To Voydan*] Why don't you go for a little walk?

[*Voydan doesn't move.*]

CLAUDIA. I've been on your trail for days. You're good at hiding. So this is where you prepare for the holy mission. Working on absolute physical fitness. You're very popular. They drink to your health in the Macedonian bars. Young girls treasure your photographs. The old folks swear by you. People bet on your future. Some are expecting you to get cut up into a million little pieces. Others are expecting you to put Macedonia on the map of the world. They glorify you and avoid you. Love you and fear you. Like all messiahs. I've been eager to meet you. Standard-bearers with their head in the noose are always attractive. I've been wanting to ask you ***which*** map of the world exactly you're intending to put Macedonia on. Is it something real or something imaginary?

TSIBRA. What is it that I can do for you?

CLAUDIA. You've done enough already. Now you'll have to stop. I'm Claudia Rogoff. Ex-Kostadinka Rogova. Daughter of somebody you know well, namely Steven ex-Stavré Rogoff. I have a letter here from his lawyer. As of today, you are forbidden to visit my father or communicate with him in any way whatsoever. There'll be no more watching football games from his special box. You'll have to go back among the masses. There'll be no more stealing money.

TSIBRA. Miss Rogoff!

CLAUDIA. You convinced my father to state in his will that he wished to be put in deep freeze after his death. And that you would take care of his body and bury it in the old country when it was liberated. You charged him the total sum of three thousand two hundred dollars in three payments for this service. You're nothing but a common crook making a business out of the nostalgia of helpless old men.

TSIBRA. It was his idea. I simply agreed that it was an excellent one.

CLAUDIA. You must be simple-minded. How do things stand as regards the "liberation" of our motherland?

TSIBRA. They don't.

CLAUDIA. So?

TSIBRA. So I practice my pistol-shooting. Your father wanted to buy up our motherland, as the Americans bought up Alaska. I told him it would be expensive and impractical. We ended up with this alternative.

CLAUDIA. You sold him lies.

TSIBRA. He paid for them. So he must have needed them.

CLAUDIA. What qualifications do you have for being his national adviser? We checked up on you. You left the country as a small boy. You don't have any memory of it even. You grew up in America. How did you become the model Macedonian?

TSIBRA. Tarzan grew up among the monkeys in the jungle, Miss Rogoff, but he remained a man. And how did you, who grew up in the old country, become the model American? We did some checking-up, too. You donate money to the Fund for the Protection of Seals and Other Endangered Wildlife. You're ***their*** messiah. It's a question of taste!

CLAUDIA. No, a question of common sense. Both seals and small nations are in danger of extermination. But the seals can be helped, whereas the fight for the small nations has been lost. And is out of date, anyway. They don't know whether we're from — Yugoslavia, Czechoslovakia, Czechoslavia, or Yugoslovakia. Belonging to a small nation means floating on a raft in a rough sea, while the world, up on its luxury liner, is sunbathing, drinking gin and tonic and not even feeling the waves. I've abandoned the raft. I've gone over to the liner. I can't complain. I don't feel guilty about it. Everyone does it.

TSIBRA. I'm staying on the raft.

CLAUDIA. Good luck to you.

TSIBRA. And I'll blow the liner sky high.

CLAUDIA. You think you've got a chance?

TSIBRA. No.

CLAUDIA. So?

TSIBRA. I don't have a chance of living forever, either.

CLAUDIA. So why do you deliberately back a losing horse?

TSIBRA. So it won't give up the race completely. This way it knows that someone out there's cheering it on. It does its very best. It runs. It knows it'll lose, but it doesn't give in.

CLAUDIA. Charming!

TSIBRA. When we used to play Cowboys and Indians, I was always an Indian. I had to be an Indian if I wanted them to let me play with them. They tied me to a tree. They circled round me, whooping and shooting. Once it started raining. They all ran home. They left me tied up in the rain. I decided then not to leave the raft. It's not a question of small nations and big nations. Only of Cowboys and Indians. [*Pause*] Don't look at me like that. You'll take pity on me. And then you'll fall in love with me. That wouldn't be a bright idea. I'll just love you and leave you.

[*Pause. Exit Claudia and the bodyguard. Pause. Voydan looks at Tsibra with disdain. Pause.*]

VOYDAN. ***Goodbye***! [*He leaves angrily. Pause. He returns.*] I don't want to have anything to do with you from this moment on.

TSIBRA. What have you had to do with me so far?

VOYDAN. Do you know I could lose my job if they get to know I've been hanging round with you? I could end up in jail. Even our own people avoid you. You mess things up for everyone. I didn't know who you were! I'm going to pack my bag. I'm leaving!

TSIBRA. To go straight into legend.

VOYDAN. I feel sick.

TSIBRA. Perhaps you're pregnant.

VOYDAN. Don't touch me. You'll contaminate me.

TSIBRA. You're a doctor who's afraid of disease. How're you going to cure people? [*Pause*] Let's drink to our parting.

SCENE 13

[A night club. Both drunk, Tsibra and Voydan are sitting at a table covered with bottles and glasses. The dancer is doing a belly-dance. The music is played by a band with a clarinetist, drummer, etc. Voydan is gazing at the dancer. The dance ends. The musicians retire. The dancer sits down at the table next to Tsibra.]

TSIBRA. Pretty good. [*He kisses her on the cheek.*] I don't have any money on me.

DANCER. Never mind. Just call me sometime.

VOYDAN. Kitsch! [*Pause*] This is kitsch! [*Pause*] Disgusting! [*Pause*] I'm ashamed to watch!

TSIBRA. You weren't ashamed to watch while she was dancing. Why didn't you leave?

VOYDAN. I wanted to see just how low she'd go.

DANCER. Ah, the gentleman would prefer something more in the way of art?

TSIBRA. No, the gentleman would prefer you to dance for him in private, so he can shove both his hands in his pockets.

DANCER. Giselle? Romeo and Juliet? Swan Lake? Or something not so classical?

TSIBRA. She knows them all. She's a trained ballerina. No work at the moment. She's got an audition on Broadway tomorrow.

VOYDAN. Liar! You're all liars! Everybody's been lying to me from the moment I set foot in America. From the porters at the airport. The stewardesses on the plane. They lie to me at all the desks. On the street they give me wrong directions. I'm not so gullible! I wasn't born yesterday. [*To the dancer*] Go on, get out of here! Go away. Get out!

DANCER. Who ***is*** this creep you've picked up, Tsibra?

VOYDAN. I'm his assistant!

DANCER. You might just about be able to assist him to take a leak. But I doubt even that.

VOYDAN. I am a research assistant!

DANCER. Then assist yourself a little.

VOYDAN. What exactly are you after?

DANCER. What are ***you*** after exactly?

TSIBRA. He knows what he's after, except he doesn't know what he's after!

VOYDAN. Get the hell out of here!

DANCER. [*Slapping Voydan's face*] Don't worry. I'll get as far away as I can from you, Mr. Kitsch.

VOYDAN. [*He goes to strike her, but Tsibra holds him back with one arm.*] Let me go! Leave me alone!

TSIBRA. Good luck at the audition. If they take you, I'm going to drink champagne from your shoe!

DANCER. The left one or the right?!

[*She blows him a kiss. Exit.*]

VOYDAN. The middle one! Whore! Jesus, the people you hang around with!

[*Tsibra lets go of him. Voyan collapses on the table. Pause. He realizes that he is drunk.*]

VOYDAN. We've had enough.

TSIBRA. You mean ***you've*** had enough. Why don't you leave? There's nobody stopping you.

VOYDAN. Plenty of time. Tomorrow's another day.

TSIBRA. You sure? [*Pause*] Is that what they teach you? We should teach our children there's no future. The future just won't come, the past just won't go — and we're left here acting out the present.

VOYDAN. When I look at you, I begin to wonder whether I really exist. You don't understand me, and that makes me stop understanding myself. It's like talking to a foreigner and starting to stumble over words myself. How can I explain to you who I am and what I am?

TSIBRA. No! Don't! Don't try to explain anything to me!

VOYDAN. We're different, but that's what I like about you. But you, you'd like to kill me. Let me explain. You're a man who's just repeating well-known formulas, well-worn myths, hiding in them like in a glove — where it's nice and warm. I'm free of your complexes and frustrations. I've finished with origins, nations, all that shit. History's junkshop. It's all poison. "Nationide." Local anesthetics! We sit here after Freud and Einstein playing hide-and-seek and saying who's going to be on whose side. You say my father was better than me? I don't deserve him? Who gives a fuck about him? We don't belong to anyone. All causes are dead! All theories wrong! [*Pause*] I look on the world as the arena for cultural competition among the nations.

TSIBRA. You'll have to put a lot more weight on you, guy, before you're allowed to say that.

VOYDAN. Everything's much more complicated than you think.

TSIBRA. And simpler than ***you*** think.

VOYDAN. I'm an intellectual. A cosmopolitan.

TSIBRA. You don't like dogs ***or*** cats. You're a tourist on safari. A bit of an intellectual, a bit of a jerk-off. A bit of a hero, a bit of a traitor. A bit left, a bit right.

VOYDAN. What about you? You're a typical example of a recruit from the industrial proletariat! From a sardine-can town. You went to bad schools; your family had no time or love for you. You grew up on the street by the law of the survival of the fittest. Your stomach and your head are full of junk literature, junk food, junk films, and junk ideas. You dream of being the voice of your people. You're exploited. You don't decide anything. You don't affect anything. You're alienated from any kind of normal society. Nobody asks your opinion on anything. I can see you clearly. You're totally predictable.

[*Tsibra punches him. Voydan collapses. Pause. There is blood dripping from his mouth.*]

VOYDAN. I predicted ***that*** would happen, too. You think I didn't know you were going to do that?

[*Pause. Tsibra collects all the glasses and bottles up in the tablecloth and makes a bundle out of them. He swings it and strikes the floor hard with it several times. Pause.*]

VOYDAN. I don't want to get involved. I want to stay clean. I don't have the facts. I don't know what the real story is.

[*Tsibra lifts up his shirt to reveal the map of the full borders of his homeland tattooed on his chest.*]

TSIBRA. Here's the real story! Our true homeland! In black and white! You want to know which is the winning ticket so you can buy that one! You've turned into a monkey because they offered you bananas! Make a break! A complete break! Make a complete break with everything! Sieve the sand down to the gold! Temper the iron into steel! Develop the flesh into muscle! Raise your head up, furrow your brow, frown on the world! Call an end! No more weakness. No more silence. No more fear. Call an end to it! Be the best or nothing! Become an astronaut! Make an atom bomb! Death or freedom! Look at your enemies! [*He takes out a pistol and points around with it, turning a complete circle.*] There they are! There they are! There they are! There they are! The whole world is against you! A bullet in the head for all of them. No mercy! No forgiveness!

SCENE 14

[*Altana's bar. Altana is scratching Kolyo's back.*]

KOLYO. Up a little. A little more. There. Hard.

ALTANA. Is this why you want to marry me?

KOLYO. Why else? Why don't they ever fart, or belch, or scratch each other's backs in romance movies? Because they're only in love. Purely of scientific interest. [*Pause.*]

ALTANA. I keep seeing the same picture. [*Pause*] A stream, poplar trees, the smell of roasted peppers and cottage cheese. I'm sleeping in a railway compartment, in my father's lap. A whistle blows in the distance. Someone goes past, knocking the wheels of the cars with his steel hammer. Autumn. [*Pause.*]

KOLYO. Perhaps the best thing is to go on standby after all. You can't reserve a seat, but it's cheap. Even if you have to wait three days, it's worth it. [*Pause. He sobs, then stops.*] I can see myself doing this lousy crying and it looks so funny. An old, grey-haired man crying. It's funny. [*Pause*] But it's frightening, too, isn't it? What can I do to stop myself wanting to cry? How can I start thinking in a different way, somehow, living in a different way, somehow? Why should I be like this? [*Pause*] I can't tell you, Altana, how much I wish I was someone else.

[*Enter Voydan, drunk, in a bad mood. He takes a can of beer out of the fridge and opens it. He starts drinking.*]

ALTANA. Where've you been?

VOYDAN. Out.

ALTANA. What's it like out?

VOYDAN. Dark.

[*Pause.*]

KOLYO. Well, I'll be on my way.

VOYDAN. Why exactly would you be on your way? Because I've come? Huh? You've all started avoiding me now, too. I feel like I'm looking at you all through a magnifying glass. I've got a bird's-eye view. I hold you all in the palm of my hand. I'm your common denominator. Why didn't anyone tell me Tsibra was a hoodlum, a pimp, and a drunk? You want him to get me mixed up in it all as well. And bring about my downfall. Tsibra is a moral and political undesirable.

ALTANA. You must have had a bad dream.

KOLYO. Let's talk about something else. [*Pause*] Why don't you tell us what it's like in the old country?

VOYDAN. Terrible. Soon we won't have anything to eat.

KOLYO. You don't look underfed to me.

VOYDAN. I know how to get by.

KOLYO. How come they gave you a grant to come here, if you don't even have enough to eat over there?

VOYDAN. That's why we haven't got enough to eat. Because they sent me over here on a grant, instead of forcing me to work.

KOLYO. But why did you accept?

VOYDAN. Well, if they are fool enough to give the money, why shouldn't I take it?

KOLYO. This isn't what it says in the papers.

VOYDAN. People like ***me*** work for the papers. They're liars!

KOLYO. You really don't like us, do you?

VOYDAN. ***Like*** you? You're such likeable people! You don't like ***me***, either, but who cares. I want to feel good. I want to feel ***great.*** I want colors, smells. I want everything clean around me. A self-confident smile, nice white teeth. I want things to look nice. Toilets that smell of fresh herbs. Public clocks that work and show the right time. I don't like inane faces. I don't like greyness, or lousy food. Crumbs in my bed. Sweaty armpits, smelly breath. I don't like them changing my address three times a year. I don't like life as a natural disaster. [*Pause*] I was trying to get away from people like you. I didn't know you'd be lying in wait for me here.

ALTANA. You run right into what you're trying to get away from.

KOLYO. I hope to God you'll never know what it is to have a heart as heavy as mine.

VOYDAN. You got the monopoly on heartache, or something? Huh? The whole world must come to you to borrow it for a while! Hey, did you ever think ***I*** might have a heavy heart sometimes? If you're pining away so much for the old country, why don't you go back there, for God's sake! Anybody else with such a tortured soul would have swum the Atlantic Ocean by now. You just read airline timetables! I've had enough of your fairy tales. You don't have such a bad life here. This is the feature film for you. The homeland's just the news reel that's on first. You've come to like sitting on the fence. You can have it both ways — there's nowhere like home, but I was a clever fellow to get out. You can be swimming and holding on to the bank at the same time. You used to tell us you took your own teeth out with a nail when they hurt. And put garlic and salt on the wound. You used to tell us how you hurled bombs and grenades. How you tightened your belts, girded your loins. And now you whimper about your heavy hearts like schoolboy sissies. Fuck your hearts!

[*Pause.*]

ALTANA. Why d'you talk like that? Why torture yourself? That's only a way for God to talk, engraving the ten commandments on blocks of stone. You're a simple mortal. You have to try to understand. D'you think I just sit here, smoking a cigar and dreaming about my homeland? D'you know what else I think about? Deposits, loans, credits, business contracts with catches in the fine print, bookkeeping, leases, taxes, duties, social security, immigration departments, fire regulations, police, insurance, meat deliveries, checks, bills, bank clerks, drunk customers who can cut your heart out in a flash, black men, yellow men, red men, and green men.

[*Ruzha enters through the back door. Pause.*]

VOYDAN. Ruzha. Let's get away from here.

RUZHA. Where to?

VOYDAN. Far from this cruel world.

RUZHA. Right now?

VOYDAN. Yes.

RUZHA. I can't. Can I, Aunt Altana?

ALTANA. No. [*Pause.*]

VOYDAN. Don't leave me alone.

SCENE 15

[*Tsibra and Claudia in bed together, half-dressed. Claudia is smoking. Tsibra puts his boots on.*]

CLAUDIA. So it was all true.

TSIBRA. You should see me when I'm in shape.

CLAUDIA. Motel passion. I feel so cheap.

TSIBRA. Story of my life.

CLAUDIA. And now you're in a hurry. Ready for a quick exit. You've finished the job, done your time, earned your permit to leave. You don't make love, you take revenge. You don't want to come, to give in. You're saving yourself. Life isn't a duty, you know. It's meant for a different purpose. Do you actually like women at all?

TSIBRA. I stopped liking them when I went into a bathroom just after a really fantastic-looking woman had come out. It stank as if a hippopotamus had had a shit.

CLAUDIA. And now you're going to leave me to rot in this tired, sweaty bed. You're going to throw yourself on the world. And never get in touch with me again. This is like a movie.

TSIBRA. Story of my life.

CLAUDIA. We just exchanged spit.

TSIBRA. And trichomoniasis.

[*Claudia comes up behind him and massages his forehead. Tsibra closes his eyes.*]

CLAUDIA. I've got an antique shop. I lied about being modern. I have to do with old things just like you. I buy clothes from expensive boutiques, but I feel as if I'm wearing rags and clogs. You can't dress up your soul. You can only be superior if you're not aware of it. All the rest are inferior. I ***am*** on that liner, but deep below. In its entrails. Near the engine. It's stifling. Dirty. There a thousand little Indian rafts are floating about in the grease. One of them's mine. [*Pause*] What do I have to do to keep you?

TSIBRA. Hijack a plane.

CLAUDIA. Why?

TSIBRA. So the United Nations'll put the question of small nations on the agenda.

CLAUDIA. A terrorist group. What're we going to call ourselves?

TSIBRA. We'll have to think up some catchy name for the newspapers and TV. It's the packaging which sells the product. If Coca-Cola had been called something different, nobody'd drink it. Imagine if they'd called it Choca Chola. Bet your life people wouldn't drink it.

CLAUDIA. Well, let's call ourselves Coca-Cola, then.

TSIBRA. Don't! It reminds me of Voydan.

CLAUDIA. Pepsi-Cola! Hello. This is the Pepsi-Cola Group. We take responsibility for the hijacked jumbo jet. All the passengers and crew have been safely drowned in the Pacific. Death or freedom. [*Pause*] We could let all the animals out of the zoo. Lions, snakes, hyenas let loose on the city. Panic.

Nobody'd know how we got away. It'd be a complete mystery. [*Pause*] What's your job?

TSIBRA. I'm a truck driver. Ten-tonners. I drive for weeks on end. Up and down. All over the country. I keep a lookout for my people. I can't find them. They've gone underground somewhere. Making money to save for rainy days. Eating dog food. I try to drag them into getting up on their feet. They try to drag me down on my knees. This [*showing his pistol*] doesn't have to be put to work, but this [*knocking himself on the forehead*] must be. Something's died in here! How can anyone take us seriously when ***we*** don't take ***ourselves*** seriously? How can I make them see? [*Pause*] How can I make ***you*** see?

CLAUDIA. I'll be sorry when they kill you. [*Pause*] Are they gonna kill you? [*Pause*] Who? [*Pause*] When?

TSIBRA. I'm tired. Lost my strength. I thought Strezo's son would come on a white horse with cartridge belts crossed on his chest, a flag in his hand and a knife in his teeth. I was expecting a captain, and I got a mouse escaping from the boat. There was an imitation hiding behind the label advertising the genuine product. Give me hordes of distant enemies, just don't give me one close one. I'm in exile among my own people. I hit out at the air. I wanted something, but it wasn't this.

CLAUDIA. What does he mean to you?

TSIBRA. I don't know. That's the problem. We're just waiting for our turn to come, for the right time, and then when they both come, we miss them. We wait for another turn, some better time.

[*Pause.*]

CLAUDIA. I'd like to meet your wife.

TSIBRA. She wouldn't let you in.

CLAUDIA. What about our traditional hospitality?

TSIBRA. It's dead. It never existed, anyway. Hospitality? It was just fear. When they welcomed strangers with bread and salt, they were just opening up their doors before evil. That's wisdom, not hospitality. Nobody ever knocked on doors in our country bringing good. It was always rob, kill, rape. They opened up the doors so they wouldn't be smashed in. My wife doesn't open up. She waits behind the door with her pistol cocked.

CLAUDIA. I love you.

TSIBRA. Love me.

SCENE 16

[Voydan's room. Voydan's sitting up in bed. He knocks on the wall. Pause. He knocks again. Pause. Footsteps can be heard. Voydan quickly lies down and pretends to be asleep. Enter Ruzha. Pause.]

RUZHA. Voydan?

VOYDAN. Yes.

RUZHA. Was it you knocking?

VOYDAN. No.

RUZHA. I heard knocking.

VOYDAN. You must've been dreaming.

RUZHA. I'm sorry. [*Pause*] Good night.

VOYDAN. Wait a minute. [*Pause*] Perhaps you thought you heard me knocking because you ***wanted*** me to knock. Let's consider that possibility. What if there is some kind of "chemistry" between us? You know what that is? Shall I tell you about yourself? I know all about you. I can read your life like a textbook. You're *virgo intacta*.

RUZHA. What?

VOYDAN. A virgin.

RUZHA. Yes.

VOYDAN. Of course. Virginity as the prerequisite for marriage. There's a nice point for a bibliography! Perfectly clear. You're not married. You've received a proposal and soon you'll accept. You're embroidering the sheets for your bottom drawer. Those traditions survive tenaciously. I'd like to see the patterns you're using. I'm interested in certain recurring themes. I understand people too clearly. That's why I can't learn to love them. Is there anything I've overlooked?

RUZHA. No. [*Pause*] I was born here twenty-six years ago. My mother died when I was six. Brain cancer. She screamed a lot. My father died of alcohol when I was sixteen. He beat us a lot. Aunt Altana brought us up. After my father's funeral I ran away from home. I hitch-hiked as far as Iowa. I met Frankie there. He was a farmer. We got married. I helped him when the farm caught fire. I had his baby. It had no arms or legs. I ran away from him and the baby. In North Dakota I met Tom. A Korea veteran, disabled. He couldn't have an erection. He promised, if I married him, he'd give me satisfaction in other ways. We got married. It wasn't bad. One day Harry called. My first lover, before I ran away from home. He was calling from a prison in Oregon. He asked me to help him get out. He sent me the fare. I left Tom. I waited for Harry in a Corvette 66 deluxe convertible. We went west. The cops were on our heels. He was scared. He was mean to me. We went across to Canada. We didn't have a dime. I went out tricking for him for six months. Harry got unbearable. I ran off to California. Lived alone. Did some yoga and transcendental meditation. Harry turned up again. He asked me to marry him. He'd made millions drug-trafficking in Florida. We lived on champagne and caviar. The night before the wedding he took the car, a Mazda RX-7 GS two-seater, and drove into a wall at a hundred miles an hour. The autopsy showed large quantities of cocaine in his blood. [*Pause.*]

VOYDAN. That it?

RUZHA. Wasn't it enough?

VOYDAN. You want me to believe you?

RUZHA. I don't want anything.

VOYDAN. You said you were a virgin.

RUZHA. Yes, I did.

VOYDAN. What did you mean, a virgin?

RUZHA. I didn't ***mean*** anything. I ***am*** a virgin. [*Pause.*]

VOYDAN. Look, I've consulted plenty of specialized studies. The behavior types of our people have long been covered very thoroughly. There are defined, strictly delineated models. The exception just proves the rule. Your story is bizarre. Even if I were to analyze it, it'd just represent an insignificant statistical thousandth of an aberration from the established principles. Scientifically speaking, your life is of no use whatsoever. [*Pause*] Pity. [*Pause*] I'm sorry.

[*Pause. He grabs her breasts. Ruzha does not react. Pause. The door opens. Altana stands there. Pause.*]

VOYDAN. Leave me alone. You all fuck around with me. I'm getting the first plane home!

SCENE 17

[*An open area. Tsibra and Voydan. Voydan has a suitcase with him and is ready for a journey.*]

VOYDAN. I want to go straight to the airport.

TSIBRA. You've still got three hours till take-off.

VOYDAN. I'd rather have to wait for the plane than it for me. What can this man tell me I don't already know?

TSIBRA. If he says anything. Sometimes he doesn't say a word for weeks. Here he is.

[*Enter Strezo. He is wearing something between a long hospital gown and a dressing gown.*]

STREZO. I don't have much time. It's the Holy Martyrs Proclo and Ilarion today. You heard of them? Proclo and Ilarion? [*To Voydan*] I was talking to ***you***.

VOYDAN. No.

STREZO. What about Julian Thars.? That's Thars. period. Some kind of abbreviation. Of what? The devil only knows. I found it in the Orthodox Calendar for this coming year. [*He gives Voydan a flask.*] Want some? [*Voydan starts drinking.*] Your finger. [*He positions Voydan's little finger sticking out straight.*] Your arm. [*He positions Voydan's arm at 90 degrees to his body.*] This is the earth. Zero. [*Pointing to Voydan's finger*] If you fall, it gives you something to land on. [*Pointing to Voydan's arm*] This must be at an angle of 90 degrees. So your blood is equally distributed throughout your body and you won't get drunk. [*He takes a drink in the same position.*] And who were the 45 martyrs of Nicopolis? Or the 20,000 martyrs of Nicomedia? One should know these things. Life passes by. There was a man who wanted to be a miner, but he was afraid of going underground. Another man wanted to be a pilot, but he was afraid of heights. A rebel is not the same thing as a revolutionary. Why didn't they make us into a kingdom? The whole world would have recognized us. They have to go and make a republic! What's your speciality?

VOYDAN. How do you mean?

STREZO. Why does my leg hurt? It didn't hurt before.

VOYDAN. You've got rheumatism.

STREZO. Yes, I got rheumatism all right. It's ***money*** I don't have. And I went to Kratovo yesterday. I wrote to them three times, but they pretended not to know what it was all about. So I went there in person. Come out here, my lovelies, I said to them. They came out looking frightened. The children were crying. The women peeping out from behind. The men lined up. What can we do for you, sir? What you can do, I said, is give me the money. Please, sir, give us till Monday. I looked hard at them. I said, you've got till Monday, but don't let me have to use other methods later on. They bowed down to the ground, kissed my hand, offered me coffee, brandy. I came back by way of Shtip. Stavré said, let's have a drink together, but I said, no, I'm in a hurry. They're expecting me back.

VOYDAN. What's it like in Shtip?

STREZO. Hot. There's a drought. The vines have dried up.

VOYDAN. Things'll get better.

STREZO. Why d'you think they'll get better?

VOYDAN. I hope so.

STREZO. Don't hope so at all. No use hoping. You know who Julius Caesar was?

VOYDAN. Yes.

STREZO. Who?

VOYDAN. A Roman emperor.

STREZO. Did you know he was a Macedonian?

VOYDAN. No.

STREZO. He was. Scientifically established fact.

VOYDAN. Who established it?

STREZO. Science. And Mozart?

VOYDAN. What about him?

STREZO. Same thing.

VOYDAN. A Macedonian?

STREZO. From round Debar. We're working on William Shakespeare at the moment. We've got the proof. Just need to collate all the facts. And that's not all.

VOYDAN. What else have you got?

STREZO. Him!

VOYDAN. Who?

STREZO. There'll be proof who was the greatest Macedonian of all.

VOYDAN. Who?

STREZO. God! [*Pause*] The Lord God! What's so funny? You think black has no white in it? You're wrong. Everything is the other way round. I've got to go. Be seeing you. At least we've broken the ice. Don't tell anyone about this, okay? [*He moves off, then comes back.*] We're stuntmen right now. The shrinkage. We're sort of "pretend" at the moment. Off the record. A moving wound. The Past Continuous. You think Marx was a Skopje gypsy and the Paris Communards a singing group from Valandovo? European democracy! It's just a Paris fashion. All completely haphazard, all at random. The knife at the throat. But we've got a trick up our sleeves. We're going to win! We'll ride into the square on white horses. They'll throw flowers in our path. I've got a plan for the parade. A list of medals. Not one of you has been forgotten. We just need to hold out a little longer. Just a little longer.

[*Exit.*]

VOYDAN. [*Sighing with relief*] This guy's totally crazy. [*Picking up his case*] Who is he?

TSIBRA. The real story . . . [*Pause*] Strezo. [*Pause*] Your father.

[*Voydan drops the case.*]

SCENE 18

[*Voydan's room. Voydan in his coat, with his case.*]

VOYDAN. So who ***is*** that man, if he's not my father?

ALTANA. He could be anybody!

VOYDAN. You're all trying to drive me crazy. I talked to him for half an hour. His name's Strezo. My father's name was Strezo!

ALTANA. Tsibra found you some madman. He was playing a joke on you.

VOYDAN. Why would he want to do that?

ALTANA. Perhaps you played some joke on him.

VOYDAN. Where is my father?

ALTANA. He died ten years ago.

VOYDAN. Where?

ALTANA. You see now it would've been better if I hadn't let you come in that night?

VOYDAN. Where did he die?

ALTANA. In the street in front of the bar. I was cleaning up before opening, early in the morning. Your father had got up earlier than usual. He sat there for a few minutes, thinking about something. He asked me for a white shirt. I asked him what he wanted a white shirt for to go to work. He didn't say. He had a strange light in his eyes. Like a gold miner. I ironed a white shirt for him. He put it on. He got up. He said, "I'm off, then." He collapsed in the middle of the street. The doctors said death was instantaneous.

VOYDAN. Where did you bury him?

ALTANA. He was cremated.

VOYDAN. Where're the ashes?

ALTANA. Here. [*She points to a vase on the counter.*]

VOYDAN. What kind of a man was he?

ALTANA. An angel. God-fearing, modest, hard-working, frugal, quiet. He never grumbled. He sacrificed himself for others without asking anything in return. Everybody loved him. He was a strong man, but he never hurt a fly. He hadn't a stain on his conscience. As pure as the driven snow. He didn't drink, he didn't smoke, he didn't gamble and he didn't chase after women. Perfect in every way. The kind God takes before the others.

VOYDAN. That same angel abandoned me and my mother in that wilderness and came here to be perfect in every way.

ALTANA. When we set off for America, we broke jugs in the traditional way. If the neck fell facing the house, that meant the person would return. If it fell facing the road, that meant he would stay in foreign lands. We could never find the neck of your father's jug.

VOYDAN. This is a conspiracy. A horror show. Why don't you just finish me off instead? We'll go and see Strezo together.

ALTANA. Why don't you believe me?

VOYDAN. Why ***should*** I believe you? First Ruzha says she did six months' whoring in Canada, and then that she's a virgin.

And she's surprised when I don't believe her. How can I believe her? Was she married?

ALTANA. Ruzha?

VOYDAN. To some Frankie in Iowa, then some Tom in North Dakota, and then some Harry? She didn't actually marry him. He escaped from prison. You don't know anything about it, of course. Now you're going to tell me she's a virgin.

ALTANA. Yes.

VOYDAN. [*Trying to keep calm*] Was she away from this city for years?

ALTANA. What do you care?

VOYDAN. I have to clear a few things up.

ALTANA. What are you going to clear up? You can't clear up that kind of thing.

VOYDAN. It's my life we're talking about!

ALTANA. What about ours?!

VOYDAN. Did Ruzha run away from home? Was she away for years?

ALTANA. Ruzha was a nun. In a convent in Montana.

VOYDAN. Ruzha? A nun?

ALTANA. In a convent in Montana.

VOYDAN. And then she came back and became a cashier in a supermarket?!

ALTANA. What's so strange about that?

VOYDAN. Why did she stop being a nun?

ALTANA. Voydan!

VOYDAN. Answer me! This is getting serious! Why did she stop being a nun?

ALTANA. She didn't know which religion to choose. She didn't know whether she wanted to be a Catholic, or a Lutheran, or Orthodox, or an Evangelist, a Calvinist, a Baptist, a methodist, an Adventist, a Jehovah's Witness, a Pentecostalist, a Muslim, or a Nazarene, or a Mormon.

VOYDAN. What is it you want from me?

ALTANA. What is it you want from ***yourself***?

[*Pause. Exit Altana. Enter Tsibra. Pause.*]

VOYDAN. When did Strezo go into the mental hospital?

TSIBRA. It's a home.

VOYDAN. When did Strezo go into the home?

TSIBRA. Ten years ago.

VOYDAN. Was he wearing a white shirt when he left?

TSIBRA. Yes.

VOYDAN. How come you remember?

TSIBRA. He didn't want to go without a white shirt on. Altana ironed it for him.

VOYDAN. Did he say, "I'm off, then," before he left?

TSIBRA. I can't remember.

VOYDAN. Try.

TSIBRA. I can't remember. What I remember, I remember. What I don't remember, I don't remember.

VOYDAN. You took him there. Did Altana watch you go?

TSIBRA. Yes.

VOYDAN. So Altana's lying? She says my father's dead.

TSIBRA. Of course she's lying. She was in love with him. She cut her wrists once for him. She used to wash his feet for him and then drink the water. Perhaps he loved her, too, but he couldn't show it. He ran away from her, back to the old country. Back to your mother. He had you. Then he ran away from you two and came back to her. When there was nowhere else for him to run to, he slipped off to the home.

VOYDAN. Hasn't she ever visited him?

TSIBRA. How can she visit him when he's dead?

VOYDAN. What d'you mean, dead?

TSIBRA. To her he's dead. You know she's a virgin?

VOYDAN. Not another one!

TSIBRA. She had an operation last year. They had to break her hymen to do it. I just happened to find out. She doesn't know I know. You're to blame for her life. You're the son she should have had. She both loves you and hates you. [*Pause.*]

VOYDAN. What was my father like?

TSIBRA. A devil. Irresponsible, lazy, always fooling around. He was never sober. He used to sing "What's the use of getting sober, when you gotta get drunk again?" An ace at gambling. He had a wanger like a calf's foot. The women in New York,

San Francisco, and Los Angeles went crazy for him. He left a trail of havoc behind him. Like a hurricane. Or a plague. If he'd gone on operating for a few more years, he'd have had the whole of North America in mourning. He'd've had to move to South America.

VOYDAN. This is totally the opposite of what Altana said.

TSIBRA. The opposite, of course.

VOYDAN. Which is the truth?

TSIBRA. The gentleman would like to know the truth?

VOYDAN. How can I live if I don't know it?

TSIBRA. Make it up! [*Pause*] As I understand it, you are faced with a problem with three sub-problems: a) Is your father a sage? b) Is your father a madman? c) Is your father your father anyway?

VOYDAN. Either all of you are crazy, or I must be.

TSIBRA. Either you are or we are. [*Pause*] Was it you who made Ruzha have plastic surgery?

VOYDAN. No. Why?

TSIBRA. Because she's had it.

[*Tsibra starts to leave.*]

VOYDAN. Where're you going? Stay with me.

TSIBRA. What d'you want ***me*** for?

VOYDAN. Please. Tsibra! [*Pause*] Tsibra!

[*Exit Tsibra. Pause. Enter Kolyo. He sits down. Silence. Pause.*]

KOLYO. I bought a ticket yesterday. I was supposed to leave this morning. I didn't go to the airport. Just to spite you, I didn't go. You're not going to push me into it. I've been here for 40 years. ***You're*** not going to tell me when to go back home. I'm going to decide for myself. [*Pause*] And I'm going to decide for myself how long I'm going to sit here and when I'm going to leave. [*A long pause. They look at each other.*] **Now** I'm going to leave.

[*Exit. Pause. Enter Altana.*]

ALTANA. There're a couple of characters waiting for you downstairs.

VOYDAN. What kind of characters?

ALTANA. Ugly. They said, tell Voydan to come down, so we don't have to go up and get him.

SCENE 19

[*An open space. Tsibra is walking along lost in thought. Enter The Boy.*]

THE BOY. Tsibra.

TSIBRA. You again.

THE BOY. They want to kill you.

TSIBRA. I know.

THE BOY. Two men took Voydan under the bridge an hour ago. They worked him over a little. He went green with fear. They made him fix it so you'll meet them. They pretended you owe them some money. Did Voydan tell you anything? Don't go. They'll kill you. You listening? Voydan's a useless assistant for you. I want to be your assistant. I've learned some more guns. Mauser, Luger, Webley, Mannlicher, Schwarzlose, Walther, Colt, Cooper, Starr, Nagant, Parker-Hale, Kalashnikov. [*Pause*] I don't know anything, but I really want to. Voydan may know it all, but he doesn't really want to. [*Pause*] Is it true you've got nine bullets bouncing round in your body?

SCENE 20

[*A modern art museum. A well-lit spacious arena. Panels of modern paintings. Voydan and Tsibra are looking at them.*]

TSIBRA. You've really decided to educate me today, haven't you?

VOYDAN. Shall we go?

TSIBRA. Why? I find it interesting. [*He stops in front of a painting.*] This is something really abstract.

VOYDAN. This is something really realistic! Take a picture of a cow, for example. You have a head, a tongue, a body, a tail, an udder, grass, everything. Is that a realistic picture? You think it is, but it isn't. You can't milk a cow like that. You can't hear it moo. It doesn't exist. It's a pure abstraction. But these pictures you think are abstract are real paint on real canvas. They're realistic. See?

TSIBRA. What about you?

VOYDAN. What about me?

TSIBRA. Which are you? Abstract or realistic? [*He points to a panel of paintings.*] Imagine that behind this abstract picture there are a couple of realistic characters who for certain abstract reasons want to kill me realistically.

VOYDAN. This is a trap.

TSIBRA. I know.

VOYDAN. Why did you come if you knew?

TSIBRA. I wanted to see if you'd tell me it was a trap. I've spent my whole life running away from traps. This time I've decided to see what it's like close up.

VOYDAN. I told them I didn't want to get involved. They told me they'd cut my balls off and stuff them in my mouth. They said it was about some small debt to be paid.

TSIBRA. It's always about some small debt to be paid. [*Pause.*]

VOYDAN. What happens now?

TSIBRA. I'm off, then.

[*He turns the panel round. Two gangsters are standing behind it. Tsibra looks at them calmly. The gangsters are surprised. Pause. One gangster hits Tsibra over the head with his pistol-butt. Tsibra collapses. The two gangsters carry Tsibra outside.*]

VOYDAN. Not here. This is a shrine of art. Should I come with you? Take me with you. [*Pause.*]

[*Enter The Boy.*]

THE BOY. You betrayed Tsibra, you motherfucker. [*He punches Voydan in the stomach.*] He gave you a free ride! You're dying to get fucked, but you don't want it to go in!

SCENE 21

[*Voydan's room. Ruzha is sitting with her face wrapped in bandages. Pause. Enter Voydan.*]

VOYDAN. Ruzha!

RUZHA. You recognized me.

VOYDAN. It's not my fault.

RUZHA. No, it's all my fault. I went to some quack. The poor always pay twice. The wound got infected.

VOYDAN. Does it hurt?

RUZHA. It itches.

VOYDAN. What happens now?

RUZHA. We'll see.

VOYDAN. It'll be alright.

RUZHA. No, it won't.

VOYDAN. Why won't it?

RUZHA. Why should it be alright?

VOYDAN. It has to be. Nobody can have it in for us that much. [*Pause*] I didn't mean for you to take it like that when I mentioned plastic surgery.

RUZHA. Like this, like that. What does it matter?

VOYDAN. I declare you Miss Macedonia of America. The jury consists of one man. Me. [*Pause*] I betrayed Tsibra. And he let me. Why? Am I such a curse? He'll be back. He'll forgive me.

God! I'll wash your feet. I'll drink the water. Do you know any prayers? Say a prayer.

RUZHA. Uproot all heresies, sects, and deviations. Strengthen the true faith and the holy life everywhere. In this coming year keep our homeland, our city, and all Thy world from hunger, pestilence, earthquake, flood, hail, fire, and the sword, from foreign attacks, wars, fatal diseases and wounds, accidents, and grief. Dispel all manner of hostility, unrest, and civil strife from our country. Grant us peace, strong unfeigned love, an ordered life, health, and success in all good things.

[*Voydan takes her hand, kisses it, and strokes his cheek with it.*]

SCENE 22

[*A richly and tastefully furnished drawing-room in Claudia's house. Claudia and Voydan.*]

CLAUDIA. Something to drink? Whisky?

VOYDAN. Yes, please.

CLAUDIA. Straight? On the rocks? Water?

VOYDAN. Yes.

CLAUDIA. [*Bringing him a drink*] Are you a Virgo?

VOYDAN. Excuse me?

CLAUDIA. In the Zodiac.

VOYDAN. Yes. I was born on September 7. How did you guess?

CLAUDIA. Virgo Nine. I'm Cancer. We don't get along. In your stars for this week it says, as far as work's concerned, you'll achieve something more than you expected on both the private and business planes. As far as love is concerned, two girls dream of winning you. You know them both and it all depends on you which one you choose.

VOYDAN. Is there anyone normal in this city?

CLAUDIA. You're the only one. That's why we're not going to let you go just like that. Did you know that there's a kind of rooster that is so puffed up with pride when it crows that it falls over backwards? [*Pause*] Have you heard what happened to Tsibra?

VOYDAN. No. What?

CLAUDIA. I don't believe it. They must be lying.

VOYDAN. What?

CLAUDIA. Strange you haven't heard. [*Pause*] You will.

[*Enter the Tattooer, with The Bodyguard behind him.*]

TATTOOER. Good evening.

CLAUDIA. You're here. Would you like a drink?

TATTOOER. I don't drink on the job.

CLAUDIA. This is the gentleman [*indicating Voydan*].

TATTOOER. How are you doing? I'm at your service. We can start right now if you're ready.

VOYDAN. Start what?

TATTOOER. The tattooing!

VOYDAN. Tattooing?!

TATTOOER. Your shirt, please.

VOYDAN. There must be some kind of misunderstanding. What tattooing? I don't want a tattoo.

TATTOOER. [*Getting his instruments ready*] It's nothing to be afraid of. We just have a bad reputation. We're all tattooed in some way or other. Some with sex, some with drugs, some with rock'n'roll. Those who think they're not, they're tattooed under the skin. They have it worst of all. Your shirt, please!

[*The Bodyguard tears Voydan's shirt off, and Voydan stands there naked above the waist.*]

VOYDAN. What're you trying to do to me? Please leave me alone!

TATTOOER. It doesn't hurt. And even if it did, you're a man. It's just like a mosquito bite.

VOYDAN. What right do you have? This is coercion! I don't need my country tattooed on my chest! I have a different life. You can't do this.

TATTOOER. You're not excited about the idea now, but when it's over you'll be pleased. You'll be proud. When you go to the beach, all eyes will be on you. When you're a grandfather, you'll take your grandchildren on your knee and show them your chest. What's five minutes of pain compared with eternity?

VOYDAN. What's eternity compared with five minutes of pain?

[*The Tattooer starts working.*]

VOYDAN. No-o-o-o-!! It hurts!!

TATTOOER. Let it hurt! It's supposed to hurt! And it's a good thing it hurts. Just don't faint on me. I can't work if the subject's unconscious.

SCENE 23

[*An open space. Voydan and Strezo. Strezo is dressed exactly as in Voydan's description of his father in scene* 6.]

VOYDAN. That's how I've imagined you dressed all my life. I spent the whole of my grant to buy it all. Now I'm through. It suits you.

STREZO. Is this a present?

VOYDAN. From Santa Claus.

STREZO. They say he's gay.

VOYDAN. I'm Voydan. [*Pause*] I've come here from the old country. On a scholarship. [*Pause*] Do you understand?

STREZO. Voydan. From the old country. On a scholarship. I understand.

VOYDAN. Does it mean anything to you?

STREZO. It does indeed.

VOYDAN. What does it mean to you?

STREZO. It means a lot to me.

VOYDAN. Where are you now?

STREZO. Home. Sweet home. I couldn't stand it in America any longer, so I came back.

VOYDAN. Are you in an old folks' home or a mental hospital?

STREZO. We play baseball there. I don't know the rules, so they don't let me play. I collect the balls that bounce out.

They're not much good at it either, so their balls are always flying all over the place. So I get to play the most, in fact.

VOYDAN. Why are you there?

STREZO. Because of Charlie. He's an electrician. He connects wires without using insulating tape. Don't ever touch wires Charlie's connected. Whatever you do.

VOYDAN. Are you my father? [*Pause.*]

STREZO. You've got the best view from here. There's Lake Ohrid over there and Lake Prespa over on this side. [*Pause*] See?

VOYDAN. No.

STREZO. How come? Look.

VOYDAN. I can only see smoke.

STREZO. From a ship?

VOYDAN. From factories.

STREZO. Don't look at the smoke. Behind the smoke. [*Pause*] You still can't?

VOYDAN. No.

STREZO. You will. There's time. [*Pause.*]

VOYDAN. Am I your son? [*Pause*]

STREZO. But the father said to the servants: Bring forth quickly the best robe, and put it on him; and put a ring on his hand, and shoes on his feet: And bring the fatted calf, and kill it, and let us eat, and make merry: For this my son was dead, and is alive again; he was lost, and is found.

VOYDAN. Am I Voydan?

STREZO. Yes, yes.

VOYDAN. Your child and Ivanka's?

STREZO. We all belong to someone. If I was your father, it'd be easy, you'd have found me. But it must be someone else. Did you look in Kavadartsi?

VOYDAN. No.

STREZO. Try there. [*Pause*] What about in Kumanovo, or Probishtip?

VOYDAN. No.

STREZO. Well, where ***have*** you looked? You haven't looked anywhere. How d'you expect to find him if you haven't looked anywhere?

VOYDAN. Are you dead?

STREZO. That's something else we can discuss, if you like. It wouldn't be hard for me to be your father. I can be anything that's required of me: father, cousin, cherub, butcher, jeweler, Albanian, Chicano. I can be dead, too, if you want. It doesn't make much difference. You pay the piper, he plays the tune. But I don't want to deceive you. Why should I want to deceive you? [*Pause.*]

VOYDAN. I had you all put in the computer, in files, on diskettes, all packed up nice and neat. And then some resistor must have blown. Now we've just got the lights on. There's no one at home. [*He lifts up his shirt to show his tattoo.*] Look what they've done to me. They've tattooed a bottle of Coca-Cola with a straw in it on me. Serves me right. I can't cry "Death or freedom." Only "Death or fun."

STREZO. Thousands of tattooers lie in wait around the world with their styluses and needles and inks. They're looking for healthy, smooth young skin to defile.

VOYDAN. Did you have a son called Voydan?

STREZO. Yes. [*Pause*] But he'll never come to see me. Never. Never.

VOYDAN. What about me? Who am I?

STREZO. You'll grow up and it'll come to you of its own accord. Who will ever be able to get to the bottom of us people.

SCENE 24

[*Altana's bar. Ruzha, her face in bandages, Altana, Kolyo, and Voydan are sitting in silence. Long pause.*]

KOLYO. In a circus once I volunteered to chain up an escape artist and lock him in a chest. They lowered the chest into the water, and he was supposed to get himself out in two minutes. I had the key. The audience was looking at me. They thought it was all fixed. That I was his assistant and we worked together. Time passed. Nothing happened. The man didn't come out. Some of the circus people rushed up. They opened up the chest. The man inside looked like a boiled rabbit with staring eyes. Dead. He couldn't've been more dead. I thought I'd killed him. They tried to comfort me. They said he'd done it himself. He'd been doing that trick all his life — there couldn't have been a mistake. [*Pause*] Why did he have to pick ***me*** to help him kill himself?

[*Pause. Enter Tsibra. His shirt is bloody over his chest. He goes to the fridge slowly and takes out a beer. He opens it and sits down, gazing blankly in front of him. Pause. Enter Mary.*]

MARY. Of course. It didn't require much intelligence to imagine how you'd end up! I'll load you onto the pick-up like a hunk of wood. Pity they didn't take your head off so we'd at least have you at home for a few days. You'll get better. But what am ***I*** going to do? You put your white shirt on on Sunday and go and beg forgiveness of people. [*To Voydan*] You left these forms behind. I read them. You don't understand a thing. It can't be too easy for you. My little girl threw up chocolate over one of the pages. There's at least one speck of life in there now. She got her first tooth this morning. Top left.

[*Pause. Enter The Man.*]

THE MAN. Good evening. I heard you'd suffered a misfortune in the house. I just wanted to apologize. I suspected Mr. Tsibra of something. It turned out to have been someone else. I tore his eyes out. We wish you a speedy recovery.

[*Pause. The man sits down. Enter The Boy. Pause.*]

THE BOY. The world is wallowing in a refined kind of boredom. Between dead causes. Looking after the environment. That's fashionable. They're still flaying us since we're unfashionable. [*Pointing to Tsibra*] They skinned his chest. Along the borders of his homeland. [*Pause*] I'm off. I'll keep the last bullet for myself. If anyone comes to his senses before it's too late, I'll take him on as an assistant.

[*Exit. Pause.*]

ALTANA. This is no way to live. Millions of people live in bunkers. They peep out through narrow gun-slits. There's no life if you think everyone's against you. That the world's a big conspiracy. There's love and goodness and honest people in the world. We think we're the only ones who've been moved out and resettled. The whole world's been resettled. Everybody thinks there's something missing in their lives. They all feel surrounded by enemies. They all think they're at the end of the world. The Earth's round. Wherever you start from, you're always on the edge. The South doesn't like the North, or the East the West; Europe doesn't like America, or Ireland England; people from Prilep can't stand the people from Bitola; two areas of the same city hate each other, and two buildings in the same area; two different entrances to the same building are at loggerheads and two different apartments in the same entrance; two different families in the same apartment can't stand each other, or two people in one family — and those two people hate themselves in turn. The Indians try to be Cowboys at any price, while the Cowboys are sorry they're not Indians anymore. Where does it all lead to? If that's the way things are, there's no deliverance. And without deliverance, no life. And without life . . . nothing. Only death.

[*Pause. Voydan starts slowly tearing one of his forms into small pieces.*]

VOYDAN. Ruzha. [*Pause*] May I ask you to be my wife? [*Pause.*]

RUZHA. I don't know what I'll be like when I take the bandages off.

VOYDAN. I've taken mine off. And look at me. [*Pause.*]

RUZHA. Can I, Aunt Altana?

[*Altana starts to cry.*]

KOLYO. Altana, don't start that again.

VOYDAN. Tsibra?

[*Tsibra raises his beer can and drinks down the beer. He puts the can back on the table. Pause.*]

VOYDAN. Kolyo?

KOLYO. I'll think about it a while. [*Pause*] All we need to do now is ask to be hired by a circus. As unidentified flying people.

ALTANA. They wouldn't take us. Who's interested in that kind of thing nowadays?

KOLYO. Then we could always try swimming. And see what happens.

[*Pause. Voydan throws the pieces of his forms up in the air. They flutter to the ground.*]

CURTAIN

4

CASABALKAN

For Pat, Igor, and Yana

CHARACTERS

ZORA 36, a Balkan woman

KONSTANTIN 36, her husband, a patriot

YANA 12, their daughter

MICK 43, an English war reporter

GAVRO 45, owner of the ship

LUKA 30, a militia man

PRAJAPATI 47, an Indian U.N. observer

TANYA 23, a Russian croupier

DUDA 50, a gypsy cleaner

PART 1

[A room in London. Yana and Zora are sitting at a table. Yana is drawing a picture with felt tip pens. Zora is drinking coffee. She's looking at the envelope of an open letter. She inspects the stamp, the writing of the address.]

ZORA. You never believed your father was dead in the first place.

YANA. And I was right.

ZORA. And you were right, too.

YANA. I thought he had many lives. I was imagining him on the Circle Line from dawn to midnight, trying to get to us, but he didn't know where we lived so he didn't know where to get off.

ZORA. Poor daughter.

YANA. Poor mother.

ZORA. *[Opens the letter. Takes a polaroid photograph from the envelope. Looks at it.]*

YANA. Will you tell me everything?

ZORA. Should I?

YANA. Don't you think the time has come?

ZORA. You first.

YANA. What?

ZORA. You tell me a secret first.

YANA. Then you?

ZORA. Then me.

YANA. Promise?

ZORA. I promise.

YANA. I taught the children in my class a game. It was called "It ***can*** happen here." We pretended we were living in a siege. I showed them how to crouch "under the windows" to escape bullets. I asked them to imagine living without water in the heat of summer and without heat in the dead of winter. I told them what it was like to live on a diet of nettle soup, cooked snails, and wild plums. I rolled them cigarettes out of dry chamomile. They loved it. Mrs. Jones took me to one side and said: "For heaven's sake, Yana, don't freak them out! You should be grateful you're in England now. Leave your misery behind and don't bring it here to us." I was taken to see the headmaster. He was with someone who looked like a psychiatrist. They asked me why I thought it could happen here. I said, if it could happen there, it could happen here and everywhere." I told them I'd been killed. That I was shot in the head by a man with boots. But that was a long time ago. And I was much better now. And would they please not tell my mother because you'd be ever so worried. [*Pause*] Your turn now.

BLACKOUT

[*Lights up on the hull of a ship. Midnight. A storeroom. Bales of cargo covered with tarpaulin, crates of wine and beer, a freezer. A rickety table, folded up deckchairs. Cold and not very clean space. Bluish light. The door opens. Light comes in from the brightly lit hallway that leads right into the casino. Zora comes down a flight of steep steel stairs. She carries a traveling bag. Konstantin follows her on crutches. Zora helps Konstantin down the stairs. Konstantin is wearing a winter coat under which he is wearing pyjamas. He is unshaven.*]

ZORA. [*Looking round*] It's here.

KONSTANTIN. What's here?

ZORA. The man will come here.

KONSTANTIN. What man?

ZORA. He's bringing our passports here at midnight.

KONSTANTIN. You must be joking!

ZORA. [*She takes a deckchair. Opens it up.*] Sit down.

KONSTANTIN. [*Sits down.*] You didn't pay him, did you?

ZORA. I did.

KONSTANTIN. In advance?

ZORA. Everything is under control.

KONSTANTIN. I can't believe this. Who told you about me?

ZORA. They rang. They said, we think your husband's alive.

KONSTANTIN. They ***think*** I'm alive?

ZORA. You ***think*** he's alive, I said? We think it's ***him***, they said. You ***think*** it's him, I said?

KONSTANTIN. I think it's me, too.

ZORA. I hope it's you. He's wounded, they said. He's at the seaside in a refugee center — which used to be a hotel. What seaside? What center? What hotel? They couldn't say. I was so lucky to find you! I've been looking for you for ages.

KONSTANTIN. Where are we going?

ZORA. London!

KONSTANTIN. I don't like London. There's fog in London.

ZORA. There isn't any fog in London. There used to be fog in London in the times of Oliver Twist. It's all been cleared since.

KONSTANTIN. They've sent it all down to us. How do we get to London by ship?

ZORA. Across to Italy first. I wanted to avoid going by land. We're too vulnerable.

KONSTANTIN. That we are.

ZORA. When you died I left for London. My only desire was to get as far away from the Balkans as possible. Ruth sent me an invitation. Yana's with her now.

KONSTANTIN. We should have left when Ruth first invited us. The war had just started then. You begged me to go. I couldn't leave then. I was a patriot then.

ZORA. You were a father too.

KONSTANTIN. I'm sorry. [*Pause*] How's Yana?

ZORA. She never believed you were dead. She expected you to come home any minute.

KONSTANTIN. Who told you I was killed?

ZORA. First I heard you were arrested. I went round in circles trying to locate you. Then two policemen confirmed you'd been shot. [*Pause*] My mother died.

KONSTANTIN. No!

ZORA. No insulin. She went blind. The end was terrible.

KONSTANTIN. How did Yana take it?

ZORA. Yana doesn't believe she's dead. She expects her to come back any minute. [*Looks at her watch. She goes up the stairs. looks to the right, down the corridor.*] Are you worried?

KONSTANTIN. Should I be?

ZORA. We'll be alright now.

KONSTANTIN. You must have been relieved when I disappeared. Was it awful to hear I wasn't quite dead yet? [*Pause*] I'm not ready, Zora.

ZORA. Ready for what?

KONSTANTIN. Look at me.

ZORA. What were you doing under the tree? Gazing at the sea? Why didn't you go back home?

KONSTANTIN. Where?

ZORA. To our house.

KONSTANTIN. Other people have moved into our house. Nice people. I went to see them. They haven't touched any of the furniture. All our things are there, just as they were. Only we have gone. They were very kind. Their own house was burnt to the ground. They apologized. They asked me if I wanted to stay. I drank a glass of brandy with them and left.

ZORA. They live with our photo albums?

KONSTANTIN. And the books and the diaries and the beds and the underwear and the kitchen utensils and the toilet seat. [*Pause*] Are you married to an American diplomat? And living in New York?

ZORA. What?

KONSTANTIN. Are you living in New York?

ZORA. No, I'm not!

KONSTANTIN. I heard rumors. Why didn't you look for me earlier?

ZORA. Look for you where? Why didn't you get in touch earlier?

KONSTANTIN. Get in touch with you where?

ZORA. I thought you were dead.

KONSTANTIN. I was. My eyes've been messed up. My balance's been messed up. [*Hits his head with his hand*] It's like an old TV. You hit it, it turns itself on.

ZORA. Don't.

KONSTANTIN. It's only a cheap black and white set.

ZORA. [*Kisses him*] You'll be fine.

KONSTANTIN. [*He lies down.*] Enjoying the cruise, darling? Shall we have an aperitif and look at the sunset? [*Pause*] I can't go anywhere.

ZORA. I promised Yana to get her father back to her.

KONSTANTIN. What's she like?

ZORA. [*Gives him a photograph*] She'd ask me why people go to war. I'd say, sometimes they just go crazy. She'd ask what if they got crazy in London. I'd say they wouldn't. She'd ask how I knew. Her teachers told me they were alarmed at her behavior. And would I not tell her that. We watched the news together. Interviews with raped women. A girl of eight with blood running down her legs. I was sick to my stomach, I couldn't breathe. What do I tell my daughter if she starts asking questions? She insisted we sleep in the same bed. “Don’t go crazy, Mom.” “I won’t, Yana.” “Promise?” “Promise.” “Goodnight now!”

KONSTANTIN. [*He wipes his eyes.*] My eyes get sore.

ZORA. You’ve changed. [*Pause*] What have they done to us?

KONSTANTIN. Nothing we didn’t ask for.

ZORA. They destroyed our lives.

KONSTANTIN. We fucked up so tremendously.

ZORA. What happened to you?

KONSTANTIN. I’m tired. I think I can fall asleep.

ZORA. Do.

KONSTANTIN. I haven’t slept for months. I see people with half faces. We’re in no man’s land on the front line. In smoke and fog. I don’t know whether we’re attacking or retreating. Are we moving? We’re afloat.

ZORA. We’ve put to sea.

KONSTANTIN. You shouldn’t have bothered with me, Zora. This is a trap. Your man won’t come. We’ve been duped.

ZORA. I’ll find him.

[*Zora goes out.*]

KONSTANTIN. [*Shouting after her*] Duped, conned, and betrayed!

[*Pause. Enter Luka. He’s a big man, wearing an elegant black suit. He pays no attention to Konstantin. He opens a cardboard box. Produces a metal detector. He puts the earphones on his ears. Konstantin looks at him.*]

KONSTANTIN. Are you the man?

LUKA. [*Not turning*] Yes.

KONSTANTIN. My wife went out to find you.

LUKA. Did she?

KONSTANTIN. Where are they?

LUKA. What?

KONSTANTIN. The passports?

LUKA. What passports?

KONSTANTIN. The passports she paid you for.

LUKA. How much did she pay me?

KONSTANTIN. Who are you?

LUKA. [*Turning to Konstantin*] Who are you?

KONSTANTIN. I'm Konstantin.

LUKA. I'm Luka. I am the ship's security guy. I like your pajamas.

[*Tanya comes in. She's dressed in a Charleston-style short dress, a cap, and long gloves. She's smoking a cigarette in a long cigarette holder.*]

TANYA. [*Singing in Russian*] *Shto ti guljaesh moj sinochek*![1]

LUKA. We're happy tonight.

TANYA. I've got a padlock.

LUKA. You've got what?

TANYA. A real padlock. Fake gold, I think. I've got it on down there.

---

1. "Why do you stray from me, my boy?"

LUKA. Down where?

TANYA. Down there.

LUKA. No!

TANYA. Gavro's got the key. It's like a chastity belt. His anniversary present to me. I pretended I loved the idea. He'll unlock me at crack of dawn.

LUKA. He's insane.

TANYA. I know. Could I tell him that? Why don't ***you*** tell him that? You couldn't tell him that either, could you? Save me, Luka.

[*Enter Prajapati. He's an Indian, an observer in parade in uniform. He's gloomy and drunk.*]

TANYA. [*To Prajapati*] Stop following me around, man. Gavro thinks I'm screwing you. He'll slit your throat.

PRAJAPATI. I'm a gambler, Tanya, not a lover. He knows it and you know it too.

[*Tanya goes out.*]

LUKA. On a losing streak again?

PRAJAPATI. Again? Have I ever won?

LUKA. Blackjack?

PRAJAPATI. Roulette.

LUKA. You have my sympathy.

PRAJAPATI. Can I have some cash too?

LUKA. No way.

PRAJAPATI. We split in half.

LUKA. Last night this Greek lost the shirt off his back in the casino, comes up to me and says "If you don't give me the money back, I'll jump out of the window."

PRAJAPATI. And?

LUKA. I opened the window for him and said "Go for it."

PRAJAPATI. Did he go for it?

LUKA. He went for it, yes.

PRAJAPATI. Do you know what my name means in Hindi?

LUKA. It's the name of a god.

PRAJAPATI. Have I told you this before?

LUKA. Yes, you have. So what?

[*Prajapati goes out.*]

KONSTANTIN. Never a dull moment.

LUKA. [*Takes a booklet out of his pocket*] Do you speak Danish? I can't read this. It's an instruction manual. For the metal detector.

KONSTANTIN. [*Looks at the booklet*] This isn't Danish.

LUKA. Isn't it?

KONSTANTIN. This is Norwegian!

LUKA. Is it?

KONSTANTIN. Unless it's Swedish. Anyway, this is not a manual for a detector! It's a manual for a hoover. Look at these pictures. Take it back to the shop where you bought it.

LUKA. What shop? Some Bulgarians palmed it off on me in the fish market, from the back of a van with Turkish registration plates.

[Zora comes in. Luka puts the booklet away and looks at Zora.]

LUKA. What did you bargain for?

ZORA. Two British passports.

LUKA. Six thousand?

ZORA. Eight.

LUKA. And a passage to Italy? Three thousand?

ZORA. Five.

LUKA. Prices are going up. You've been had. You're not the first.

ZORA. Is this a ferry to Italy?

LUKA. This is a floating casino. It goes up the coast a bit and then drops anchor. At dawn it goes back to port.

ZORA. We can't go back to port. We have no money. No documents. We must get to England. Our daughter is waiting for us there. My husband needs a doctor. We can't go back to port.

LUKA. Oh!

ZORA. Could you help us?

LUKA. I could arrest you as stowaways.

[Enter Duda. She's a big, fat, motherly figure. She's grinding coffee in a manual copper grinder.]

DUDA. Arrest me, arrest you, that's all you hear these days. Kill, rape, and steal! You've soiled your tongues, you've soiled your minds, you've soiled your souls. Why don't you think of nice things sometimes.

LUKA. What nice things, Duda? There aren't any nice things left. We've screwed up all the nice things up, twice.

DUDA. Think of your house. Did you have a kitchen dresser in it?

LUKA. I did.

DUDA. Did you have quinces on top of the dresser?

LUKA. I did.

DUDA. Did you have chickens in the yard?

LUKA. I did.

DUDA. Aren't those nice things?

LUKA. They are.

DUDA. Well then. Think of them. Grind some coffee for me.

[*Luka takes a crate of wine. He goes out.*]

DUDA. You're never too busy to refuse a cup. [*She turns to Konstantin.*] Please? [*She gives him the coffee grinder. Konstantin starts grinding.*] I like it the old way. The village had sooner perish than its customs. You're staying for breakfast, aren't you? For my borsch? Killer of hangover and giver of life. Out to impress not only as a soup, but as a meal too. Root vegetables, beets, swedes, turnips, carrots. Plus my secret spice! You must be cold here. The teeth of Uncle February! But the sky is starry, and the sea is calm. Aren't you going to the casino?

ZORA. We're not very presentable.

DUDA. Shall I read your palm?

ZORA. No, thank you.

DUDA. It's for free.

ZORA. I don't believe in any of that.

DUDA. Don't you? What do you believe in? Your name's Zora, right? Do you believe now? [*She takes Zora's palm.*]

ZORA. How did you know my name?

DUDA. It's all over your face. You have suffered a lot. At the border all your documents were taken away from you. You've left a man feeling bitter and betrayed. You have separated and will be reunited. You have loved and lost. He's coming your way.

ZORA. He's here. This is my husband.

DUDA. Another man, perhaps. A foreigner. English, I believe. A war reporter.

ZORA. Who are you? Have we met before?

DUDA. We've all met before. [*To Konstantin*] Your palm says you need some clothes. Come with me.

KONSTANTIN. Where?

DUDA. We'll make a new man out of you. Come on.

[*Konstantin and Duda go out. Pause. Zora lights up a cigarette. Mick appears at the door. He's wearing a white dinner jacket. He stands there for some time. Then he comes in. He has a bottle of drink in his hand. Zora looks at him in bewilderment. Pause.*]

MICK. Camel?

ZORA. Sorry?

MICK. The cigarettes?

ZORA. Yes.

MICK. No filter.

ZORA. No.

MICK. You always smoke them?

ZORA. Yes.

MICK. I like that.

ZORA. Me too.

MICK. Your hands are shaking.

ZORA. I know.

MICK. I like that, too.

[*They look at each other. Pause*.]

ZORA. Mick!

MICK. It's a compliment! You remember my name. Welcome to the snakepit. My surrogate mother, Duda, recognized you. She said: Your lady's here. She's seen your face before. I keep your photograph under my pillow. It's wet for all the tears I cry in the night.

ZORA. What are you doing here?

MICK. Am I interrupting something? I'll go. Who's the man?

ZORA. Konstantin. My husband.

MICK. You got married? Congratulations.

ZORA. I was married before I knew you.

MICK. Were you?

ZORA. He was killed.

MICK. Was he?

ZORA. It's a long story.

MICK. Obviously. Where are you going now?

ZORA. London.

MICK. Of all places?

ZORA. My daughter is waiting there for us.

MICK. Daughter too. Well, well. She's not mine, is she?

ZORA. She's twelve years old.

MICK. You made such a fool of me!

ZORA. No Mick!

MICK. Yes Zora! You never told me a thing.

ZORA. I couldn't talk, Mick. I felt so guilty.

MICK. I hope you did. I hope you do.

ZORA. We're terribly stuck. You must help us.

MICK. Oh no, I won't. I help nobody but myself these days. It's a lesson I learnt in your part of the world. It's a lesson I learnt from you.

[*Konstantin comes in. He's now wearing an old suit.*]

ZORA. This is my husband, Konstantin. This is Mick.

KONSTANTIN. Hello, Mick.

MICK. Hello, Konstantin.

ZORA. We met in the siege.

KONSTANTIN. What a small world!

ZORA. After you disappeared, I needed money. Every morning I would cross "sniper alley" to get to the Holiday Inn. I worked as an interpreter for the foreign press corps.

MICK. The "designer fatigues" crowd.

ZORA. Mick is a war reporter.

MICK. Was.

KONSTANTIN. What are you now?

MICK. A cynic.

KONSTANTIN. Welcome to the club.

MICK. Are you a member too?

KONSTANTIN. I was an enthusiast for a few seasons. I was shouting on my underground radio station for people not to give in to the nationalist beast.

MICK. The "underground radio station!" I've heard about you.

KONSTANTIN. My enthusiasm withered away. People went to their tribes. Multi-ethnic wasn't cool anymore. Chauvinism was chic again! Overnight I became old-fashioned and cynical.

MICK. It was a brave thing not to lose hope!

KONSTANTIN. It was stupid to lose everything else. I kept my family hostage.

MICK. I cut my teeth in a few wars. Zimbabwe, Lebanon, Angola. Everywhere I'd go it'd take me three days to suss out the situation and get bored with it. I've been here forever, and I still don't have a clue.

KONSTANTIN. About what?

MICK. Who's killing who and why.

KONSTANTIN. Give it up.

MICK. I have. I've taken up drink instead. I've become a resident barfly on this ship, drowning my sorrows in whisky and gin under the pretense I'm writing a book. Would you like a drink?

KONSTANTIN. I thought you'd never ask.

MICK. Zora?

ZORA. Hit me.

[*Mick pours drinks. They drink.*]

MICK. Cheers!

KONSTANTIN. Your good health! [*He drinks.*] What's your story?

MICK. A milkman father made good, sent me to a private school. I side-stepped university for the university of life. I married a posh bird. Manor type. Her parents disapproved. We spent our honeymoon in a villa her friend owns on a Greek island. Daughter came. We retreat to the countryside. I get a desk job in London. She's happy, I think I'm happy too. One day Gerard appears, my crazy photographer comrade from a few wars back. He takes me on a night out. I wake up with him and two naked girls in the same bed. I realize what it was I'd been missing. I tell my wife I'll piss off to Afghanistan for "my last fling." Make friends with the mujahidin. My wife keeps quiet. Stiff upper lip and all that. Six months later I come back.

Passionate reunion, etc. Then I wander off again. A year later she divorces me. For the chap who owns the Greek villa. I have no right to see my daughter.

KONSTANTIN. So we find you in our siege.

MICK. So I find myself in your siege. I go to the Holiday Inn. There's a chambermaid comes every morning to clean our rooms, with her daughter of eight, looks just like my daughter. I can't take my eyes off her. She clings to her mum, won't talk to me. Her eyes are very bright. It's later I realize that's because she's hungry. It's later I realize she doesn't come anymore because she's been killed. I get furious. This is new to me. I spent years bumming around through wars, women, and wine, feeling no excitement. Nearly got killed in Beirut. Nothing. Lost close friends. Nothing. Here, suddenly, I get emotional. I'm helpless. I'm frustrated. The man of no commitments and no politics is suddenly taking sides? What's going on? Am I getting old? Am I losing it? Midlife crisis? Closing doors panic? That's when she appeared.

KONSTANTIN. Who?

MICK. A woman.

KONSTANTIN. Oh, no!

MICK. Oh, yes! I fell in love. Head over heels, in a dying city, during raging battles, with rockets crisscrossing the sky, leaving trails like comets. I thought she loved me, too. But soon she left me. I walked through the burning streets, calling her name louder than the shells, hoping to be cut in two with an endless volley of bullets.

KONSTANTIN. Where is she now?

MICK. Here. In my heart. One day I might figure out what happened. It's like history. Finding rational explanations to irrational events. Like war reporting.

KONSTANTIN. We're keeping you from your business.

MICK. Please do. Tonight on the ship we have assorted army commanders, politicians, nationalist cheerleaders, agents and couriers, delegates, deputies, and diplomats. A convention of friends and foes. Opposites that are fatally attracted. Plus a few American ladies seeking romance. This ship glides along the coasts and borders of three warring nations. Nobody ever shoots at it. Enemies meet here for a drink, a quiet chat, a civilized game of cards, a reassuring glimpse of humanity. Then they go back to their respective front lines and go on murdering each other. They are all here in a bunch. Like eels entwined with each other when the south wind blows.

[*Gavro appears at the door. He's short and pompous. He is also wearing a white dinner jacket. He sits down. He unwraps bread, sausage, and onion out of greasy paper.*]

GAVRO. You won't mind me having my dinner here. I don't like to eat out there with the "caviar" clientele. [*He eats in a crude manner.*] Would you care to join me?

ZORA. No. Thank you.

MICK. This is Gavro. This is Zora and her husband Konstantin.

GAVRO. I told myself: "One day, when I get rich, I will not forget my humble beginnings. I will stick to my simple diet." Enjoying the party? The anniversary of my venture?

ZORA. We are indeed.

GAVRO. Good. What do you do?

ZORA. Before the war I was an assistant lecturer in English Literature. I wrote my M.A. on the female characters in Jacobean drama.

GAVRO. What's an M.A?

ZORA. I wonder myself.

GAVRO. What will you be after the war?

ZORA. Will there be an "After the War?"

GAVRO. What do you have in your bag?

ZORA. [*Takes the bag and gives it to him*] You want to have a look?

GAVRO. Tell me. I trust you.

ZORA. I have a gun.

GAVRO. What make is it? [*Pause. He shows his gun.*] This, for example, is a Colt. You don't have a gun. What ***do*** you have?

ZORA. A book of bedtime stories. Sunglasses. Three packs of cigarettes. A lighter. Medicines. An old tourist guide. A pack of cards.

GAVRO. Cards?

ZORA. My grandmother's cards. She taught me to play patience. She died when I was 12.

GAVRO. Is that all?

ZORA. A couple of stones, a shell, an old earring, a leaf, a twig, a fluffy keyring. Used lipsticks.

GAVRO. You don't wear makeup.

ZORA. That's because it's all used up.

GAVRO. What else?

ZORA. A little cassette radio. With a tape of bird speech. My father was an ornithologist.

GAVRO. Was he really? What's that?

ZORA. Bird scientist. He went into the dark forest at night to record the birds. One day he didn't come back. We found his things in a neat pile. With the tape.

GAVRO. Isn't that terrible? What do you do, Konstantin?

KONSTANTIN. I'm a graphic designer. I'm making an ink drawing of Zora exposed on a sea cliff as a morsel for the hungry marine monster. What do you do?

GAVRO. I supply.

KONSTANTIN. What?

GAVRO. Whatever's in demand.

KONSTANTIN. Like?

GAVRO. Boxer shorts, whisky, perfumes, jeans, CDs. Genuine imitation stuff. Tobacco. Russian 5-125 ground-to-air missiles. One of those warhead jobs. They come dirt cheap these days. Bootleg country.

ZORA. Where they've thrown the baby out with the bath water.

GAVRO. I heard about your trouble. [*He takes out a photograph of himself. He signs it. Gives it to Zora.*]

MICK. Lucky you. That's a don't-mess-with-me photograph, credit card, and universal pass. With the picture alone you could get into a shop and ask for anything. With the signature as well, you could get into a shop and ask for the shop.

ZORA. Thank you very much.

GAVRO. Mick is my biographer and PR adviser. He promised to get me married into the English royalty. We failed with a fake Romanian princess. He's alright. Except for his soft spot for the refugees. He's syphoned off more money to charities and relief agencies than all of the European Union put together. [*To Mick*] You think I don't know about your "clean" dealings.

[*Luka comes in. He brings Gavro a mobile phone.*]

GAVRO. [*Gavro picks it up.*] Yes. No. [*Listens. He gets angry about something. Shouts.*] Tell them to sell the family silver. They've got two companies. One for soda ash and chemicals on the Black Sea. The other for urea fertilizer, ammonia, and industrial gases. I'll wait. [*Pause*] No? Tell them to fuck off, then! I want to hear you tell them that. [*Pause. He gives the phone to Luka. He looks at Zora.*] Sometimes you make a profit from the violence of war, sometimes from the deceit of trade. "Unto everyone that hath shall be given, and he shall have abundance; but from him that hath not shall be taken away even that which he hath."

ZORA. Gospel according to St. Matthew.

GAVRO. [*Gavro lights up a huge cigar.*] Is it? No idea! I heard it from the village priest. When the war came, I took it by the horns. The old regime died. I was amongst the first to smell the rat. I went where nobody dared. Uncharted territory. Like Christopher Columbus. This is my ship and it's sailing into the future!

[*Gavro puffs at his cigar.*]

[*Enter Tanya.*]

TANYA. Are you refugees? I mean, dressed as refugees, for this evening's theme?

ZORA. We didn't know there was one.

TANYA. I am Tanya. [*She extends her hand.*]

ZORA. I'm Zora. [*Shakes Tanya's hand.*]

TANYA. I am Russian. I have a headache. Here, here, and here. Are you a healer? [*Tanya takes Zora's hand and puts it on her cheek. Closes her eyes.*] So soft. It smells of wild thyme. I came here with the first batch of strippers, posing as Bolshoi ballerinas. Now I'm a croupier. We organize evenings on a theme. "The lesser-known rituals of the Egyptian pharaohs." "The secret life of Alexander the Great." "The shady side of the leaders of the Russian Revolution."

ZORA. What's the theme tonight?

TANYA. "Casablanca — Capitalism for Beginners." Mick's Bogart. Gavro's Bogart, too.

GAVRO. I'm Bogart One, he's Bogart Two.

TANYA. The rhinos are on the verge of extinction. Their horn is in great demand.

GAVRO. [*To Tanya*] You're so funny.

TANYA. He paid hundreds of dollars for a couple of ounces. He also uses vacuum pumps and hormone injections. He promised to give me a job if I gave him a blow job. Then he set fire to my passport.

GAVRO. She's drunk.

TANYA. I lived near Krasnouralsk. There's a copperworks there. Tall smokestacks raining pollution. There's lead in the earth, the water, and the air. It gives people brain damage. They can't leave. There's nowhere to go. The jobs may kill them, but they feed them, too.

GAVRO. Don't listen to her.

TANYA. My little sister got sick. We gave her wine to strengthen her blood. She refused to take it. We put sugar in the wine. She still wouldn't take it. Then I'd wake her up, at night, in her first sleep, to force a tumbler of wine into her. Then she died. I left for Moscow where I was a star in a film. Then I came here.

KONSTANTIN. The Tera Camp.

GAVRO. The Tera Camp?

KONSTANTIN. You would come at dusk. In a 1930s replica Mercedes. Get out crates of booze, go up to the upstairs rooms, party to death.

GAVRO. What are you talking about?

KONSTANTIN. I saw you through the cracks in the wood. We could hear the orgies through the night. Their screams and the loud music. The loud music and their screams.

GAVRO. I don't know what you're talking about!

KONSTANTIN. Oh yes, you do!

GAVRO. I've never killed anybody.

KONSTANTIN. You came for the women.

GAVRO. You're a comedian.

KONSTANTIN. Many times, all through last summer.

GAVRO. What were you doing in the Tera Camp?

KONSTANTIN. I was a prisoner there.

GAVRO. It was a camp for Them. I thought you were one of Us.

KONSTANTIN. I was.

GAVRO. So you couldn't have been with Them! All the male prisoners in that camp were executed, anyway.

KONSTANTIN. I was left alive to tell the tale.

GAVRO. I went to camps for volunteer work. I helped with the catering. We're at war.

KONSTANTIN. You went in those random missions! Blitz balaclava affairs. Pop across the border, rape a few women, set a village on fire, kill a few suspects, loot video recorders, and run. It was the thing to do on the weekend. Macho business. Boys will be boys.

GAVRO. There was a job to be done! Your country calls!

KONSTANTIN. Who?

GAVRO. Your country!

KONSTANTIN. Oh, yes!

GAVRO. No! You wouldn't know what that means! The General of the Army gave me a medal. There was a reception in my honor. I kissed the flag. [*Takes his gun out. He points it at Konstantin.*] Are you fucking with me?

[*Duda comes in with the coffee.*]

DUDA. Coffee break!

GAVRO. Answer my question! Are you fucking with me?

MICK. Take it easy, Gavro!

GAVRO. Stay out of this, Englishman! [*To Konstantin*] What are you doing on my ship? This is a private party! You're trespassing on private property! [*He takes the photograph he gave to Zora and tears it to pieces.*] When we get to port, I'll throw you to the police! Fucking spy!

[*Enter Prajapati. He has a cocktail drink in his hand. Prajapati looks at Gavro.*]

GAVRO. What the fuck are you looking at me for? Who gave you a drink?

[*Prajapati quickly spills the drink on the ground and puts the glass down.*]

GAVRO. I want my money back. I want it all and I want it by dawn.

PRAJAPATI. Please, Gavro.

GAVRO. The money! Or jump in the sea and drown.

[*Gavro goes out. Pause.*]

LUKA. He's angry.

DUDA. Have some coffee.

LUKA. He's very angry.

[*Luka goes out after Gavro. The others drink their coffee.*]

DUDA. Slurp, Mick. You must slurp.

MICK. Sorry, Duda. I always forget.

DUDA. You don't drink my coffee without slurping.

MICK. Bad habits die hard.

[*They slurp in silence.*]

PRAJAPATI. Do I look like a gypsy?

DUDA. Yes, you do.

PRAJAPATI. These children saw me in the street this morning. Must have thought I was a gypsy. They threw stones at me. Bloody racists. [*He starts crying.*] Forgive me.

MICK. [*Mick takes out some money and gives it to Prajapati.*] I can't stand your uniform, Prajapati.

PRAJAPATI. I know, Mick.

MICK. You're neither an officer nor a gentleman.

PRAJAPATI. [*Gets up to go*] You just saved my life again.

DUDA. Finish your coffee first.

[*Prajapati gulps the coffee down. He goes out. Pause.*]

TANYA. Now if this isn't the best cup I've ever had.

[*Tanya goes out. Pause. Duda gets up to go.*]

DUDA. Mistletoe's got little berries like white moons. When they get dry, they turn golden. It's poisonous. But — don't tell anyone — if you know what to do with it, it's a good witch's brew!

ZORA. Thanks for the coffee.

DUDA. Stay away from Gavro.

[*Duda goes out. Pause. Konstantin gets up.*]

KONSTANTIN. You must stay away from me. It's dangerous for you to be near me. It was irresponsible of you to come here in the first place. You're risking your life. I'm leaving you. You must go back and take care of Yana.

ZORA. You can't do this to me, Kosta!

KONSTANTIN. Yes, I can. I'm doing it to you, Zora!

[*Konstantin goes out.*]

MICK. Not a good season for sacrifices!

ZORA. If we go back to port, that'll be the end of him.

MICK. Then you can make a brand-new start!

ZORA. Does it give you pleasure to insult me?

MICK. Yes!

ZORA. Go on then!

MICK. Where was I?

ZORA. Are you only fascinated by the banality of evil, or have you become banal and evil yourself?

MICK. I was offered work in other swamps. I didn't take it. I stayed around the Balkans waiting for a miracle.

ZORA. I want to have a teacup which is mine. And a hook on which I can hang it. A little pot of flowers. Hot croissants and coffee. And full observation of table manners. I'm sick and tired of going to bed and waking up with the BBC World Service on a little radio plugged into my ear. [*Whistles the BBC world service jingle*] The soundtrack of my misery.

[*Enter Luka. He carries a big black plastic rubbish bag. Leaves it in the middle of the room.*]

MICK. Don't leave it here.

LUKA. It's just arrived.

MICK. Take it to Gavro.

LUKA. I don't know where he is.

MICK. Find him!

LUKA. I can't walk around with this!

MICK. Don't leave it with me!

[*Luka leaves the bag and goes out. Pause. Zora is looking at the bag.*]

ZORA. What's that?

MICK. A trash bag.

ZORA. What's in it?

MICK. Ears. Noses. Fingers. Dicks. Depending on the local custom.

[*Zora opens the bag. She takes out a fistful of banknotes.*]

MICK. It's Gavro's laundry.

ZORA. Crumpled-up notes. What does he do with them?

MICK. He irons them.

ZORA. How did it come here?

MICK. In a speed boat. It's a con. Funny money.

ZORA. What do you mean?

MICK. You wouldn't understand.

ZORA. Try me.

MICK. Private banks. Shell-company deals. Triangular trade. Diversion of corporate funds. Fraudulent invoices. Company formation. Offshore incorporation, registration, domiciliation, and management.

[*Zora starts laughing.*]

ZORA. When I was a girl, I watched the partisan films. I believed if the Nazis were to return to torture me, I would be brave and heroic. I was wrong. Now brute force has come into my life, it has nothing to do with anything I know. I have no weapons. It's too late to learn how to handle a gun or get a killer's instinct. [*Zora opens her bag and produces a gun.*] This was thrown in free with the bargain. A decent girl shouldn't be seen without one in this jungle of macho patriots, patriarchal warlords, launderers, and rapists!

MICK. And cynics!

ZORA. Exactly!

MICK. I'll trade you that for this! [*He takes a British passport out of his pocket.*] Your own forged passport. I didn't tell you I'd ordered one for you. It was to be a surprise. I wanted to ask you to live with me the day you didn't turn up. [*Mick produces a crumpled piece of paper from the passport.*] "Mick, I cannot see you anymore. Now or ever. I love you. Forgive me. Yours always. Zora."

[*Mick gives Zora the passport and the note. Zora gives Mick the gun. Mick puts the gun in his belt. Zora looks at the note.*]

ZORA. That was the day my daughter went missing. I looked for her for four frantic hours. I found her in the woods, miles from our home. She said she'd gone out to look for her daddy. She'd heard I had a lover and didn't want her anymore. We left a few hours later. We walked through the tunnel, out of the siege. Over the mountains. We hitched a truck. Then we were on a bus. Then trains across borders. Then Dover. I asked for political asylum. I got it. Two days later we were in a council estate in London on 40 pounds a week. I was in shock. I couldn't sleep, I couldn't eat. I felt so perverse. That I should fall in love with a complete stranger. My husband barely gone. My mother dead. I blamed it all on myself. I was paralyzed. I thought I smelled of rotten fish.

MICK. Did you think of me?

ZORA. No.

MICK. Never?

ZORA. Never.

MICK. Making love among the falling shells? In the abandoned floors of the hotel? Where the chambermaids never went?

ZORA. Never.

MICK. In desolate cold rooms, with broken windowpanes, with sinks that ran mud, in dirty unmade beds, left in a hurry by the last civilian guests?

ZORA. Never.

[*Pause.*]

MICK. We've anchored.

ZORA. Now what?

MICK. Now I won't let you go away again.

ZORA. Don't.

MICK. Never.

ZORA. Ever.

[*They kiss. Blackout.*]

PART TWO

[*Hull of the ship. A few hours later. Luka has nearly finished sorting out the cash from the black bag. He puts rubber bands around wads of banknotes and puts them in stacks. Zora comes in. She looks at him. She lights a cigarette.*]

ZORA. In the casino Gavro set free a hundred doves. They all flew out of the windows. But one of them got stuck. Must have had a bad wing. It started banging about from one wall to the other. One of the colonels got his gun out and shot it. One hit. No mistake. There were rounds of applause.

LUKA. We go out of our way to keep you entertained.

ZORA. Do you always count money publicly in front of strangers?

LUKA. Why not? If they were to tell anyone, who'd believe them? Ask me the exchange rates. I know all of the exchange rates.

ZORA. I'm not particularly interested in the exchange rates.

LUKA. But ask me.

ZORA. The Japanese yen.

LUKA. As opposed to what?

ZORA. To the Spanish peseta.

LUKA. 100 yen equals 14.7 Deutchmarks. 100 pesetas equals 11.8 Deutchmarks. 100 yen equals 124 pesetas! That's no problem. The problem is that both Belgian and Swiss francs are called francs, but are otherwise totally different. We don't get many of them, though. Mostly dollars and German marks. On some nights the odd British pound. Depends on the tide.

ZORA. Lovely ship this!

LUKA. For fifty years she was a minesweeper. Ex-Italian navy, built in Genoa. 10 yards in the beam, 20 knots average speed. Her original name was "Balkan." When Gavro bought her, he wanted to change the name to "Casablanca." But the painters messed it all up. They started writing "Casablanca" and wrote "Casabalkan" instead. Gavro was furious at first, but then he rather liked it. She was registered under this hash of a name.

ZORA. Gavro's a bastard, isn't he?

LUKA. Of course he is.

ZORA. Why do you do what he says?

LUKA. I'm a poor peasant. They took me from my field. You must do your patriotic duty, they said. I must plough my field, I said. Patriotism first, ploughing later, they said. I lay in a trench day and night, summer, and winter. Now I've been promoted to security. In the meantime, Gavro made millions. He says we're in the same boat. The problem is, one day we'll be comrades with Them again. There'll be brotherhood and unity again, we'll start building railways and bridges again, and it'll be me working again and Gavro smoking his cigar. But that's how it is. That's how God planned it. You've got to serve somebody.

[*Zora puts the metal detector earphones on her ears.*]

LUKA. [*Takes out a map from his pocket*] I've got this secret old map. A Venetian ship was transporting Dutch gold and diamonds. The Turks sank the ship and took the loot. The Slavs went after them. The Turks hid the treasure. The Slavs started fighting among themselves. The riches are still there somewhere.

ZORA. Go for it.

LUKA. The map could be fake.

ZORA. Follow your intuition.

LUKA. Will you follow yours? Mick or your husband? Your husband or Mick? Which of them will your intuition take you to?

[*Enter Duda. Luka goes out.*]

DUDA. Your husband is fast asleep. He watched me prepare food. I was telling him a story. He dozed off. I put a blanket over his shoulders.

ZORA. What was the story?

DUDA. My daughters left with their families when the shooting started. They all crammed into two cars. Children, toys. I couldn't leave. Who was going to feed the animals? I sat and smoked in front of my house. The village was deserted for three days. They came at dawn. They took fridges, videos, sewing machines, everything. Then they set fire to the houses. They didn't touch me. As if I was invisible. I went to the stable to let the animals out. The mare was standing over her dead foal. Someone had shot it. Not the mare. Only the foal.

ZORA. What am I going to do, Duda?

DUDA. What are any of us going to do, child?

[*Enter Tanya, disheveled. She has been beaten up. She wears a red scarf around her neck.*]

ZORA. What's happened to you? Did someone beat you up? Gavro? Look at you! Is this your school scarf? I had one of those myself. We all got our red scarves when we became communist pioneers. We were given flowers and badges. We felt so important, so proud.

TANYA. They told us about the battle of Sverdlovsk. About the importance of sacrifice. My film starts with me asleep in a room. I'm naked except for the scarf around my neck. Three men in overalls come in through the window. They rudely wake me up. I put up some kind of resistance. But they take me one after the other. I scream and shout, but the audience is to believe it's from pleasure. Then they leave and I fall into a sweet sleep again. The film was called "Perestroika."

[*Pause. Gavro appears at the door.*]

DUDA. Back to work. There's the washing to do.

[*Duda goes out.*]

ZORA. What did you do to her?

GAVRO. You wanted to see me.

ZORA. Did you do that to her?

GAVRO. I never touch her. Not that she doesn't ask for it.

[*Gavro looks at Tanya. Tanya goes out.*]

GAVRO. What do you want?

ZORA. I need help.

GAVRO. That was what my wife said. "I need help," she said. She was one of Them. The Others. Actually, she was half and half. Her mother was one of Us, her father was one of Them. When the war started, she wanted to cut herself in two with a chainsaw. "Cut your bad part off," I said. "I will," she said. "Shall I cut horizontally or vertically? Or diagonally?" she cried. I knew I had hit a sore point. I left her in the siege. With the daughters. Later I tried to get them out. They refused to come with me.

ZORA. It's awful.

GAVRO. Life's awful.

ZORA. You're awful. If you could only see yourself.

GAVRO. I can see ***you***, though. When the war started, you left to brown nose Europe, I stayed to fight. You were scrounging asylum seeker's allowances in Britain, while I was organizing the import of oil so that schools and hospitals could stay open. When your international "peace" criminals were choking this country, I was helping it stand on its own two feet! What is it that makes traitors like you so goddamn superior? This is my country, I run it the way I see fit, and if I'm wrong, ***in my country***, I have the right to be wrong.

ZORA. You have the right to walk over the dead bodies of hundreds of thousands of people? You have the right to act out your filthy fantasies on innocent civilians? Right to be wrong, you call it! I call it fascism!

GAVRO. Has anybody ever hit you for no reason? Just to cause you pain? Like this. [*He slaps her face.*]

[*Zora throws the drink in his face.*]

GAVRO. The end of reason and the beginning of passion. Now you're on my turf. What do you want from me?

ZORA. I want you to leave my husband alone.

GAVRO. I want to fuck you. You think "It only happens to peasant women." That "Only bad girls get raped." You know that I know that "Women ask for it." That "Any woman can resist rape if she really wants to." That "When a woman says no, she really means yes." I'm not after your body. I can get sex anywhere! I want to fuck your mind. To show you you're nothing!

[*Enter Mick. Pause.*]

GAVRO. Let me know what your answer is.

[*Gavro goes out.*]

ZORA. I shouldn't have given you my gun.

MICK. Did he want to screw you? I know his standard negotiating procedures. We must leave while the ship is still at anchor. The driver of the speedboat is waiting for us. He's loyal to Gavro, but for cash he'll make an exception.

ZORA. What about Konstantin?

[*Enter Konstantin.*]

KONSTANTIN. I'm a new man. I had a nap. I dreamt I was walking on the sea on crutches.

MICK. Would you like a drink?

KONSTANTIN. Is there any left?

MICK. Zora?

ZORA. Please.

[*Mick pours three glasses. They all drink.*]

KONSTANTIN. Cheers.

MICK. Cheers!

ZORA. Cheers!

KONSTANTIN. To our future, whatever that means! [*He drinks.*] Do you know what my nationality is? I'm a Martian. That's what I wrote under the heading "Nationality" in the last census. Zora's a Martian too.

MICK. Rather nice.

KONSTANTIN. That's what we thought at the time. We met at university. We fell in love. We got married. And for a few years we were very happy. I worked as a book designer. I thought the place of words was very important. There wasn't Us and Them then. All of our friends were Martians. But we had enemies and they sent us warnings! My father was a respected historian. He had a school named after him. With the monument to him in the schoolyard. A few weeks before the war started, we found the bust of my father lying in our living room. Ripped off the pedestal and thrown in through the window. Zora thought we should leave immediately. I told her not to be hysterical. I shouldn't have done that. And then, coming home one night, I was rounded up with a group of citizens at a street barricade. A few jerks with guns asked us to declare whether we were Us or Them. I could have simply told them I was one of us. I could have said my name. Shown them my identity card. They would have let me go.

ZORA. What did you do?

KONSTANTIN. I said I didn't understand their question. I refused to answer it. I asked them who gave them the right to ask such stupid questions. I said I was one of ***Them***.

MICK. What did they do?

KONSTANTIN. They hit me in the head with a rifle butt. When I came round, I was in a camp with ***Them***. I had plenty of time to think about it all and ***then*** say who I really was. But I was half-blind. Who was I supposed to ask for mercy? The people who put me there? Were they really ***my*** people? I was one of ***us***, imprisoned with all of ***them***. Now I know what we did to ***them*** because we did it to ***me***. Later, they realized I was the odd man out. They let me go. I stumbled to the front line. And stole a tank.

MICK. A tank?

KONSTANTIN. A nice, shiny tank, left in the fields.

MICK. Where did you learn to drive a tank?

KONSTANTIN. I did my military service. A tank with two dead soldiers in it. One inside and the other one perched on the top. I drove for twenty miles down the freeway. Dozens of checkpoints, militia, U.N. troops, nobody stopped me. They waved me by. Me and the dead soldiers singing songs of freedom. Then I ran out of gas. Some army unit surrounded me. I told the captain I'd got a couple of his guys, would he bury them and notify their next of kin. They put me in a makeshift tent prison. I crawled away in the night. I reached my goal. Nonexistence. A vacuum. *Die Kunst ist tot.*[2]

[*Pause. Silence. Zora starts weeping. Mick quickly goes out. Konstantin starts humming a plaintive tune. Pause.*]

[*Enter Prajapati.*]

PRAJAPATI. [*Scratching a stain on his uniform*] Wine stain. I must keep my uniform pristine. That's the only interesting part of me. I watched too many cowboy movies in Bombay as a child. I wanted to be a cavalry officer. Arriving to the rescue, announced by the trumpet. By the time we were deployed our mandate was already obsolete. My soldiers do a little paragliding. A little wine tasting. A little smuggling on the side. I was demoted. Blunders were made elsewhere. Lots of people died. It had nothing to do with me. Lack of coordination, design flaw.

---

2. Art is dead.

[*Enter Mick.*]

PRAJAPATI. We lost everything.

MICK. You can say that again.

PRAJAPATI. My name is that of the god Prajapati. He was the primordial being. Everything was contained in Prajapati. He was the universe, Time, and the sacrificial altar. He put order into the unseen unity. [*Pause. He starts crying.*] Forgive me. [*Prajapati gets up to go.*]

ZORA. Prajapati, you don't want to do that! [*Prajapati stops and turns to Zora.*] You don't want to jump in the sea and drown!

[*Prajapati goes out. Pause. Zora looks at Mick.*]

ZORA. I love your dinner jacket. It suits your invisible imperial baggage. Your aura of untouchable immunity. The ease with which you "request and require"[3] that some of us "pass freely without let or hindrance." In case of chaos, danger, or emergency, there's always a British consul conveniently nearby. You get hurt, you shout international scandal, a helicopter whisks you to safety! Of course, that doesn't diminish your empathy for us who are being butchered wholesale.

MICK. It's murder everywhere I look. My cup of coffee takes me directly to the slave plantations in Colombia. My shirt takes me to the sweatshops in Honduras. My watch to the cheap labor boats in Singapore. My sneakers to the Chinese prisoners. It's all a swindle.

---

3. Zora is quoting the words on the inside cover of a British passport: "Her Britannic Majesty's Secretary of State Requests and requires in the Name of Her Majesty all those whom it may concern to allow the bearer to pass freely without let or hindrance, and to afford the bearer such assistance and protection as may be necessary."

ZORA. Is that what they teach you in your fancy schools? "All this world is but a swindle, be thou a joyful swindler!" They teach you the craft of how to govern losers like us, how to atomize a few tribes, remove and manipulate some headmen and chiefs. How to loot the place and leave it to stew for centuries in futile ethnic conflicts and secessionist troubles. How to make artificial borders with the use of trigonometry and rulers, with dead straight lines and no concessions to rivers, mountains, and natural habitats. Let alone people. Or peoples, rather.

MICK. Are you blaming me for the sins of my forefathers?

ZORA. Are you telling me those sins died with your forefathers? It was easy for my forefathers, though. In their wars the bad guys came from foreign lands and spoke a foreign language. My enemy is my neighbor. We wasted all of our energy fighting Stalinism. We didn't know nationalism would creep up on us from behind our backs.

[*Zora goes out. Pause.*]

KONSTANTIN. You must do me a favor. Help her get to London. I can't go. I don't want my daughter to see me like this.

MICK. You must go together. You need each other. You're a witness. You must get out and testify.

KONSTANTIN. What use is a witness? They've killed for years, "live," on world television. There's no shortage of witnesses, there's a shortage of resolve to bring them to court. The Son of God has been hanging on a cross for twenty centuries as a witness. So what? There's a cosmic principle called indifference! You're in the wrong profession. Maybe the world really would be a better place if the killing went on and nobody knew anything about it.

[*Luka appears at the door. He gives Mick a British passport.*]

MICK. [*To Luka*] That was quick. [*He gives the passport to Konstantin.*] This is yours now. It still has my name on it, but it's got your photograph. The one Zora used to search for you. A speedboat will take you to Italy. You must leave immediately.

[*Konstantin inspects his picture in the passport.*]

MICK. Neat, isn't it? There are magicians on this ship. Zora's got one of those as well.

[*Enter Zora.*]

KONSTANTIN. I can't take this. Where shall I go?

MICK. The Hague.

KONSTANTIN. Where's the Hague?

MICK. Somewhere out there. In Europe.

KONSTANTIN. Where's Europe?

MICK. Roughly northwest, last time I saw it.

KONSTANTIN. Was it busy? Feeding the butcher with one hand and the victim with the other?

MICK. Sure was!

KONSTANTIN. I must stay here. Evil should be lived with, like viruses and germs. I've killed my instinct for justice. Morality is a private luxury.

MICK. Try the hard sell approach. In justice, like in business, you don't get what you deserve, you get what you negotiate for.

KONSTANTIN. I'll find you and give you your passport back.

LUKA. You've got to hurry.

[*Luka helps Konstantin up the stairs. Zora looks at Mick.*]

MICK. I request and require that you pass freely without let or hindrance.

ZORA. And you?

MICK. I'll go to Tunisia. And work as a tourist rep in a hotel. In the morning I'll take the German ladies for a fitness course; at lunch I'll entertain their children; in the evening I'll be the disc jockey.

ZORA. And the snake charmer's assistant.

MICK. This reminds me . . .

ZORA. . . . of a film . . .

MICK. . . . I once saw.

ZORA. We saw it together.

[*They look at each other. Zora quickly goes out. Mick lights a cigarette. Duda comes in.*]

DUDA. [*To Mick*] Do you know that washing machines eat pieces of laundry? Every so often a sock is missing or a pair of underpants is nowhere to be found. Where do these items go to? Ever thought about that? We are talking millions of pieces here. Where do they all congregate? And to what purpose? There's food for thought. If it's not a conspiracy — what is it?

[*Exit Duda. Enter Gavro.*]

GAVRO. What's going on? Where is he? Where are they?

MICK. They're gone.

GAVRO. Gone where? How do you mean, ***gone***?

MICK. They went for a cruise.

GAVRO. A cruise? What do you mean a cruise?

MICK. In your speedboat.

[*Gavro goes to the door. Mick stands in his way.*]

MICK. Wait!

GAVRO. Get out of my way.

MICK. I don't think so.

[*Gavro pushes Mick to the side.*]

[*Mick takes out his gun.*]

GAVRO. Where did you get that? Do you know how to use that? [*He takes out his gun.*]

[*Mick shoots at Gavro.*]

GAVRO. Beginner's luck.

[*Gavro falls down dead. Luka comes in. Luka looks at Gavro's body.*]

MICK. Have they gone?

LUKA. They've gone.

MICK. Is he dead?

LUKA. He's dead.

MICK. Fuck.

LUKA. He shot himself. Too much cocaine. Depression. Mafia business. He was complaining to me about it. He fell in the sea. We never found his body. Guess who took over his business?

MICK. You?

LUKA. You.

MICK. Me?

LUKA. You know more about Gavro's affairs than he ever knew himself.

MICK. What if I refuse?

LUKA. What if you shoot yourself, too?

MICK. What if I accept?

LUKA. Eighty for me — twenty for you? [*Pause*] Sixty for me — forty for you? [*Pause*] Fifty-fifty?

[*They look at each other in silent agreement*.]

MICK. Poor Gavro.

LUKA. Poor Mick. You're one of us now.

[*Enter Tanya. She looks at Gavro's body*.]

TANYA. Beautiful corpse.

MICK. Take the dead away. I'm the king now.

[*Luka and Mick take the corpse out. Pause. Duda comes in with the borsch*.]

DUDA. Where are you taking him?

LUKA. To the sharks.

DUDA. Wash your hands when you're done and come and have breakfast.

[*Pause. Duda and Tanya put a white tablecloth over the money on the table. They pour the borsch into plates. Enter Luka and Mick. They all sit down. They eat. Pause. Enter Prajapati. He's drenched to the bone. He has a lifebelt around his waist.*]

DUDA. You jumped in the sea with a life belt on?

PRAJAPATI. I was trying my best. I was drowning properly. Suddenly a motorboat passed by. Zora threw me this and wagged her finger at me. Then they swooshed off.

[*Duda pulls him in to her by the shoulders and gives him a long, sloppy kiss.*]

DUDA. You've become a real man!

[*She lets go of him. Pause.*]

PRAJAPATI. Am I really worthy of divine intervention?

DUDA. Shush! Eat now.

[*Prajapati sits down. They all eat in silence. Pause.*]

PRAJAPATI. I sank all the way down to the propeller. I saw bodies.

DUDA. What bodies?

PRAJAPATI. The dead. That the rivers carried down to the sea. From towns and villages, valleys, and mountains.

DUDA. [*She crosses herself.*] God have mercy on their souls.

[*They eat in silence. Pause.*]

LUKA. I found a creature minced up in the air-conditioning system. Fur and feathers in the goo. Must be one of the doves. Or a seagull.

TANYA. Doves and seagulls? With fur?

LUKA. Alright. A vulture then?

TANYA. Seen any vultures round here?

LUKA. Alright. Maybe it was a rat?

TANYA. With feathers?

LUKA. I've seen a picture of a rat with wings. In a book.

TANYA. You've read books about rats?

LUKA. It wasn't a book to read. It was a picture book. "Favorite Vermin," or something. [*Pause. He looks at Tanya.*] Will you stay with me?

TANYA. Do you want me to?

LUKA. Do you want to?

TANYA. Will you be good to me?

LUKA. Will you marry me?

TANYA. Yes.

LUKA. Are you joking?

TANYA. Are you?

LUKA. Not at all.

TANYA. He threw the key to the padlock in the sea.

LUKA. I'll cut it off with my teeth.

TANYA. How romantic!

LUKA. Mick will be our best man.

TANYA. Duda will cook a feast.

LUKA. We need a priest.

TANYA. There must be one in the casino.

LUKA. Then he's undercover. Prajapati will find him.

MICK. You mean we do it now?

DUDA. Now?

PRAJAPATI. Now?

LUKA. Oh, yes now!

TANYA. Why not now?

[*They look at each other. They smile.*]

BLACKOUT

[*Lights on room in London. Zora and Yana are sitting at the table, looking at each other.*]

ZORA. Now you know everything.

YANA. I'm a big girl now.

ZORA. It's been a year since all that happened.

YANA. So Daddy went back to the Balkans to give Mick his passport.

ZORA. And to take Mick away from that ship.

YANA. Daddy wasn't very happy here in England.

ZORA. He said he was too old a dog to learn new tricks.

YANA. He thought the English sky was too low.

ZORA. I don't think he can live without the Balkans.

YANA. He's gone back to finish the war.

ZORA. The war has finished.

YANA. His war hasn't.

ZORA. At least his health is better now.

YANA. Do you think Daddy would like the fact you told me this?

ZORA. [*Shows Yana the back of the polaroid photograph*] He's written here: "To Yana and Zora." He wanted you to see this.

YANA. [*Looking at the photograph*] Daddy and Mick. Look at them.

ZORA. They look happy.

YANA. They look drunk.

ZORA. They are drunk.

YANA. I think they'll set up house together.

ZORA. I wouldn't be surprised.

YANA. They'll get on together like a house on fire. They'll play chess and quarrel about politics.

ZORA. Maybe they'll come and see us one day.

YANA. We'll ask them round for a Sunday roast.

ZORA. Only if they bring us flowers.

YANA. [*Gives her the drawing*] This is for you.

ZORA. Nice and bright. Is this your new phase?

YANA. A house in the sun.

ZORA. Flowers in the windows.

YANA. Four figures. One woman, two men, one child. "To Mom. With love."

ZORA. Thank you.

[*Pause.*]

YANA. [*Looking out.*] I'm not sure about the sky here in London, either. I mean, look, it's on top of my head most of the time. I can touch it with my hand. Yes, we had clouds in the old country too, but they were up there, minding their own business. [*Pause. Yana takes her mother's hand.*]

ZORA. I think this is the beginning of a beautiful friendship.

[*They look at each other. They smile.*]

BLACKOUT

CURTAIN

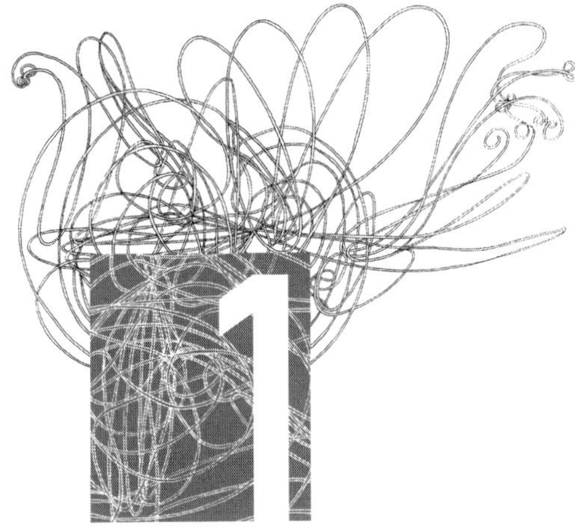

EX-YU

A scene for the theater

CHARACTERS

MAYA 18

NIKOLA 50

MARTIN 30

WAITER 65

FATHER 60

[A separate room in the restaurant of what once must have been a grand hotel in a provincial town in Ex-Yugoslavia. Ex-imperial delusions of grandeur clash with contemporary neglect and poverty. A cold winter evening. Nikola and Maya are sitting at a table in their coats. Nikola is a sturdy peasant. Maya is a lively teenager. A bottle of red wine in front of them. They raise glasses.]

NIKOLA. To your father. [*They drink.*] I'm sorry he shot himself.

MAYA. Whenever I pass by this hotel, I have a feeling he's inside reading his newspaper and drinking coffee. This was his favorite place.

NIKOLA. What's wrong with the heating in here?

MAYA. There *is* no heating. Energy rationing. When I was a child, my parents would bring me here for dinner. I would look at the chandelier in the lobby and think I was Cinderella. Now the hotel's full of refugees huddling in cold rooms.

NIKOLA. What did you want to talk about?

MAYA. I don't know really. I just wanted to meet you.

NIKOLA. How did you find me?

MAYA. I asked around. Some people from your village showed me where you lived. Thank you for coming into town to see me in this weather.

NIKOLA. It happened in the early days of the war.

MAYA. Four years ago.

NIKOLA. You must have been a kid then.

MAYA. You actually saw him do it?

NIKOLA. Yes.

MAYA. Please tell me about it.

NIKOLA. Tell you what?

MAYA. What it was like.

NIKOLA. What is it like to blow your brains out with a gun?

[*Pause.*]

MAYA. Where were you at the time?

NIKOLA. Right behind him.

MAYA. I mean, what was the place?

[*Maya produces a map. She puts it in front of Nikola. Nikola looks at the map.*]

NIKOLA. [*Putting his finger on the map*] That's the general area. But it's 30 miles across.

MAYA. Would you be able to recognize the place now?

NIKOLA. No way. [*Looking at the map*] Impossible.

MAYA. You were mobilized at midnight.

NIKOLA. We traveled all night. At dawn we got off in wheat fields somewhere. Unharvested, scorched crops. Very hot September it was. They told us we were at the front line.

[*Pause.*]

MAYA. And?

NIKOLA. What?

MAYA. What happened when they called you up?

NIKOLA. How do you mean?

MAYA. When they called you up, you just went to war?

NIKOLA. Yes.

MAYA. Nothing stopped you? Nobody stopped you?

NIKOLA. Who could stop me?

MAYA. What did your wife say?

NIKOLA. She packed some food for me.

MAYA. That was it?

NIKOLA. That was it.

MAYA. Did you shoot?

NIKOLA. Did I shoot?

MAYA. Did you shoot?

NIKOLA. I did.

MAYA. Did you kill?

NIKOLA. I didn't let them kill me. [*Pause.*] Everybody killed.

MAYA. My father didn't.

NIKOLA. True. Your father didn't kill anybody. [*Pause.*] Anybody ***else***, that is.

MAYA. And the enemy that everybody killed? We lived together in — what was that catchy phrase — "Brotherhood and Unity." ***They*** used to be ***us***.

NIKOLA. Used to be, yes. Then they became the enemy. Do you know they have skin between their toes? Like ducks. Did you know that?

MAYA. No.

NIKOLA. They're not as fully developed as we are. They're a primitive tribe. I'm glad we've cut ourselves free from them.

MAYA. Did it have to be so bloody?

NIKOLA. Do you like pork chops?

MAYA. I'm not hungry.

NIKOLA. I mean, you ***have*** eaten pork chops and sausages in your life? Yes. And have you killed a pig in your life? No. You see, I have. You can't cut the pork chops and sausages off the pig without blood. You can't be nice about it. Winter comes, you want food, you slaughter a pig. And pigs, when you kill them, they squeal. Are you sorry for them? Perhaps. But you are also hungry.

MAYA. You can choose to be a vegetarian.

NIKOLA. Not if you sweat in the fields, you can't. You can choose to be a vegetarian if you sit and read books all day long.

MAYA. That's my father for you. Too many books. Too much thinking.

NIKOLA. What was there to think about? He should have taken up arms and fought like a man.

MAYA. But it was an ugly civil war.

NIKOLA. So?

MAYA. There wasn't one clear issue about it.

NIKOLA. He was a teacher of history. He should have known better.

MAYA. What does fighting like a man mean?

NIKOLA. What does killing yourself mean? My country called. I took up my gun, like my father before me. I believe in God. I trusted the authorities.

MAYA. And what if they are a bunch of gangsters?

NIKOLA. And what if they aren't? You've got to trust somebody.

MAYA. What about my mother? [*Pause.*] She's one of them. I don't think she has skin between her toes, but she's one of ***them***. [*Pause.*] The primitive tribe.

NIKOLA. Is she?

[*Maya nods.*]

NIKOLA. Oh, well. Now it makes sense, doesn't it?

MAYA. What?

NIKOLA. It all makes sense.

MAYA. Does it?

[*Nikola and Maya look at each other.*]

NIKOLA. Sorry.

MAYA. No, ***I*** am sorry. [*Pause.*] What does this make me?

NIKOLA. What?

MAYA. When my father is one of us and my mother is one of them, what does it make me?

NIKOLA. One of us.

MAYA. How do you know?

NIKOLA. The father's line is what matters.

MAYA. Are you sure?

NIKOLA. Yes.

MAYA. Oh, good. [*Pause. She drinks.*] You buried him on the spot?

NIKOLA. "Buried" him is not the right word. We didn't have time to dig too deep. It was a makeshift grave. We had to move on.

MAYA. And Martin helped you? The young man who helped you dig — his name's Martin. I located him, too.

NIKOLA. You've done your homework, haven't you? He was one of those deserter bastards. There was no one there to court-martial them.

[*Martin comes in. He has had a few drinks too many.*]

MARTIN. Good evening! Hi! Hello! I'm Martin.

MAYA. Martin! Hello! I'm Maya.

[*Martin and Maya shake hands.*]

MARTIN. I'm late.

MAYA. Thanks for coming. This is Nikola.

[*Nikola and Martin shake hands.*]

MARTIN. Haven't we met before? It's murder out there.

MAYA. Still snowing?

MARTIN. Snowing? The sky has collapsed. Icy sleet and wind.

MAYA. Would you like a glass of wine?

MARTIN. Absolutely. [*He sits down.*]

NIKOLA. [*To Maya*] You didn't tell me he was coming.

MARTIN. It's pitch dark on the main street. There are horse carts stuck in the snow. Steam coming out of the beasts' nostrils.

[*Martin downs his glass. He pours himself another one.*]

MARTIN. Cheers! [*Pause*] Well?

MAYA. Well.

MARTIN. You're just like I imagined you.

MAYA. Is that good or bad?

MARTIN. How can you tell? You were talking, I interrupted you. Time for the serious stuff. Where are we? The general subject is war and peace. [*To Nikola*] Did you have a good war?

[*Pause. Nikola does not react. Martin drinks.*]

MAYA. What do you do, Martin?

MARTIN. What do I do? I don't do much. I've retired here to the provinces. Convalescing. Reading comics. Post-traumatic stress disorder. My mother makes me chicken soup with dumplings.

NIKOLA. Nice.

MARTIN. I know.

NIKOLA. Who kills the chickens? [*Pause. They look at each other.*] Do ***you*** kill the chickens?

MARTIN. She buys them at the butcher's. Do you still do yours manually?

[*Nikola and Martin look at each other. Pause.*]

MAYA. What is your line of work?

MARTIN. Was. Computers. I worked in the capital. I engineered software viruses.

MAYA. You've been pretty hard to get hold of. I left messages.

MARTIN. My mother has instructions to vet callers. I keep aloof like a sultan. I sit in my room behind closed curtains and play on my Gameboy. The irony is, I came here to keep a low profile. But what do you know? They start mobilizing the provinces first. They gave me a gun, shoved me on a truck, told me I had volunteered! I made a stink. They said fight or leave. I left.

NIKOLA. Deserted!

MARTIN. Deserted. Thank you. I ran to find someone to surrender to. I got on a freight train. Walked across the border. Then Europe took me in. I know some English. I emigrated to swinging London.

MAYA. Wow!

MARTIN. Yes! I went sightseeing. Lunar House in Croydon — the immigration theme park. Choice council estates in Crawley. A grand tour of the streets of London Town. I was the dishwasher in radical chic, left restaurants. Watched the intelligentsia smoke, eat, drink, and discuss moral issues all at the same time. They kept asking me: "What can *we* do, what *can* we do?" They felt ever so guilty about our war. More than we ever had. I went to seminars and symposiums about us: "The artistic challenge of cultural diversity." "Is multiculturalism still possible in the Balkans?" I went to theaters which put on little plays about our problems. I was hot property in London. But only for a short while. As the war ended, my popularity waned. I returned home.

NIKOLA. Whoever granted you amnesty?

MARTIN. Now I'm waiting for the next war to put me in the spotlight again.

MAYA. You refused to fight. Did you have any doubts about it?

MARTIN. It was the right thing not to fight in that war. Yes. [*Pause.*] No. There isn't any ***thing*** I would fight for, any cause I would defend. Isn't that rather selfish? Yes, it is. Would I still think the same if I had children? Yes, I would. My parents didn't care much when they passed the buck on to me.

NIKOLA. Poor boy.

MARTIN. There ***is*** something I would fight for, though: instant gratification of my whims. Pleasure I wouldn't give up without a fight.

MAYA. But you can't be that selfish. You helped bury my father.

MARTIN. Oh, that was a pleasure.

MAYA. Why didn't he join you and run?

MARTIN. He must have been uneasy about the old baggage. Patriotism and all that bullshit. Not full of it enough to fight, not empty of it enough to run. [*To Nikola*] Yes? You were going to say something?

NIKOLA. Fuck off.

MARTIN. I thought so. I don't blame you. You're on automatic pilot. People are hierarchical animals. Do you understand what I'm talking about?

NIKOLA. No.

MARTIN. [*To Maya*] I think we're doomed. What are you going to do? Study history like dear papa? Try not to repeat his mistakes?

MAYA. Do you think he was a moral man?

MARTIN. Moral? That word rings a bell. What does that mean exactly?

MAYA. It means: ethical, right, good, pure, honest, proper, upright, honorable, decent, respectable, virtuous, righteous, principled, scrupulous, incorruptible, noble, just. That's what it means, exactly!

MARTIN. Touché!

MAYA. Why do you think he did it?

MARTIN. Wrong diet. He liked novelty dishes: democracy *au gratin*, justice *flambée*, equality *surprise*. Mad scientists invent those specialties in Western laboratories. Your father's refined palate suffered in this backwater inn, where the preferred cuisine is still one of manual butchery and cholesterol. You don't seem impressed with my explanation.

MAYA. You're trying hard to be cynical.

MARTIN. Yes.

MAYA. Why?

MARTIN. It gives me a kick.

MAYA. Trying to care might also do the trick.

MARTIN. Not really. I've tried a bit of that. Care about what, anyway?

MAYA. About erections! About men having erections as they rape little girls! How come they have erections? What gives them an erection? What the hell is it in them that gives them an erection?

MARTIN. Why ask me? I've never raped anybody. Ask him. [*He points at Nikola.*]

NIKOLA. You ***are*** asking for it, aren't you?

MARTIN. You think this whole war was about you and your papa, don't you?

MAYA. Well, I'm sure it wasn't about you and London Town.

MARTIN. We buried him for you. He's gone.

MAYA. Not for me, he isn't.

MARTIN. He's dead, dear. His blood splattered all over my shirt!

NIKOLA. Shut up!

MARTIN. I wasn't talking to you, hero!

NIKOLA. If it splattered over anybody's shirt, it splattered over mine!

MARTIN. You told him: "Come on teacher. Lead us into battle! Show us the way! Tell us this is a holy war, or you are a traitor and a coward and you'd better shoot yourself."

NIKOLA. That's a lie!

MARTIN. That's what you said.

NIKOLA. I said nothing! I was sitting down having my bread and garlic for breakfast. You said: "Come on, Mister Historian, explain to these peasants this war is dirty. Tell them to refuse to obey commands. If not, you'll be responsible for the massacre." You gave him the goddamn idea.

MARTIN. You moron!

NIKOLA. What did you say?

MARTIN. You illiterate, homicidal moron!

[*Nikola gets up ready to fight. Martin gets up. The Waiter comes in and looks at them.*]

MARTIN. Hit me! Hit me!

[*Nikola restrains himself.*]

NIKOLA. They told me I should leave. Please go home, they said to me, you're too old to fight. But I stayed. I have three sons and seven grandchildren. One of the sons is missing. And you're playing with words! If I hit you, I'd knock your fucking head off.

[*He slowly goes out. Pause. Martin and the Waiter sit down.*]

MARTIN. Well, I've had my kicks for today! [*He drinks up his wine.*] Some of my nationalist compatriots in London broke one of my ribs and two of my teeth. I have a daughter of five. My wife won't let me get anywhere near her. My ex-wife, that is. *"About suffering they were never wrong, The old Masters."* How it always happens while someone else is fucking about.

[*He goes out. Pause. The Waiter sits down.*]

WAITER. Men!

MAYA. I know.

WAITER. Who's paying?

MAYA. The women, as usual.

[*The Waiter scribbles down her bill. She gives him money.*]

MAYA. We were talking about my father.

WAITER. I knew him well. You know, if you're a decent human being, there are two things you can do in a war. Shoot yourself, or go mad. Your father shot himself. We others, we went mad. [*He collects the bottle and empty glasses.*] It wasn't particularly hard for me this time, though. I still hadn't recovered from the last war.

[*The Waiter turns half of the lights off.*]

WAITER. We're closing in a minute.

[*The Waiter goes out. Maya is left alone. Pause. Silence. Maya's dead Father comes in. He is wearing a white summer suit and a summer hat. He has the looks and mannerisms of an absent-minded professor. He is carrying a cup of coffee in one hand and a briefcase in the other. He puts the coffee down on the table and the case on the floor. He takes his hat off and then takes a newspaper from his pocket. He sits down, puts his glasses on, looks at the newspaper. Pause. Maya and Father don't look at each other.*]

MAYA. I'm trying my best, but it's not easy. The data is hard to come by. Documents have been destroyed. Witnesses give me contradictory stories. I traveled some of the way by bus, and then I walked. Men in various uniforms stopped me at checkpoints. There was one long stretch of land I wanted to investigate, but the U.N. wouldn't let me. They say it's a minefield now. They're digging for mass graves. [*Pause.*] Then the snow came. [*Pause.*] But I'll find you, minefield or no minefield. [*Pause.*] Why did you do it?

[*Father sips his coffee and reads his newspaper.*]

MAYA. You don't want to talk about it.

[*Father turns a page. Pause.*]

MAYA. I stumbled upon a book. I don't understand any of it. Categorical imperative. Absolute universal law of moral conduct. Humanitarian society based on reason and free will.

FATHER. Immanuel Kant.

MAYA. That's the one!

FATHER. *Grundlegung zur Metaphysik der Sitten.*

MAYA. The book is still lying open on your desk.

FATHER. *Groundwork of the Metaphysics of Morals.*

MAYA. Don't tell me you remember the year of the first edition?

FATHER. 1785.

MAYA. [*Maya shakes her head in amazement.*] Why, Father? Was that a choice or an accident? [*Pause*] Dad?

FATHER. Do you have a boyfriend?

MAYA. No.

FATHER. [*Looking at his paper*] How's Mom?

MAYA. She's coping.

FATHER. Take care of her, won't you?

MAYA. I will.

FATHER. And take care of yourself.

MAYA. I will.

FATHER. Do you hear me?

MAYA. Yes.

FATHER. Go now.

[*Pause. Maya resolutely goes out. Father turns a page.*]

BLACKOUT

SILYAN THE STORK FROM THE DEBAR DISTRICT

By Slobodan Unkovski

1. NOTHING

Goran Stefanovski slipped into the small rehearsal room in the Skopje Drama Theater in what was then the Republic of Macedonia, part of Yugoslavia, in the autumn of 1971. He was nineteen and in his first year studying English at the University — tall, shy, long-haired, hesitant, both in his manner and his ideas, there to observe our rehearsals. I had graduated from the Faculty of Dramatic Arts in Belgrade and was working on my second professional production, Chamber Music by Arthur Kopit, using the Grotowski Method. I thought I knew everything and the world was mine. At that moment, I was twenty-three — much, much older than Goran.

In fact, the Director of the Drama Theater, Risto Stefanovski, had insisted on one of his nephews coming to see me, the one who wanted to study playwriting in Belgrade. I hate meeting such candidates. Especially because, as a candidate myself for theater directing, I had come to the same theater to see a director in the flesh; I'd never had any contact with professional theater beforehand. The most avant-garde director of the time turned up — in a wolf-skin jacket, bearded, smoking, looking just as a director should, particularly if his name is Liubisha Georgievski.

I showed up as I was, my main feature being my long hair. I might know this nephew from somewhere, I'm not sure. He stayed for the rehearsals, as I thought that was the best way for him to see things from the inside. He soon became an important part of our team. He was good at taking delight in what we'd achieved in the day; many of the actresses asked for his opinion. He was smart and had direct experience of theater. He was writing and gave me some things to read. At that time, I thought it would be good to do something with our folklore. I can't remember who mentioned Tsepenkov — I would like it to have been me, but I'm not sure it was.

In contrast to some other authors who liked to complicate things and drag out the process for years, Goran worked fast and with precision. He quickly drew up a concept for a theater piece called Petré, the name of the protagonist, an outline of a dozen or so scenes. That was to remain the basic structure of his first text, Yané Zadrogaz. And, of course, there were those who claimed to have had the same idea but hadn't actually written anything down.

Everything conspired towards making Goran Stefanovski a playwright: the real-life drama of his extended family, refugees from Western Macedonia before World War II, who had ended up in Skopje; his childhood growing up in the theater in Prilep and in the so-called Debar Maalo (Debar District) of the city; his actor-director parents, who had been banished from Skopje for political reasons and later moved back; and Macedonian literature, which was entering its mature period during that time, precisely through the genre of drama. Nevertheless, I would say it was, above all, his innate talent, his enormous curiosity about all aspects of life, his openness towards world literature and music, the deep-seated restlessness and excitability of his mother Nada, an actor with a profound knowledge of life, together with his theater-director father Mirko's analytical nature, his determination and enigmatic, vibrant ambiguity, both of them on high adrenaline.

Goran was to begin his playwriting studies as one of the best in his year in Belgrade but, after only a year, still one of the best, he left and came back to Skopje. I never asked him why. Afterwards he started writing plays and I started directing them, as did many others in various countries and in various languages. All very sweet and simple. In fact, it was neither.

2.
MIRKO

It was a pre-war building. Like the set for a Chekhov play, perhaps: high ceilings, slight draft, nurses, doctors, white metal benches painted over with ivory-colored oil paint. I don't know which of us was more scared — Goran or I. His father was sitting down and didn't look terminally ill. I can't remember the date, the time of year, nor why Goran and I were in Belgrade. I do remember a particular light in Mirko's eyes, which I've only ever seen in that family. That's how Ibsen must have looked when he said his last line: "Tvertimod" (on the contrary). Characters from Mirko's productions were scattered about the corridors, from his personal dramas between Skopje, Prilep, and Celje, an all-encompassing view of Life and the Theater. Not a trace of self-pity. If I ever want to draw a centuries-old sycamore, he could be my model.

3.
IDADIA

I start thinking what I can possibly say to Goran in November 2018 which I haven't already said from November 1971 up to that day. What part of our conversations isn't finished? What topic hasn't been touched on, what are the secrets we haven't shared? What emails haven't we exchanged, usually written in pseudo world languages we didn't speak? I never went to see Goran and Pat in Canterbury.

I wanted to believe his stay there was temporary and he was about to come back to Skopje, to Debar Maalo, where his soul lives.

I have a picture in my head of Goran walking around Canterbury on the route he once told me about, looking like Dubrovnik in this part of the world; him going to the university, chatting to various acquaintances on the way, dropping into his favorite café on the way back, the one whose owner had known Pinter personally, never missing a visit to the record shops, stopping at the newsagent's. I never learned the correct name of his university, the names of his new colleagues who meant so much to him, the titles of the courses he taught. It was all just temporary, you see. But when he started to write his plays in English, when that language became his native tongue, I realized that my selfish wishes for his return were never to come true. When he came to Skopje from time to time for a few days, weeks, or months, he completely dissolved into the city, called to say he would be with me in a while after he'd taught his course, done his research, met contacts, been to his special haunts, which had to include the old Turkish quarter and his favorite restaurant, Idadia.

He was like Silyan the Stork from the best Macedonian folk tale about a man who turned into a stork and flew home every year to sit on the chimney of his house, unable to speak, watching his nearest and dearest living their lives out with moments of suffering and of joy without him, certain he had gone forever. In *The Black Hole*, Goran's thrilling metaphorical play about the end of a regime, of a civilization, the protagonist Silyan experiences the fate of Silyan the Stork in the folk tale; in Part Two of the play, he is present but invisible, watching how events in which he had taken part now unfold without him, and without his being able to influence them. That's how I see Goran today.

4. NEW PLAYS

Goran would usually finish a new play towards the end of the summer, sometimes a month or two later. I would be sitting in the theater café with actors Atso Giorchev and Stevo Spasovski in June when Stevo would ask: So when are we going to start rehearsing Goran — October or November? We'd all smile, but we knew that's what would happen.

When Goran was a young writer who was developing and making his way, he would give me hard copies of his texts. I would read them over for a few days and then we'd meet up so I could tell him what I thought of them, and when we'd start rehearsals. This was hard for him because he wanted to know my opinion immediately, whereas I'd been conditioned to read a new play when I was completely prepared for it, when I could concentrate on the material. When Goran became a distinguished playwright, some things changed. We'd come across each other one evening at the MCM Club, or in another of our haunts, and he'd ask me, out of the blue, if I was ready to hear his new text. We'd go to his flat and he'd read it out loud to me, so that I couldn't even touch it. He usually had just one copy, which meant I couldn't take it home with me to reread it, either. I used to think that the fact that he gave me his texts to read, or read them aloud to me, was a huge privilege. And so it was. But then I'd be in town and say to our leading actor Nenad Stoyanovski: Goran's got a new play, it's great, and he'd reply: Right, I know. It's excellent. Or Chorevski, another leading actor would add: I haven't read the latest version, but it's great. And then Goran's childhood friend from the Faculty of Engineering, or a relation from some other place, would confirm they'd read it, too, not to mention his close friend at the Criminal Court, whose opinion Goran particularly valued. Sophia was interested to know which direction the plot would take, because Goran had told her both options. I'd complain to Zoki, the owner of MCM, that Goran had a new text, *Shades of Babel*, for example, and that everyone had read it . . . and Zoki would just add: It's good — just the end's a bit weird. Risto the Director would ask me: Is the writer writing anything? And just when I thought I'd found one of Goran's fans who didn't know the text, Risto would add: It's a bit hermetic for my liking and seems a bit long. Before that, people would meet me in the street and, being the one responsible for this particular writer, I had to know the answer to the question: Is Goran writing something? Where's he got to with it? I'm pretty sure I never asked Goran whether he was writing anything and where he'd got to with it.

5.
THE KARPOSH HOTEL

I'm sitting in the Karposh Hotel, next to the Drama Theater, with Goran's brother Vlatko, a guitar virtuoso and a big name in European music, next to the several actors who will be orphans without Goran's future texts. We're remembering happy moments with our great author. The commemoration ceremony for Goran has just finished.

And I'm imagining looking down with Goran, impossible as that is, on his body lying in an English hospital room, a scene from an English war film like *The English Patient*, or from an English play like Pinter's *A Kind of Alaska*, his perfect Oxford brogues under the bed, the doctor from Ian McEwan's *Saturday* working here, English notices in black Latin letters in relief on white enamel plaques, staff whispering in an English I can't quite follow, his bed Prospero's isle from Shakespeare's *Tempest*, and around him, in the room, in the corridor, all the way to the car park full of Land Rover Series IIIs and Mini Morrises, their steering wheels on the right, a Citroën 2CV6 lost in the middle of them, its steering wheel on the left, the one he left Macedonia in for England with Pat, everywhere standing at ease hundreds of anxious characters from his plays and screenplays, holding their passports with their British visas in their hands, furtively wiping their tears away, recognizing each other, getting to know each other, for the first time in their existence outside the space of their plays, each whispering their name in Macedonian: ***Silyan***, soon to become a stork; ***Svetlé*** with her heavenly body; ***Sania*** in a silk kimono; ***The Father*** watching "snow" on the TV; ***Makso*** with his jeep; ***Pero*** listening to a symphony; ***Anna,*** wife and lover; ***Magda,*** who didn't want to be anyone's girlfriend; ***The Mother,*** come to give advice; Goran's friends from *Long Play* — ***The Rolling Stones, Bob Dylan, The Animals, The Monkees, Aretha Franklin, Tom Jones, Yoko Ono, Rudi Dutschke, Ernst Fischer***, and others; ***The Father,*** who's a train driver; ***Yoné,*** who listens to Radio Luxembourg; ***The Sister,*** who wants to be Rita Pavone; ***The Mother,*** who likes the Radetzky March; ***Bond*** with all his suspicions; ***Hakim*** with all ***his*** suspicions; ***Mr. Jones,*** who has visions; ***Jane***, who doesn't know and doesn't understand; ***Harding,*** the lonesome hobo; ***The Secretary***, the Youth Organization's fervent music activist; ***JFK*** and ***Marilyn Monroe*** in a motel room in Baltimore; ***Angie*** waiting for her nineteenth nervous breakdown; ***Sister Morphine, Cousin Cocaine; Valentina Tereshkova*** and ***Comrade Vastok*** trying to make a baby in space; ***Che Guevara*** with his beard and cigar; ***Sergeant Pepper*** with his girlfriend, ***Eleanor Rigby; Rina,*** who is great at chess, who has come back from England and has healing hands; ***Damian,*** who doesn't understand the play he is in; ***Blaga,*** his sister; ***Todor*** and ***Marko,*** cementing up barrels full of toxic materials; ***Victor,*** history in motion; ***Nevena*** looking for her lost brother; ***Petar,*** the father, sick in the head; ***Ghosts*** of the past; ***Marta,*** the girl with green hair who wants to go to London; ***The Boy*** with no imagination; ***The Father,*** who doesn't know anything; ***The Mother*** in amazement; ***Rampo Prtseski,*** the Director and nothing; ***The Chinese Interpreter***; ***Chuang Li*** and the ***Second Chinese Businessman***, who cherish their traditions; ***Chorbé,*** the lyrical lover from Burgas; ***Mr. and Mrs. Balbakov***, the married couple; ***The Woman Soldier*** and the confidential dossier; ***Itso,*** the untalented actor; ***Slaveykov,*** the theater manager under pressure; ***Tsvetko, Neda, Jafer Aga*** from another play by Goran; ***Alexander*** and ***Katalin,*** an unforgotten love; ***The Music Teacher*** at the wedding; ***The Man in Tails*** from the village of Seltsi; ***Sara,*** researcher and architect; ***Rudi*** the postman; ***Gorchin*** as Gavrilo Princip; ***Hamdia*** as Andrich and Tito; ***Fata; The Chorus of Dubrovnik and of Vukovar; Sulio,*** the cook and other things; ***Azra,*** the woman at the window; ***Muyo*** the taxi driver; ***Maya*** the journalist; ***Sarajevo***, the city; the god ***Dionysus***; the prophet ***Tiresias; Agave***; ***The Chorus of Maenads***; everyone from the Yugoslav Wars; ***Zora,*** the mother, telling the story in London; ***Konstantin,*** the father, convalescing from the continuing war; ***Yana,*** the daughter, who doesn't believe her father is dead; ***Mick,*** the Englishman, war correspondent and lover; ***Gavro,*** war profiteer with a ship; ***Prajapati,*** the pitiable U.N. observer; ***Marko Tsepenkov,*** who will be ***Todé the Wise***; ***The Queen,*** a Macedonian before they existed as such; ***Yané Zadrogaz,*** the soul of Macedonia; the very wicked and dangerous ***Dragon***; ***Yankula, Sekula, Petrula,*** the Queen's half-witted sons; ***Tasé,*** the musician; ***Dafina,*** the village woman; ***Bozhin,*** the baker; ***Magda*** and ***Naidé the Leech***, the village doctor; ***Vaska*** and ***Dimché,*** the blacksmith; ***Kostadinka*** and ***Itso,*** the tailor; all the enthusiastic villagers on their holiday; ***Dimitri Andreyevitch***, father, invalid, mason, announcing the war; ***Maria,*** the mother who recognizes wild flesh; ***Andrei,*** the grocery shop assistant and revolutionary; ***Stevo,*** his brother and employee of an automobile dealership; ***Simon*** the waiter, an alcoholic and loser; ***Vera,*** the housewife who wants to get pregnant; ***Herzog,*** director of the automobile dealership, a Jew; ***Sara,*** his daughter, the widely read, stunningly beautiful Jewish woman; ***Hermann Klaus,*** the visitor from Berlin headquarters; ***Sivitch,*** the adviser; ***The Prostitute***, ***The Priest; Mihailo*** and ***Evto***, the fresco-painter brothers; ***Sultana,*** their mother, who remembers tragedies;

Raina, Evto's wife, who's having a baby; ***Panaiotis***, a Greek merchant among other things; ***Elena,*** his wife, who will steal the baby; ***Kiro,*** a former teacher; ***Gavril,*** his rebel-fighter brother; ***Angelé,*** the professional performer, juggler and palm-reader; ***The Pasha***, the Turkish authority with the wisdom of a Great Power; ***Ostoitch,*** a Serb passing through, among other things; ***Velkov***, a Bulgarian priest, among other things; ***Boris,*** the father and grandfather, an ex-convict; ***Matei***, his hi-fi grandson; ***Sonia***, daughter and mother; ***Mira,*** the girlfriend; ***The American*** passing through; ***The Russian*** passing through; ***The Arab*** passing through; ***Jacob,*** high-energy artist; ***Bozho,*** the minister of culture and writer; ***Paraskeva,*** wife and mother; ***Novey,*** a civil servant; ***Voydan,*** an ethnologist in free fall; ***Tsibra,*** his dangerous half-brother; ***Kolyo,*** a traveler going nowhere; ***Strezo,*** who may not exist; ***Altana,*** mother and pillar of strength; ***Ruzha*** with no support; ***Mary,*** as dangerous as Tsibra; ***Claudia,*** an unknown entity; ***The Tattooer***, a threat; and yet many others I can't recognize in the distance.

And through that great throng, I seem to see the Beatles, all of whose songs Goran knew by heart, with his Fan Club membership card no. 2003 like some kind of entry ticket, and the theater audiences from Skopje, Belgrade, Ljubljana, Sarajevo, Podgorica, Zagreb, Moscow, London, Stockholm, Antwerp, Vienna, Paris cover the 15km road from the hospital to his Canterbury. Goran and I are looking down on all this and, even though he can't speak and appears not to hear, he smiles enigmatically, hugs me with one arm and delivers one of his deadly sarcastic sentences, which we will never know. A group of people from Debar Maalo have turned up late, are pushing through the crowd and shouting out his local nickname. . .

And back in reality, in the evening, Pat, Jana, and Igor Stefanovski are alone with Goran in his hospital room. Igor leans his mobile phone next to Goran's ear and I say to him from Skopje: Unko here. You know how very much . . . Or perhaps I don't say anything because I seem to be talking to myself as I lie dying.

6.
PETRÉ

When Goran started writing his first play *Petré*, later to be called *Yané Zadrogaz*, the most significant playwrights in the previous century of Macedonian drama were the following: J. H. Jinot with his didactic plots with religious and symbolic themes, Voydan Chernodrinski with *Macedonian Blood Wedding*, Dimitar Molerov with *The Dragon's Bride*, Vasil Ilyoski with *Guv'nor Teodos* and *The Runaway Girl*, Risto Krlé with *Money Kills*, Anton Panov with *Earning a Living Abroad* and Goran's direct predecessors: Kolé Chashulé with *Black is the Color*, Tomé Arsovski with *Diogenes' Paradox*, Bogomil Giuzel with *Adam, Eve, and Job*, alongside a whole string of other writers trying to articulate the modern human condition and society. Macedonian drama was late in beginning to free itself from its self-imposed task of providing the torch and herald of the struggle for national liberation, consciousness, and identity of the Macedonian people and to leave the circle of national themes in a modern setting, insofar as that was possible in the given political system for the arts.

During the almost two months of rehearsals for Chamber Music at the Drama Theater, Stefanovski was to write the synopsis and draft for his first play *Petré*, which was to be worked on in the years that followed and become *Yané Zadrogaz — A Folk Fantasia with Songs*. Taking the ten volumes of folklore, songs, tales, sayings, and customs collected by Marko Tsepenkov in the second half of the 19th century and the first two decades of the 20th, Stefanovski was to extract the essence, soul, and genome of the folk narrator and articulate a new synthesized quintessence with a gentle and careful hand.

In the 1972–73 season, we began rehearsing *Yané Zadrogaz*, the first text by this potential new playwright. The first night of a new Macedonian play is a real celebration in the theater. But the leading actors in the Skopje theater considered the play wasn't yet ready for the stage and the play was removed from the repertoire after just ten days of rehearsals. Perhaps they were right, but perhaps the reason was a big film most of them were engaged in. We stopped rehearsing and both of us fell ill from the grief of it. That's the diagnosis I'd give for the defeat of someone involved in the arts who is condemned before being given any kind of hearing.

7.
YANÉ ZADROGAZ

Two seasons later, in the fall of 1974, at the strong insistence of the Director of the Drama Theater, Risto Stefanovski, Goran's uncle, Stefanovski's first text, *Yané Zadrogaz*, was again in rehearsal, having undergone serious work and with completely new actors, and its first night was a huge success. That was Goran's debut. The production was invited to important festivals and won awards there. It toured all round what was then Yugoslavia, also going to Paris and Caracas, Venezuela. This is how Goran entered Macedonian drama through the front door with his first play and opened up his path into European drama.

That first fantasia of his was based on a simple formula. A nation has a bad queen with three bad sons and a dangerous, evil dragon. The invented national hero, Yané Zadrogaz (Jack the Joker, Jack the Tease, Jack the Bold), is his nation's only hope. Goran makes this archetypal story more interesting by having it told by Todé the Wise, with the other villagers acting out the tale on his instructions on a national feast day.

In contrast to the classic Macedonian plays of Voydan Chernodrinski, for example (in whose honor Goran was to write the tragicomedy *Chernodrinski Comes Home*), where personal dramas are the result of a socio-political situation (*The Turkish Occupation*), Yané Zadrogaz conjures with archaic language and folklore outside time and politics. In this way, his fantasia with songs avoided the trap of interpreting historical reality, causes, and consequences; even though it is deeply founded in Macedonian folklore with its wealth of drama, it isn't obstructed by fixed limitations. As in classic westerns, good wins and everything is cheerful and jolly, the hero rides off into the sunset and the audience goes home feeling positive, elated, and happy.

8. PLAYWRITING

At the Academy of Dramatic Arts in Belgrade, they recognized Stefanovski's talent and his skills. Amid strong competition, he was immediately admitted as one of the best candidates. But, after only one year of studies, he left for reasons we can only surmise — perhaps he didn't like the institution, perhaps his parents couldn't cover the costs, perhaps he missed his hometown of Skopje, or perhaps it was something completely different.

9.
WILD FLESH

In the following few years, Stefanovski wrote several TV scripts for film and drama and established himself as a major writer, but in summer 1979 he produced his family chronicle *Wild Flesh*, arguably his greatest full-length play for the theater. The first night at the end of December that year was the result of a new generation of actors at the Skopje Drama Theater, and Stefanovski and I were recognized as an important tandem in Macedonian theater. Goran was then only twenty-seven.

I can't tell you how surprised and excited I was by the maturity and completeness of the work, by the precisely executed character lines, by the structure and choice of the conflict, by the multi-layered nature of the plot. At the same time, I was worried because the history of the arts is full of examples of those who have created their best work when very young and lived out the rest of their lives in the shadow of that first great success, trying in vain to repeat it or surpass it.

Those in the know will recognize Goran's family history in many of his texts. *Wild Flesh*, set in the twilight of the approaching Second World War in Skopje, in Debar Maalo, the mythical site of Goran's childhood and the root of his happiness, speaks of the spread of fascism but, above all, of the disintegration of a family, of the demolition of their home, and of the catastrophe awaiting the country with the coming war.

10. MONOLOGUE

The apartment block where Lina and I lived on the ninth floor was the famous Block 13, behind the Green Market. Famous, that is, with the stallholders from the surrounding villages, who sometimes used it as a warehouse and sometimes as everything else. Especially the elevators.

While I was doing my military service, Goran lived there, and then, as a result of his particular lifestyle, many people got to know my apartment and, I must say, my bedroom.

Later, when we were rehearsing *Wild Flesh*, the rehearsals were hard work, although we knew we were on the right path and that we were doing something important. You can feel those things. If you've felt wrong, then the first night is very awkward.

Choré, the actor Chorevski, who was playing the role of Stevo, had a scene which he couldn't act. He understood it, he knew all about it but, somehow, he couldn't do it. I couldn't help him anymore. I was thirty or thirty-one at that time, and I'd done all I could. Now I'm older and I still don't know what to do about that kind of problem except wait. Goran and I talked about what to do. He was twenty-six or twenty-seven and couldn't help much.

Lina and I had gone to bed in the living room of our two-room apartment in the aforementioned Block 13. Did we have a baby at that time? Yes, he was asleep in the bedroom with our older son. The phone rang: Unko, can I come round? Choré liked to play jokes from time to time and would call after some late-night drinking bout with his well-known message: The Drama Theater's gone up in flames — I'm the only survivor.

So this time I replied: Choré, we've gone to bed, we're asleep. Choré said: Just a quick visit. He came. We took our famous six-piece thick-foam bed apart and sat there in our pyjamas to see what Choré wanted. He said: I've found the solution to the Europe monologue (. . . Stevo Andreyevitch from Debar Maalo now sits astride his white charger . . .). I said: Great. He said: If I don't show you now, I won't be able to sleep and I won't leave till you've watched me. We sat down to watch. That was my first rehearsal at home. Choré acted it perfectly, as well as that monologue could ever be played. Instead of getting up on a chair, as he would in the performances, he got up on one of those thick-foam bed sections.

He asked: How was it? I said — I don't know what I said exactly — but I was really impressed, I said fantastic, fascinating. Take a seat and let's have a drink — coffee, something stronger. Choré said No, I have to be going, and he got up and left. That's how he was then, to the point and always on the go. Lina and I stayed awake for hours.

Goran saw him do this monologue a few days later. It was still wonderful and intriguing, but it was never to be the same as it had been after midnight in our apartment. How did you do it? asked Goran. Oh, by magic, professional secrets, special techniques. Grotowski, slightly modified. Of course, everyone, including Goran, knew about the nighttime rehearsal. That's the advantage of my work. Goran's characters can come into my living room and share one of their secrets with me. Or later, when they go bad, they can forget what they had which was most beautiful and become my deadly enemies. I can't tear them up together with the pages on which their lives are written or throw them out of my memory of past events. That's the blessing and the curse of this profession, my dear Goran.

11.
THE CONTINENT OF DEBAR MAALO (DEBAR DISTRICT)

Families, lost relatives, and brothers with completely different moral and political values are always cropping up in Stefanovski's plot lines, deftly supported by short, precise speeches, thought associations, with no cheap pathos, in the best tradition of modern plays in English, especially those by his favorite playwrights, Samuel Beckett and Harold Pinter. We have the three brothers in *Yané Zadrogaz* (the Queen's sons), the three brothers in *Wild Flesh* (a businessman just starting out, an alcoholic waiter who's a loser, and the young revolutionary who wants to change the world), the two brothers in *Flying on the Spot* (fresco painters), the two half-brothers in *Tattooed Souls* (an ethnologist from Macedonia and a probable American gangster), and so on. Brothers, home, the Macedonian homeland, but not dealt with simplistically, the sense of some indefinable menace, the articulation of the universal states of the soul, the discussion of the sense of a given moment in a given place . . . a multitude of themes which we hadn't encountered up to that time in our theater.

Some analysts of Stefanovski's works try to define him as a writer who depends on Debar Maalo, where his grandfather built a house and where his father and his four brothers grew up. Debar Maalo comes up in many places in his work, from the concrete location of *Wild Flesh* to *The Demon of Debar Maalo*, for example, and part of Goran's email address.

I would say that, when Stefanovski speaks of Debar Maalo, he's not talking about a geographical space — in reality, a smaller area than a block in a modern city, bounded by two streets.

No, Goran's notion of Debar Maalo is the mythical land of the imagination, of freedom, a world which exists primarily in his mind and whose heroes have died either before Goran was born or when he was little, with just a few surviving there, like his friend Krap, to prove that Debar Maalo did in fact exist as such and meant a great deal in the unwritten history of the city of Skopje. Paradoxically, the street where the Stefanovski house used to stand is called Albert Einstein Street.

Goran's pictures of the "continent" of Debar Maalo are based on street legends, tales of powerful and dangerous groups of young men with values which only live on there, their devotion and skill in keeping pigeons, their special mentality, strong will, pigheadedness, and perseverance, about remembering injustice, always going against the grain, outwitting and outflanking adversaries, a particular type torn away from the group, with a separate language and culture, their own concept of honor and bravery, an oral passing down of stories, whether they be fact or fiction. About a closed and perhaps marginalized group, who see themselves as important and indestructible, as the essence of a part of the city of Skopje.

In practice, Debar Maalo in Stefanovski's work is a synonym for Macedonia, from whose soil he drew all of his strength, especially his creative power. Goran's plays can be divided into many phases or thematic wholes, but certainly into two which I consider the most dominant: the first Debar Maalo/Macedonian/Yugoslav/Ex-Yugoslav phase, whatever you'd like to call it, and the second, the English/European phase. This goes together with the division of his plays originally written in Macedonian and those originally written in English. And this coincides with plays written from his own free will and those written as serious commissions from producers, theaters, and festivals.

12. STOCKHOLM

When did we create our production about Sarajevo? Where? In Stockholm, in February 1993. And then we worked on it in Antwerp and in London. We needed, both of us, to say something about Sarajevo, against the war in the former Yugoslavia. Haris Pashovitch was chosen as the director; he selected his cast but then went home to Sarajevo under siege and stayed there. I took his place, but his shadow always remained over that project.

In Stockholm the dogs don't bark and, when they get on a bus, squeeze themselves under their owner's seat in a well-behaved fashion. That was the setting on the morning when Goran and I were drinking our coffee in the huge, rented apartment near the City Hall, where the Nobel Banquet is held after the award ceremony in the Concert Hall. After Skopje, where there were packs of street dogs attacking its citizens at the time, not to mention the barking with which they had seen me off a few days earlier, Stockholm was like a breath of mountain air. We were preparing for our second rehearsal.

Then Lina called to tell me my mother had died unexpectedly. At that moment, it came into my head that it was some kind of punishment for the topic we had decided to deal with. I also thought of something which I was ashamed of — the fact that I wouldn't have to pull my hair if I saw a dead cat or dog in accordance with the superstition "So your mother won't die." I wondered whether Goran and I were close enough that we could share that moment. Mothers had died several times in our productions, brothers had killed each other, some characters had committed suicide, some had lived on as pale shadows of their former selves. Weren't we both past masters of the space between fact and fiction? The last thing I remember of that morning is his face, which showed everything. If we could go through it again, would I change that light, which wasn't right somehow in the way it was coming through the window? Or would I add a little local music from the transistor radio on the kitchen table as a counterpoint? Or say Goran wasn't up and that he came in after I heard the news? Or . . . I sat at the kitchen table, he talked and swore like anything, then called his and my Patricia Marsh.

Later I reflected it was a Stanislavski situation exercise but not original enough for a scene in a play. For years I've been holding back those unshed tears from that morning, and I transfer them from one part of me to another, only for them to emerge sometimes unexpectedly, without a good reason and apparently unconnected to my mother, and they knock me out in a second. Now, since Goran is there, too, the space has become even more cramped.

13. REHEARSAL

If there was anything that annoyed me about Macedonian playwrights, it was their need to come to rehearsals. If there was anything I could completely understand, it was Macedonian playwrights' need to see how their text was progressing.

We said to Goran: When you're writing, do we come up behind you and look at what you're typing? No. Do we know all the troubles, dilemmas, difficulties, and dramas you have while you're writing? No.

The playwright expects to see a set result. Because they have a set result in the dramatic form. The stage has a different logic to it. I don't want to repeat myself here: process, development, phases, layers, elements, and wholes, taking apart and putting back together again. Moods and creative crises, and very limited time.

That's why Goran and I agreed he wouldn't come to rehearsals. We'd invite him to come when the time came. When the time was right, when we wouldn't be ashamed, either of ourselves or of him. He had his misgivings about it. Nenad, who loved him best, told him: It's your writing, our rehearsal.

He didn't come.

Then, while I'm rehearsing, I sense someone watching from the back of the theater; I turn round, but there's no one there. I turn round again and catch sight of the author's head popping up somewhere in the back rows. We stop rehearsing and all laugh. He may have said: I dropped a pen here yesterday, so I came in to find it, or he may not have said anything.

The truth is, we want to have the freedom to say various things about the text, about individual lines, so we feel relieved, so we can master them completely. So if we say: Uh, this really doesn't work, it's not a profound analysis or criticism of the style or composition of the distinguished author, but rather our safety valve, our means of making our way through the complex and complicated texts of our dear writer.

Then he would publish the texts. He never had them printed with our cuts (some trifling line here and there) but presented them as he had brought them to the first rehearsal.

In contrast to his, almost all of Shakespeare's texts were printed from the prompter's copy, as they were performed on the stage. That's all very well, but the profession of theater director was invented many years after Shakespeare's death and only a few years before Stefanovski's birth.

14.
THE ARTIST AND THE MINISTER

In *The False Bottom*, 1984, characters are clearly opposed politically and philosophically (the Minister of Culture v. the Artist), Goran opens up a heated debate about the relationship between art and politics. This play is completely different from the approach in the lyrical folk fantasia with songs of *Yané Zadrogaz*, the profoundly emotional and poignant *Wild Flesh*, the exciting and uncompromising *Hi-Fi*, in which the author first broached a political theme, untypical of his work. *The False Bottom* at first sight is a play to read, like a thesis play, a discussion in drama about the significance of art. In the three acts, the artist presents his dilemmas and standpoints about pressure and politicization in a direct conversation with the minister of culture, his superficial wife, and their impressionable daughter.

Twelve years later, in 1996, in the new Macedonian democratic state after the fall of Yugoslavia, I myself became the Minister of Culture of the Republic. Goran remained an artist. We could now conduct the hypothetical discussions based on the playwright's imagination in the real conditions of the minister's office.

15.
MOZART WAS ALSO A MACEDONIAN

It was just the next year, 1985, when Stefanovski's especially significant play, *Tattooed Souls*, appeared, closer in structure to *Wild Flesh* than those plays immediately preceding it. A young ethnologist, Voydan, goes to the United States (*The Rose Tattoo*) to do research for his doctoral thesis on the roots and condition of Macedonian migrants there. He comes into conflict with the most rigid Macedonian myths and illusions about the importance of our small nation in the framework of world civilization. Not one of the questions with which Voydan comes to the States is answered or properly dealt with until the end of the play. He isn't even sure whether what he has learnt about his father and his second American family is the truth and, even more importantly, whether what he has seen is true. From the superior, ignorant point of view he had on arrival in the States, Voydan becomes entangled in questions which have no answer, questions he can't understand; he is astonished to find how little he knows himself and his apparently strong scientific position dissolves into the fog of the complex relationships and lives of Macedonian migrants in America.

16.
CASABLANCA CASABALKAN

In contrast to *Wild Flesh*, which appeared just before the death of Marshal Tito and indirectly formulated the nation's fears for the future of Yugoslavia, and to *The False Bottom* and *Tattooed Souls*, which were performed in the years when we could see that the fall of Yugoslavia was inevitable and we dreaded a potential war, *Casabalkan*, a paraphrase of the title of the film *Casablanca*, appeared in 1997 when Greater Yugoslavia had already collapsed into a series of small states through a bloody civil war from 1991 to 1995.

In *Casablanca*, a war-romance movie made in 1942 with Humphrey Bogart as Rick Blaine and Ingrid Bergman as Ilsa Lund in the Nazi-occupied city of Casablanca in Morocco, enemies come together in Rick's café — local policemen, German officers, secret agents, and soldiers. Rick is a cynical American expatriate, and the plot revolves around whether or not he will help his former lover and her fugitive husband escape the Nazis. The film is famous for certain lines around which a whole mythology has built up ("Play it again, Sam," "I think this is the beginning of a beautiful friendship," and so on).

In Goran's *Casabalkan*, the action takes place on a floating casino during the Yugoslav Wars, frequented by leaders from the opposing sides. The ship sets sail in the evening, the supposedly implacable enemies gamble or take part in orgies, and then they go back to the battlefield the following morning. After more than fifty years since the movie came out, we can recognize its characters in the chaos of various nations and armies, but all the circumstances are different and the context is dramatically changed, even though there is a love story at the center of it. Ilsa is Zora in the play, a refugee who fled to London with her daughter Yana and husband Konstantin, though he has returned to the Balkans. He and his wife's ex-lover Mick (Rick in *Casablanca*) seem to be trying to finish their own wars, independently of the real war. Zora and Yana reveal their secrets to each other and now their lives can go on in London, the play finishing with the last line of the movie: "I think this is the beginning of a beautiful friendship."

17. STRUCTURE

A theater studies program based on high science (as their goal) and middling practice (as their reality), where the expression postmodern is used more often than Good Morning, invited me to reconstruct one of the first productions of a Stefanovski text which hasn't been preserved in any form. Partly by chance, and partly by intention, the conversation never took place. Later, I met some of the students and they told me they had done the reconstruction themselves and that it had been great, fantastic, totally successful.

That made me think. Is it enough if you have a text, some costume sketches, and photos, even a video recording (which was lacking in this case), to have a clear picture of a production from forty years ago? After many years' work in the theater, I can't tell you how fascinating Meto Yovanovski was as Yané Zadrogaz, an impossible mix of inner chaos, love, and precise interpretation of what might be called the Macedonian Soul. Where are the wonderful pauses written down in Krum Stoyanov's introductory monologue as Todé the Wise, how can you reconstruct that archetypal energy, wickedness, and charm, which radiated from Atso Giorchev's Dragon? How can I describe Todorka Kondova's acting as the Queen, or accurately convey how Kolé, Dadi, and Dukats played the roles of her three half-wit sons? Even if you could hear the songs, nobody who wasn't there then can know how marvelous the women's singing was, as Lenché, Lilé, Snezhé, Maida, Slavitsa, and Sabina opened new phases in the structure of the play.

How could I inform a cyber researcher about the position of Stevo Spasovski's body as he spoke about his character's dilemmas, or about the ironic (both funny and wise) ineffable interpretation of the play in which nothing — absolutely nothing — is sacred, and yet at the same time everything is important. Where would that performance have been without Mité's fanaticism (too narrow a term for it) or Meshko's present absence . . . and Pero . . .? Et cetera . . . How to pack up a production in a research folder? I've seen that it can be done. I just don't know whether it should be done. At the Moscow Art Theater I once watched productions which they had kept in the repertoire for decades because of their particular significance, even though none of the original cast were acting in them. They have everything: the information, authenticity, the same set, the same space — even the same costumes, now showing signs of wear — but something extremely important has been lost.

What evidence do I have that I worked on Stefanovski's texts? Some newspaper cuttings, some prize certificates, some half-forgotten photos, a recollection in my soul. The vital members of the audience who still talk about the productions. There's no process by which I'll manage to prove with material evidence that they existed, that that was actually us.

You can't be involved in theater direction and have a need to live forever. The performances exist only from 7:30 pm to 10:15 pm (or however long they last) and everything else is just an idea for a dream. Whereas the text of the play lasts. Be careful how you hold this collection of plays by Goran Stefanovski in your hands. Various personalities, people, characters, actors, dilettantes, and top professionals, children, animals, set designers, costume designers, lighting designers, and supporters who could give us an ounce of strength at the right moment, which had been lacking up to then — any of them might drop out of its pages. These are the footnotes to this book, that's the selected bibliography of the Playwright, those are the threads which bind us forever.

Shakespeare says in *The Tempest*: We are such stuff as dreams are made on . . . The life of a whole generation was special, exciting, and constantly challenging because it had its own playwright, Goran Stefanovski. The new generations are discovering him anew and transporting him into the contemporary Macedonian state of affairs. The man who created our dreams. . .

18. APPLAUSE

At the first night of *Yané Zadrogaz* in 1974 we stood in the corridor behind the stage and listened to the standing ovation. Then we went into the sewing room so we could laugh with joy. Goran's cheeks were flushed.

At the first night of *Wild Flesh* in 1979 we stood in the wings and embraced the actors as they exited the stage after the many bows they took to the long applause. I may well have pushed Goran to go on stage and bow himself. Clumsily, diffidently, for the sake of history.

When in 1980 we were awarded all the prizes possible at *Steriino Pozorie*, the most important Yugoslav Drama Festival in what was then Yugoslavia, the theater was full of a thousand people and the audience were screaming as if they were at a rock concert.

We didn't get any prizes for *Flying on the Spot*. We sat after the Festival and thought our wonderful production hadn't been understood.

I can't remember the first night of *The False Bottom*, but I know it was a joyful occasion. Goran was happy.

Shades of Babel brought us acting prizes. The first night was sincere and dangerous. We didn't embrace anymore, we didn't scream, there was no general chaos behind the stage. We were authors who had to show some decorum.

I directed *Tattooed Souls* in Belgrade with an exceptional cast. While the massive applause was going on, I drew Goran into a prop room near the stage. I remember he was shaking all over. It was his first great success in the Yugoslav capital. He was wearing a new jacket. From one first night onwards, I can't remember which one, he started wearing a jacket to first nights, colorful ties, pointed leather shoes, sometimes reddish yellow ones.

At the first night of *Tattooed Souls* in Moscow he brought me two Turkish cakes from Patricia, which we combined with a lot of champagne and a lot of vodka. I stayed in the hotel room for three days — just opening my eyes hurt.

Chernodrinski Comes Home was a play about a playwright. That was the essential thing about it, especially as the playwright doesn't appear in the play.

Sarajevo opened in Antwerp, European City of Culture, everything very formal. Actors from Sweden, Slovenia, Spain, and Bosnia.

At the first night of *Tongues of Fire*, I don't remember whether we took a bow or not. When Goran came a week before the first night of his *Demon from Debar Maalo,* he was in despair, he really didn't like it. I think we took a bow.

He couldn't come to the first night of his adaptation of Ismail Kadare's *The Successor* in Prishtina. I took a bow with my set and costume designers.

For a long time, we worked on a script for a big new educational series. Goran wrote half of it in the summer of 2018. He came to Skopje, where we discussed the structure with Sinolichka Trpkova, the co-producer, and then he went home to Canterbury, in the United Kingdom, to finish it. The rest is history.

Translated by Patricia Marsh-Stefanovska

BIOGRAPHIES

GORAN STEFANOVSKI was born on 27 April 1952 in Bitola, a town then in Yugoslavia, near the border with Greece on the Balkan Peninsula in Eastern Europe, now in North Macedonia. His father, Mirko, was a theatre director and his mother, Nada, a leading actress. Much of Goran's childhood was spent in theaters.

During his teenage years he was heavily influenced by the music of the Beatles and the Rolling Stones and went on to study English language and literature at the University of Skopje. However, the theater was in his blood. Goran was to spend his third year of studies at the Faculty of Dramatic Arts (FDU) in Belgrade and have his first play performed at the age of 22. It was directed by Slobodan Unkovski, who was to become a lifetime collaborator and friend.

Goran Stefanovski wrote 23 full-length plays for the theater in all. The most widely performed internationally are *"Wild Flesh," "Hi-Fi," "Flying on the Spot," "Tattooed Souls," "The Black Hole," "Chernodrinski Comes Back Home," "Sarajevo, an oratorio for the theatre," "Hotel Europa,"* and *"The Demon of Debar Maalo."*

In 1990 he spent six months as an Outstanding Artist Fulbright Scholar at Brown University, in Rhode Island, and began a lifelong friendship with Professor John Emigh.

In 1991 Yugoslavia began to fall apart and descended into civil war. The constantly deteriorating situation led his English wife, Pat Marsh, to decide to make a new life for the family in Canterbury, England, from September 1992. For the next six years, Stefanovski was to commute between his homeland and the UK, continuing his teaching in Skopje.

In 1992, Chris Torch of the Jordcirkus theatre group in Stockholm commissioned Goran to write a play for the Antwerp European Capital of Culture, about Sarajevo, the Bosnian city then undergoing a brutal siege. This successful venture was followed by performance scripts for the festivals of European Capitals of Culture in Copenhagen, Stockholm, Avignon, and Bologna, all in collaboration with Chris Torch.

In September 2000 Stefanovski settled in Canterbury and taught classes in screenwriting and playwriting at the University of Kent before taking up his post at Canterbury Christ Church University in 2002, teaching screenwriting there until his death in 2018. He wrote six screenplays in all and his *A Little Book of Traps (a scriptwriting tool)* has been translated and published in five languages, including Chinese.

Goran Stefanovski continued writing successful plays which were translated and produced all over the world throughout the rest of his life. He died of an inoperable brain tumor in 2018 at the age of 66.

PATRICIA MARSH-STEFANOVSKA

(Pat Marsh) is a linguist with a master's degree in general linguistics. She went to Yugoslavia to take up the post of British Council lector in English at the University of Skopje in 1974. She met Goran Stefanovski after a month there and they were married in 1976. Patricia is the author of a number of articles published in linguistic journals, especially those concerned with comparative linguistics.

As a native speaker of English, Patricia was much in demand as a translation editor from the beginning of her life in what was then the Republic of Macedonia. After she had become a competent speaker of Macedonian, she began to make her own translations of all kinds of texts, especially Goran's plays. She returned to the U.K. with her family during the Yugoslav wars of the 1990s. From 1998, Goran began to write most of his plays in English, and Patricia took on the role of his language editor.

After retirement, Patricia became an author in her own right and has published works of both fiction and nonfiction. She is also an environmentalist involved in political and community action related to the climate emergency and sustainability.

SLOBODAN UNKOVSKI (b. 1948) is a theater director and retired Professor of Theater Directing and Acting at the Faculty of Dramatic Arts in Skopje, North Macedonia. He was a visiting professor and Fulbright Scholar at Brooklyn College and the Institute for Advanced Theater Training at Harvard University. He was Artist-in-residence at the American Repertory Theater, Cambridge, Massachusetts, and at the National Theater of Greece in Athens. He has directed in many places all over the world and received several awards.

Unkovski directed at least twelve theater plays, as well as dozens of TV plays and series by Goran Stefanovski. Together and with Meta Hochevar, frequently their set designer, and Angelina Atlagich, costume designer for many of this tandem's productions, as well as with Professor Rasha Dinulovich, an expert on theater technology, they held many highly successful master classes on theater direction.

CHRIS TORCH is an independent cultural expert, project designer, and policy consultant, with extensive practical experience about audience engagement, artistic curation, and intercultural policy. He led the Artistic Unit at Timisoara 2021 — European Capital of Culture (Romania) during the StartUp Phase, February 2017–July 2019 (www.timisoara2021.ro).

In 1996, he founded Intercult (www.intercult.se), a production and resource unit focused on culture, ideas, and arts. He served as Artistic Director until February 2017. It was during his time with Intercult that multiple collaborations with the Macedonian playwright Goran Stefanovski were conceived and implemented, all of them with significant support from the E.U. Starting with *Sarajevo* (1992–1993), followed by *Bacchanalia* (1996), *Euralien* (1998), and *Hotel Europe* (2000–2001), this series of multi-disciplinary large-scale projects were designed and written by Stefanovski, produced and toured by Torch and his team. At the sudden death of the playwright, work had begun for another large-scale production, commissioned by two European Capitals of Culture (Rijeka 2020 and Timisoara 2021), to be directed by the renowned Bosnian/Croatian stage director Oliver Frljic.

Torch has conceived and led other co-productions within the European Neighborhood, reflected in long-term projects: *Seas*, 2003–2010 (www.seas.se) and *Corners*, a complex partnership of cultural initiatives at the "edges of Europe," 2011–2018 (www.cornersofeurope.org), both co-financed by E.U. Creative Europe program. He joined the artistic leadership for winning bids to become European Capitals of Culture for both Matera 2019 and Rijeka 2020. In Rijeka, he served as Program Director, until December 2016, when he was recruited to Timisoara.

Among recent tasks, he served as Senior Expert/Culture on programming the E.U. House at *SXSW 2020*, the influential festival of tech, ideas, culture, and society held annually in Austin, Texas. He initiated and curated a small local festival, *Pisciott'Arte* (www.pisciottarte.com) in a small village in southern Italy, in June/July 2021. He is presently commissioned by the Cultural Relations Platform (E.U.) to map interest by E.U.-based arrangers to present artists from South Africa and surrounding countries. He also serves as a consultant for Coimbra 2027 — one of Portugal's candidate cities to the title of European Capital of Culture.